D1393036

Long

Biology

11–14

JAY KERMISCH

EMFR

Aaron Bridges | Mark Levesley
Janet Williams | Chris Workman

Contents

Contents

Contents

How to use this book

Introduction: Each topic starts with a question. The question should help you to think about what you are going to study. You should be able to answer this question by the time you finish the topic.

Key words: Important scientific words are in bold the first time that they appear in a section. You will also find a glossary at the back of the book. The glossary has a definition of each of these words.

Quick check questions occur throughout the topic. These will help you and your teacher to check you have understood the material so far.

Fact boxes give you some interesting facts linked to the section.

SECTION 1

Cells and life processes

1.1 Characteristics of living things

What is an **organism**? The term is used to describe a separate object which carries out living processes. There are about two million different types of organisms.

How can you tell if something is living or dead? Is a robot alive? There are seven **characteristics** of living things. If something does all seven of these over its lifetime then it is living.

The seven key characteristics of living things are:

Movement. This is a change of position needed to respond to the surroundings. Animals move their whole body from place to place but plants can only move parts of their body.

Figure 1.1 *Movement*.

1 It is easy to see how large animals move. Suggest how smaller organisms such as microorganisms might 'move'. [Total 2]

food + oxygen → energy + carbon dioxide + water

Figure 1.2 *Respiration*.

Respiration. This is the release of energy from food or stored chemicals in cells for immediate use by the organism.

The male Emperor moth can detect the scent of a female from up to 11 km away. Special cells on the male antennae can detect single molecules of the scent.

Sensitivity. Individuals need information from the environment to react and carry out the other living processes. They respond to different stimuli. Plants will grow in the direction light is coming from and animals may move in response to seeing something coming towards them.

Figure 1.3 *Sensitivity*.

---

2 Food and nutrition

Summary

- Plants get their energy from sunlight.
- Photosynthesis needs chlorophyll to trap li
- Photosynthesis combines water with carbo
- Glucose and oxygen are produced by phot
- Glucose can be used to make starch, cellul

Questions

1 Copy and complete the following sentences. Plants make their own food using _____ energy, carbon dioxide from the air and _____ from the soil. The process is called _____. _____ (e.g. glucose) is produced and used to make all other substances the plant needs. _____ is a waste product. Leaves look _____ because they contain chlorophyll. The _____ traps the light energy. Most chlorophyll is in the _____ cells near the top surface of a leaf. [Total

2 Give two functions of the roots of a plant. [Total

3 List the raw materials and substances needed for photosynthesis. In a second column state where the plant gets the substance from. [Total

4 List the products of photosynthesis. In a second column state where the substance goes to when it moves out of the chloroplast. [Total

5 Name five substances that plants make from the glucose produced in photosynthesis. [Total

6 A shoot of pondweed was placed in a boiling tube of pond water. A bench lamp with a 60 W bulb shining o the tube was placed 20 cm away. An oxygen probe wa

Summary boxes: Each topic ends with a summary which will help you to draw together what you have just read. They will also help you revise.

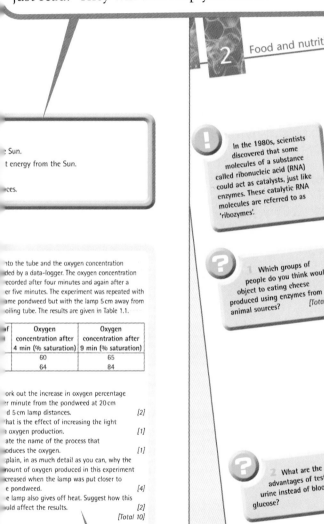

e Sun.

t energy from the Sun.

ces.

nto the tube and the oxygen concentration ded by a data-logger. The oxygen concentration ecorded after four minutes and again after a er five minutes. The experiment was repeated with ame pondweed but with the lamp 5 cm away from oiling tube. The results are given in Table 1.1.

f	Oxygen concentration after 4 min (% saturation)	Oxygen concentration after 9 min (% saturation)
	60	65
	64	84

ork out the increase in oxygen percentage r minute from the pondweed at 20 cm d 5 cm lamp distances. [2]

hat is the effect of increasing the light oxygen production. [1]

ate the name of the process that oduces the oxygen. [1]

plain, in as much detail as you can, why the nount of oxygen produced in this experiment creased when the lamp was put closer to e pondweed. [4]

e lamp also gives off heat. Suggest how this uld affect the results. [2]

[Total 10]

2 Food and nutrition

Enzymes

Enzymes in action

The properties of enzymes make them very useful in many areas of industry, and they may also be used in various ways in the home. Their ability to speed up very specific reactions under low temperatures and pressures means they can save a lot of time, energy and money.

Cheese production

Humans have been making cheese for thousands of years. The methods used have changed a great deal, but they have always relied on the action of enzymes in one way or another. Enzymes from the stomach lining of slaughtered calves or pigs were very widely used during the twentieth century, but technological advances have meant that microbes are now the main source of enzymes for use in cheese manufacture. Microbes can be grown in large vessels, and the enzymes they produce can be extracted from the liquid in which the microbes grow.

! In the 1980s, scientists discovered that some molecules of a substance called ribonucleic acid (RNA) could act as catalysts, just like enzymes. These catalytic RNA molecules are referred to as 'ribozymes'.

? **1** Which groups of people do you think would object to eating cheese produced using enzymes from animal sources? [Total 2]

Medical uses

One of the symptoms of diabetes is the presence of glucose in urine. This can happen when blood glucose levels are too high for the kidneys to cope with. Doctors use strips called Clinistix™ to test urine for glucose, as it is an easy and quick way to tell if someone might have diabetes. Clinistix™ contain two enzymes and a substance that changes colour. The strips work in the following way:

a The stick is dipped into a urine sample.
b If there is any glucose in the sample, the first enzyme in the strip acts on it, producing a new chemical.
c The second enzyme in the strip then catalyses a reaction between this new chemical and the colour-changing substance in the strip.
d The resulting colour can be compared to a chart, from which the urine glucose level can be read off.

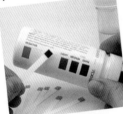
Figure 5.6 *A packet of clinistix™.*

? **2** What are the advantages of testing urine instead of blood for glucose? [Total 2]

58

Question boxes: There are question boxes at the end of each chapter and each topic. The questions towards the end of each box may be a little harder, to help you to see how well you have understood the work.

Some questions have an **R** next to them. These are research questions. You will need to use other books or the Internet to write a full answer to these questions.

In the end of section questions some questions have a **P** next to them. These questions can be used to help you plan practical investigations.

How Science Works pages: At the end of each section there are pages that look at How Science Works. Each topic on these pages is linked to part of the work in the section you have just read.

1.1 Characteristics of living things

What is an **organism**? The term is used to describe a separate object which carries out living processes. There are about two million different types of organisms.

How can you tell if something is living or dead? Is a robot alive? There are seven **characteristics** of living things. If something does all seven of these over its lifetime then it is living.

The seven key characteristics of living things are:

Movement. This is a change of position needed to respond to the surroundings. Animals move their whole body from place to place but plants can only move parts of their body.

? 1 It is easy to see how large animals move. Suggest how smaller organisms such as microorganisms might 'move'.
[Total 2]

Figure 1.1 *Movement.*

Respiration. This is the release of energy from food or stored chemicals in cells for immediate use by the organism.

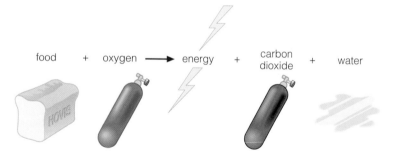

food + oxygen ⟶ energy + carbon dioxide + water

Figure 1.2 *Respiration.*

! The male Emperor moth can detect the scent of a female from up to 11 km away. Special cells on the male antennae can detect single molecules of the scent.

Sensitivity. Individuals need information from the environment to react and carry out the other living processes. They respond to different stimuli. Plants will grow in the direction light is coming from and animals may move in response to seeing something coming towards them.

Figure 1.3 *Sensitivity.*

Figure 1.4 *Growth.*

Growth. Individuals start off small and grow until 'adulthood'. Animals often have a maximum size but plants continue to get bigger over all of their life.

Reproduction. This creates new individuals. They replace those that have died and ensure the survival of the species.

Figure 1.5 *Reproduction.*

Excretion. This is the removal of waste produced by chemical reactions in cells of the individual. This includes gases (carbon dioxide), special compounds (urea) and water. Plants excrete toxins into their leaves. They then drop the leaves in autumn.

Nutrition (feeding). The organism must take in energy to keep it alive. Plants take in simple compounds and light to make their own chemicals. Animals eat plants or other animals to get complex compounds from them.

Figure 1.7 *Nutrition.*

Figure 1.6 *Excretion.*

These seven points are often remembered by a mnemonic, e.g. MRS GREN. Can you think of another mnemonic that is special to you and your friends?

Can you work out if a car is alive? It can move from place to place, it feeds on petrol, takes in oxygen and gives out waste substances. Its engine burns fuel and some cars can react to the environment by turning on lights if it is dark. However it does not grow or reproduce so it isn't alive.

> **!** A camel's hump is full of fat, not water. The fat acts as a good food store. The fat is combined with oxygen to release energy.

The list of processes shows that there are differences between plants and animals. This is because of the way they feed. A plant must trap enough light energy from the Sun by spreading out its leaves over a large area. Movement is not necessary for this form of nutrition, unlike typical animal nutrition. A comparison of the features of animals and plants is in Table 1.1.

Animals	Plants
Move whole of the body from place to place.	Only move parts of the plant.
Compact structure.	Branching structure with large surface area for both leaves and roots.
Usually grow to a maximum size.	Grow throughout their lives.
Variety of colours.	Leaves usually green.
Respond to stimuli quickly.	Respond to stimuli slowly.
Complex behaviour patterns.	Very simple behaviour.
Most animals reproduce by adult moving to find another adult.	Reproduce by pollen being moved by some agent (e.g. wind) to reach the stigma of another individual plant.
Young move away from parents by their own movement.	Young (seeds) spread by another organism or the wind.

Table 1.1 *A comparison of the features of animals and plants.*

Summary

- There are about two million different types of living things.
- Living things are described by seven life processes (MRS GREN).
- Animals and plants differ because of the way they get their food.

Questions

1 Copy and complete the following sentences.
Animals can _____ from place to place but plants only move part of their bodies. The release of energy inside cells is called _____. Sensitivity is important for organisms so that they can _____ to stimuli. Organisms increase in size when they _____. Sexual reproduction requires two _____ and special sex cells. Some plants can _____ from one parent, e.g. when a new plant develops from a cutting. Waste produced by the cells of organisms must be removed. This is called _____. Carbon dioxide, water and urine are examples of animal _____. _____ get rid of poisons when they drop their _____. _____ feed on other organisms but plants can make food out of non-living substances. The intake of the food is called _____.   [Total 6]

2 Copy out and match up the life process with the correct description.

respiration	change of position of part or whole of organism
nutrition	production of new individuals
movement	removal of waste products
reproduction	intake of chemicals for energy and growth
excretion	the release of energy in cells

[Total 5]

3 List three things that are excreted from an animal and one that is excreted from a plant.   [Total 4]

4 Explain how each of the following get their food:
a) plants   [2]
b) animals.   [1]
                                                               [Total 3]

5 a) Suggest two substances or items that you think are similar to living things but do not fit all of the seven criteria.   [1]
b) Explain how they do not fit all of the seven criteria.   [2]
                                                               [Total 3]

6 An alien landed on Earth and tried to work out if a washing machine was alive. What questions should it ask to find out if it is living?   [Total 7]

7 Describe the main difference in form between animals and plants and explain how the form helps the organism to live.   [Total 4]

8 Suggest how microorganisms fit each of the seven criteria for living things.   [Total 7]

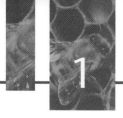
1.2 Where organisms live

How are organisms adapted to the place they live? A polar bear could not live in a hot desert because it would get too hot. A fish cannot live out of water because it cannot get oxygen from the air. Each type of organism is able to live in one kind of environment.

Habitats

To us the Earth is a very special place. Life may have started about 3500 million years ago and organisms are now able to live in most areas of the sea, land or air. Very few areas are entirely free of life. The surface of the Earth where living things can survive is called the **biosphere**.

Organisms live in specific places in the biosphere. The place where each organism can live is called its **habitat**. This is a local **environment** which usually describes the main type of plant or the structure of the environment e.g. a woodland, a pond, the seashore. The organism must be adapted to the special conditions existing in that area. Different species (types of organisms) will each be **adapted** to that particular habitat and form an interacting group – a **community** of organisms.

The organisms interact with the non-living environment. The combination of the community of organisms and the non-living (physical) environment is called the **ecosystem**. Ecosystems are often grouped together on a global scale to give **biomes** (Figure 2.2). These are large areas where similar types of plants can grow.

Figure 2.1 *A deciduous woodland habitat.*

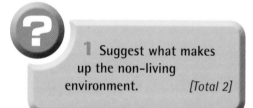

?

1 Suggest what makes up the non-living environment. [Total 2]

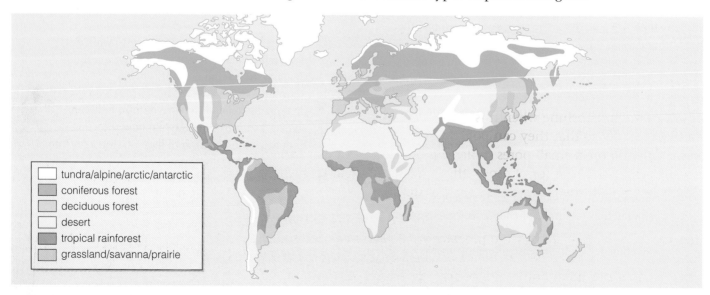

- tundra/alpine/arctic/antarctic
- coniferous forest
- deciduous forest
- desert
- tropical rainforest
- grassland/savanna/prairie

Figure 2.2 *The major biomes of the world.*

Adaptations

Each organism is adapted to live in the habitat where it is found. The adaptations often appear strange to us but are essential to the organism. In the sea, a blue whale has tail flukes to help it move through the oceans, with small arms (seen as flippers) to help direct the whale in the water. It feeds by filtering the sea water for small organisms which it swallows using its strong tongue. Its nostril (blowhole) is on the top of its head to allow breathing when swimming at the surface. It also has a special blood circulation system to ensure that the brain and heart muscle have the best oxygen supply to conserve 'air' during a long dive.

Figure 2.3 *Blue whale.*

Some cactus plants look like spiky balls instead of a 'normal' plant, but this helps them to survive in the desert. Leaves have been reduced to spines which are present to protect the cactus from animals eating it. Only the green ribbed stem is used to capture sunlight.

The ribs create some areas of shade so that carbon dioxide can enter for photosynthesis without the cactus losing too much water. The stem has a small surface area which cuts down water loss. The roots are usually long and spread over a wide area so that if it rains water can be absorbed quickly and stored within the stem.

These are just two examples of the ways organisms can be adapted to the physical environment. Some organisms need to change during the day and throughout the year to take advantage of the different conditions.

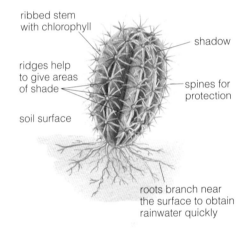

ribbed stem with chlorophyll

shadow

ridges help to give areas of shade

spines for protection

soil surface

roots branch near the surface to obtain rainwater quickly

Figure 2.4 *Sea urchin cactus.*

Daily changes

Organisms respond to the daily changes in physical factors to maximise their survival in the habitat. A crocus plant will open its flower in bright sunshine when it is most likely to be warm enough for insects to fly so that they can pollinate the flower. In sunlight, leaves will also open small pores (holes) on the surface so that carbon dioxide can be taken in for photosynthesis. Later in the day, when the light is less bright, the pores close to stop water loss.

Different organisms are active at different times of the day so that they can protect themselves from predators and gather enough food. For example, a bat has a better chance of catching insects at night when it can sense them but it cannot be seen. During the day the bat must hide in its roost to avoid its own predators.

> **!**
> Zoos help to breed endangered species so that they do not become extinct. Sometimes they can release the individuals back into the wild. For example, red kites have been released in North Wales and red-crowned cranes in Japan and north-east China.

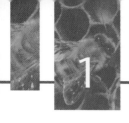
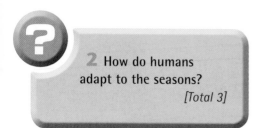

2 How do humans adapt to the seasons?

[Total 3]

Spiders and insects are among the oldest types of animals on the earth – about 300 million years old.

Seasonal changes

In an oak wood you can see how the organisms have adapted to the seasons. The oak trees burst into leaf in late spring so that they gain the maximum amount of sunshine in the warmest conditions. Underneath the oak trees, holly trees have very thick dark green leaves to absorb as much light as possible in the shade of the bigger trees above.

Squirrels are active during the day as they need light to collect their food. At night they defend themselves by resting and hiding from the nocturnal predators in the wood. The squirrels remain active all summer and find enough food to raise a family.

As autumn approaches wood mice store more of their food energy as fat to last them through the winter. When the air temperature falls the wood mouse's respiration slows down and its body temperature decreases. It **hibernates** to save energy during the cold months.

The oak tree loses its leaves to make sure that the branches are not damaged by stronger winds and so that the delicate leaves are not damaged by frost. Another advantage to the oak tree is that waste chemicals can also be lost from the tree in the falling leaves. The smaller holly tree can now receive more light and so continues to grow slowly using its better-protected leaves.

In spring, as the temperature increases again but before the oak leaves open, bluebells grow using food stored in their bulbs. They flower early so that the insects and wind can get to the flowers without hindrance from the oak tree leaves. The leaves of the bluebell use the light energy getting to the woodland floor to create a new bulb for the next year ... and so on for many years.

The flowers of the bluebell are adapted to attract insects. They are colourful and perfumed. Insects arrive to get food as a reward but they also carry the pollen from one flower to the next. Each flower must only give the insect a small amount of food so that it will fly to another flower instead of going to the hive or nest. The flower and the insect developed together millions of years ago. The insect cannot live without the flowers and the flowers cannot reproduce without the insects. This is an example of co-evolution and the beneficial way organisms can interact within a community.

Figure 2.5 *Insect pollinating a flower.*

Summary

- The biosphere is divided into biomes.
- An ecosystem consists of the non-living environment and living organisms.
- A habitat is the place where an individual organism lives.
- The group of organisms living in a habitat is a community.
- Organisms are adapted to the habitat in which they live.
- Daily and seasonal changes occur in the habitat. Organisms respond to these changes.

Questions

1 Copy and complete the following sentences. The surface of the earth where living things can survive is called the _____. The organisms can only live in the areas to which they are suited. The area that one type of organism is found in is called the _____. Several different types of organism living together is called a _____. The physical parts of the habitat, e.g. light, wind, temperature, and the community of organisms make up the _____. *[Total 2]*

2 What is the biosphere? *[Total 1]*

3 Explain the difference between a community and an ecosystem. *[Total 2]*

4 Describe how a cactus is adapted to prevent it losing water. *[Total 3]*

5 Suggest how an oak tree survives conditions in winter. *[Total 2]*

6 Explain why a flower produces only a small amount of nectar (food for insects) at a time. *[Total 2]*

7 An investigation into where woodlice live used a chamber where half was damp and half dry. The 20 woodlice in the chamber could move freely between the areas. After 10 minutes in the chamber 16 woodlice were in the damp area and 4 in the dry.
  a) Calculate the percentage of woodlice in the damp area. *[1]*
  b) Why do you think more woodlice were in the damp area? *[1]*
  c) The surface of a woodlouse allows water to pass through easily. Why is it important to stay in a damp area? *[1]*
  d) If a woodlouse stayed in a dry atmosphere for several hours, what would happen to the mass of the animal? Try to explain why. *[2]*
  e) What type of habitat is the most likely place for you to find woodlice? *[2]*
  [Total 7]

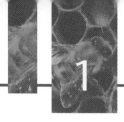
1.3 Organs

How does an organism allow all of the different life processes to go on at the same time? An individual or organism must be complex to carry out all of the living processes needed to survive. Each process is carried out by different parts of the body.

Imagine if everyone in your class tried to do their favourite subject at the same time in the same place. Trying to do a biology experiment next to someone speaking French and someone else kicking a ball around the room is not very efficient. Each activity may get done but they interfere with each other. The school's answer is to create special areas for different studies and to co-ordinate the movement of pupils between the areas. Plants and animals are co-ordinated in the same way.

The body is divided into **organs**. Each carries out one major function. The organs are often arranged into **organ systems** so that several associated functions are co-ordinated. The product of one activity can be passed directly onto another for further treatment. The activities are controlled by the body itself. For example, if you smell food you produce saliva so that you can start to break up the food and swallow it. The saliva helps the food get to your stomach. In the stomach, the food is changed again. The use of energy in the body is much more efficient if each job is done in many small steps.

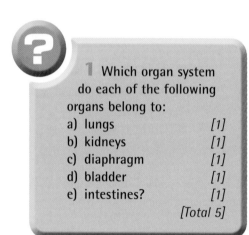

?

1 Which organ system do each of the following organs belong to:
a) lungs   [1]
b) kidneys   [1]
c) diaphragm   [1]
d) bladder   [1]
e) intestines?   [1]
                              [Total 5]

Digestive system

The digestive system takes in, breaks down, and absorbs the soluble products in food and removes undigested food. This is the way all energy and nutrients enter the body.

Breathing system

This consists of the organs associated with breathing and gas exchange. The breathing system helps supply oxygen for respiration and remove carbon dioxide, e.g. lungs in mammals, gills in fish. The leaves of plants have the same function.

Circulatory system

This transports all soluble materials around the body. The heart pumps the blood which circulates in blood vessels. Plants move water and dissolved chemicals through vascular bundles (veins) in the stem, leaves and roots.

Excretory system

Waste produced by the cells is removed from the body. Excretion usually refers to the removal of urine by the kidneys but should also include the lungs and skin as organs that get rid of wastes. Plants excrete waste through their leaves.

Nervous system

This controls the organism's response to stimuli. It includes the sense organs, brain and nerves. In plants there is no equivalent but there are sensitive regions, e.g. tips of shoots are sensitive to light.

Skeletal system

Made up of bones and muscles for support and movement. The bones can also protect the body. In plants the vascular bundles have supporting tissue next to them. Plant cells use water and the cell wall to support them.

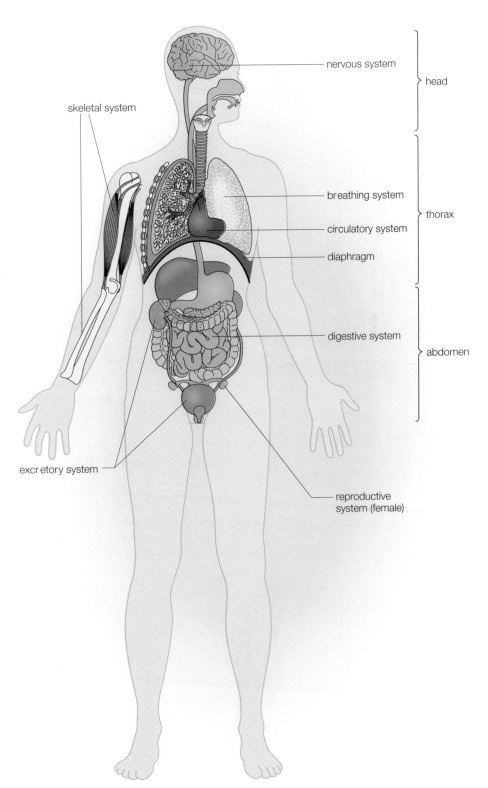

Figure 3.1 *Human organ systems.*

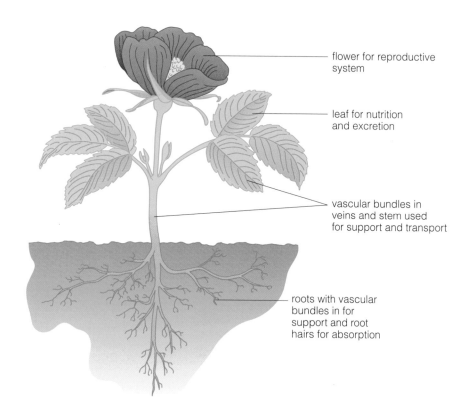

flower for reproductive system

leaf for nutrition and excretion

vascular bundles in veins and stem used for support and transport

roots with vascular bundles in for support and root hairs for absorption

Reproductive system

Organs associated with production of sex cells and development of the young. Male organs are different from female organs and are usually in different individuals for animals. In plants both sex structures are usually in the flowers.

Figure 3.2 *Plant organ systems.*

Figure 3.3 *Relationship between organ systems, organs, tissues and cells.*

Each organ is made up of a series of tissues. The **tissues** are groups of **cells** which look alike and carry out a single function in the organ e.g. the muscle cells of the heart contract but the blood cells carry the oxygen. Each cell of a tissue has a similar structure. For the different functions to be carried out the cells must be specialised. This makes the cell better at carrying out the task.

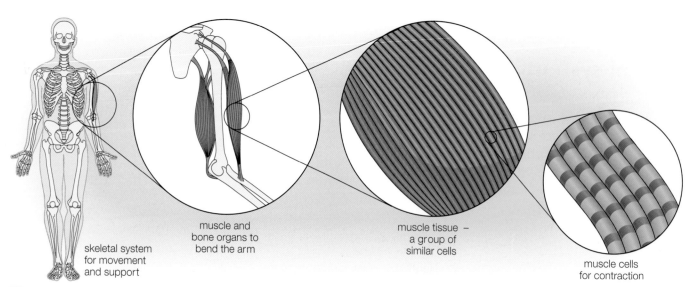

skeletal system for movement and support

muscle and bone organs to bend the arm

muscle tissue – a group of similar cells

muscle cells for contraction

Summary

- A tissue is a group of similar cells.
- An organ is made up of tissues, each of which carry out a particular function.
- Organs are grouped into organ systems to make the functions more efficient.
- The body of a mammal is divided into the head, thorax and abdomen.

Questions

1 Copy and complete the following sentences.
Organ systems are a series of _____ carrying out related activities so that one overall function is done more efficiently. The substances _____ from one organ can be used by the next to complete the function of the organ _____. The organs are made from groups of similar cells called a _____. *[Total 2]*

2 Place the following items in order of increasing size:
digestive system   organism
cell   stomach   muscle tissue   *[Total 1]*

3 What are the functions of the following organs:
a) flower   *[1]*
b) root   *[1]*
c) heart   *[1]*
d) lungs?   *[1]*
[Total 4]

4 Which organs are involved in the following processes? There may be more than one for each process. Include plants where applicable.
a) excretion of urea   *[1]*
b) thinking   *[1]*
c) movement   *[2]*
d) absorbing energy into the 'body'.   *[3]*
[Total 7]

5 Explain why organs are arranged into organ systems.   *[Total 2]*

6 The human chest is also known as the thorax.
a) What divides it from the abdomen?   *[1]*
b) Make a table to list the organs in each of the head, thorax, abdomen and limbs.   *[12]*
[Total 13]

7 Describe how the digestive system does some of the opposite jobs to the excretory system.   *[Total 2]*

8 Flowers have organs just as animals do too.
a) Name three different plant organs.   *[3]*
b) Explain what an organ is, using the words 'tissues' and 'cells' in your answer.   *[3]*
c) Why do you think bacteria cannot have organs?   *[2]*
[Total 8]

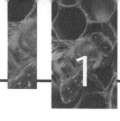

1.4 Cells

What is a cell? In 1665 Robert Hooke used a microscope to examine cork from an oak tree. He saw tiny boxes similar to a monk's cell (which is a small room) so he named the structures 'cells'. All living things are made up of these cells but what is inside them?

Cell structure

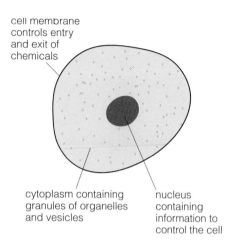

Figure 4.1 *An animal cell.*

cell membrane controls entry and exit of chemicals

cytoplasm containing granules of organelles and vesicles

nucleus containing information to control the cell

An organism is made up of **cells**. It is really like a house made of different components such as bricks, wood and glass. Each small component is arranged in a special way, and carries out a particular job, so that the house becomes a complete functioning unit. All the cells have the same overall structure that allows them to carry out the basic life processes but some are changed to carry out special functions. All cells have the following structures.

- The **cell membrane** surrounds the cell. It is very thin and cannot be seen using a light microscope. It holds the substances in the cell and acts as a 'gatekeeper' to control the chemicals that can enter or leave. The membrane is flexible and will fold or bend but if too much strain is put onto it the membrane will break and the cell dies.

- Inside the cell membrane is a soup of chemicals and complex structures which carry out all of the activities of the cell. It is called the **cytoplasm** and is usually seen under the light microscope to have granules in it. These are **organelles**, specialised areas of the cell where particular jobs are carried out. The granules can also be small **vesicles** which store food reserves or break down unwanted substances. The cytoplasm is colourless but the consistency can vary from a thick gel to runny. In some cells, like the pond organism *Amoeba*, different regions of the cytoplasm have different consistencies.

Figure 4.2 *Human cheek cells (flattened epithelial cells) stained and magnified 200 times to make them clearer. Note the light blue coloured nucleus, granular cytoplasm and folded edges. They are very thin cells. Several layers of the cells make up the inside of the cheek surface.*

Each cell has a **nucleus**, to control the activities of the cell. It stores all the information in coded form in molecules of **DNA** (deoxyribonucleic acid) found in the **chromosomes**. Relevant parts of the code are copied and then sent to the cytoplasm. There it is decoded so that the required action is carried out. For example, milk must be made in the mammary gland cell so the codes for milk production are sent to the cytoplasm to make it.

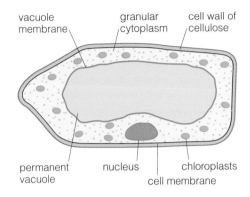

Figure 4.3 *A plant cell.*

Plant cells

Both plant and animal cells have all the three features described already but plant cells have extra features.

- The **cell wall** is made by the plant cell from a special chemical called **cellulose**. This chemical has long fibres and is very strong. It forms a wall on the outside of the cell membrane to support the cell and stop the contents bursting when it is full of water. It is quite thick and can easily be seen through a light microscope. The plant cells appear to be separated from each other. The cell wall allows substances to pass between the fibres so that they can enter or leave the cell freely.

- The **permanent vacuole** is a bag-like structure containing a dilute solution. It is seen in the middle of the cytoplasm. Its functions include the storage of waste substances, or giving colour to the cells e.g. the red of beetroot. It will also take in water from the surroundings of the cell to create a pressure against the cell wall. This is like a football when it is blown up or a fizzy drink bottle when it is shaken. The cell becomes very firm and is able to support the plant without a hard skeleton. The permanent vacuole is separated from the cytoplasm by a membrane similar to the one surrounding the cell.

- **Chloroplasts** are the structjures that contain the green pigment chlorophyll. They are not found in every plant cell but there are many in leaf cells. They are seen as small green dots in the cytoplasm of the cells. They trap light energy to make food for the plant. They are separated from the cytoplasm by a membrane but chemicals can move between the two very easily.

Figure 4.4 *The epidermal cells are separated by cellulose cell walls. The nucleus is at the side of the cells. No vacuole can be seen as there is no coloured substance in it. The cytoplasm looks rough due to the different organelles and storage substances. There are no chloroplasts as the cells are from inside the onion bulb.*

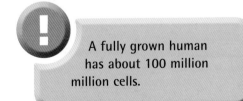

A fully grown human has about 100 million million cells.

1 a) Draw and label a diagram of a plant cell.

[Total 4]

b) What are the functions of the following organelles:

i)   nucleus
ii) cell membrane
iii) cell wall
iv) vacuole
v)   chloroplast
vi) cytoplasm?

[6]

[Total 10]

Why are plant and animal cells different?

An animal needs to move from place to place to catch its food so it needs to be light. Some of the cells must also bend (muscle cells get shorter and fatter) so that the organism can move. The animal must have some sort of rigid skeleton to attach its muscles to and give it the required shape but individual cells do not need support which would be heavy. Therefore the cells are very weak because they do not have a cell wall. They have a simple basic plan but can be modified to carry out specialised functions. Animal cells need to absorb simple but ready made chemicals as their food.

On the other hand a plant needs only to stay still and have a large surface area to trap sunlight energy. It has cells that are supported by the cell wall so a skeleton is not needed. As long as there is enough water in the cells the plant stands upright. The chloroplasts trap the light energy and the cells can use the stored energy directly.

Animal cells	Plant cells
nucleus present	nucleus present
cell membrane	cell membrane
cytoplasm	cytoplasm
no chloroplasts	chloroplasts often present
no cell wall	cell wall made of cellulose
only temporary vacuoles	permanent sap vacuole
variety of shapes	regular boxes in appearance
usually smaller	usually larger
food stored mainly as glycogen*	food stored mainly as starch*

Table 4.1 *Similarities and differences between cells. (* glycogen and starch are both made of glucose molecules linked together in a particular way)*

Unicellular organisms

Animals and plants are made up of many cells. They are **multicellular**. However they are not the only types of organism. Others are single-celled (**unicellular**). Some unicellular organisms have a nucleus surrounded by a nuclear membrane (like the nucleus in an animal or plant cell). There are also organisms with a very simple structure. These include bacteria. They are different because the DNA is in the cytoplasm and not in a separate nucleus. Scientists think that they were the first types of cells to evolve.

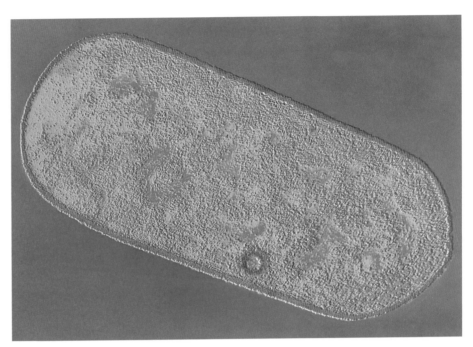

Figure 4.5 *Bacillus bacterium cell.*

Bacteria show this type of structure. They are very small (less than 0.002 mm long). They do not have a nucleus but there is a single circular chromosome which controls the activities of the cell. Some of them have fine hairs sticking out called flagella which help the cells to move. They divide into two to reproduce. This can be done as often as every 20 minutes so the numbers increase very quickly.

Bacterial cells	Animal and plant cells
no separate nucleus	have a distinct nucleus surrounded by a nuclear membrane
single chromosome made only of DNA	several chromosomes made of DNA and other chemicals
no organelles bound by membranes	separate organelles in the cytoplasm
usually smaller than 0.002 mm	usually larger than 0.010 mm

Table 4.2 *Differences between bacterial and animal and plant cells.*

Most bacteria are not harmful to humans, but, during the Great Plague of 1665, (which was caused by bacteria carried by fleas) 68 956 people died from plague in London alone.

Summary

- Organisms are made up of cells.
- The cell membrane controls which chemicals enter or leave the cell.
- The nucleus contains the coded information to control the cell. It contains chromosomes of DNA.
- The cytoplasm is where reactions take place in the cell.
- Animal cells do not have cell walls, permanent vacuoles or chloroplasts but plant cells do.
- Bacteria do not have a nucleus but the information is in a circular chromosome of DNA.

Questions

1 Copy and complete the following sentences. Organisms are made up of tiny units called _____. Cells have a _____ to control their activities. The information for control is arranged in chromosomes made of a molecule called _____. Most chemical reactions take place in the cytoplasm. The cell _____ controls what enters and leaves the cell. _____ cells also have a cell wall to support the shape of the cell, a _____ vacuole full of a solution to push against the cell wall and some have _____ to make food for the plant. Bacteria are tiny, simple cells that do not have a proper _____. *[Total 4]*

2 State the major functions of the following parts of a cell:
a) nucleus *[1]*
b) membrane *[1]*
c) cytoplasm. *[1]*
[Total 3]

3 What are the functions of a) chloroplasts and b) the cell wall of a plant cell? *[Total 2]*

4 Copy the diagram of a plant cell shown in Figure 4.6 and label the parts indicated. Underline the labels that you would also find in an animal cell. **Figure 4.6** *[Total 7]*

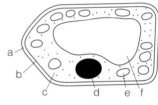

5 List four differences between plant and animal cells. *[Total 4]*

6 Where would the red colour be found in a cell from a petal of a rose flower. *[Total 1]*

7 Copy and complete Table 4.3 to show the differences between bacteria and plant or animal cells. *[Total 3]*

Table 4.3

Bacterial cells	Plant or animal cells
no nucleus	
smaller than 0.002 mm	
	contain organelles in the cytoplasm

1.5 Specialised cells

How different are some of the cells in your body? Organs are needed by an organism to carry out life processes efficiently. If they have different functions then the tissues and cells which make them up must be specialised.

Animal cells have the same three basic structures (cell membrane, nucleus and cytoplasm) but the organelles (specialist regions) and substances in the cytoplasm can vary to allow a cell to carry out different functions. The shape of a cell can also change.

Plant cells change in a similar way but the variety of different shapes is restricted by the cell wall.

Animal cell specialisms

Ciliated epithelial cells are found lining the windpipe, bronchi and oviducts. They move **mucus** (a thin layer of sticky fluid produced by cells) along the surface. The cilia are fine hair like structures produced by the cytoplasm. They beat in a rhythm to move the mucus and anything in it along the surface like a conveyor belt. Bacteria are removed from the lungs and the ovum is moved down the oviduct by these ciliated cells.

Smoke from cigarettes stops the cilia working (see Section 7.1).

1 Write down a list of as many different types of animal cell as you can think of. *[Total 6]*

2 Some single-celled organisms that live in pond water are covered by a coat of cilia. Suggest what these cilia might be used for. *[Total 2]*

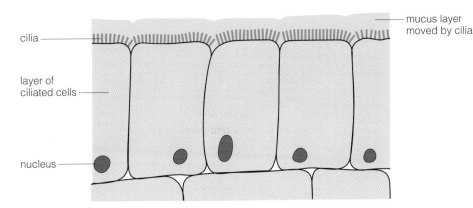

Figure 5.1 *Ciliated epithelial cells.*

cilia

mucus layer moved by cilia

layer of ciliated cells

nucleus

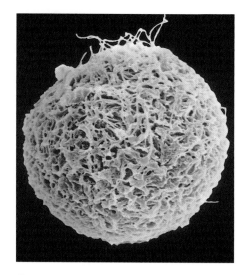

Figure 5.2 *Sperm cells surrounding an ovum.*

Sex cells (**gametes**) must also be specialised because they must fuse together to form a new individual. This means that they must have half the normal number of chromosomes in each nucleus. When a **sperm** fertilises an **ovum** the normal number is restored and the new cell can divide to produce all the other cells in the organism. The sperm must be able to swim to the ovum so it has a tail (this is like a large cilium). The sperm also has lots of energy-releasing organelles at the junction between the head and tail to power the tail. The ovum is much larger than the sperm because there needs to be a large amount of food stored for a fertilised egg to use when it develops.

Red blood cells do not have a nucleus. This is so that there is more room for the molecule **haemoglobin** to carry oxygen. Their biconcave disc shape allows red blood cells to be flexible so they can be pushed through the narrowest blood vessels. Their shape also gives them a large surface area for gas exchange.

White blood cells do have a nucleus and some can change shape to squeeze between other cells and also to move around a foreign object or cell (e.g. bacterium) and engulf it. The cytoplasm then digests the foreign object. This is one way that an animal can defend itself against disease (see Section 3.3).

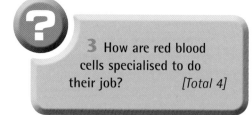

3 How are red blood cells specialised to do their job? *[Total 4]*

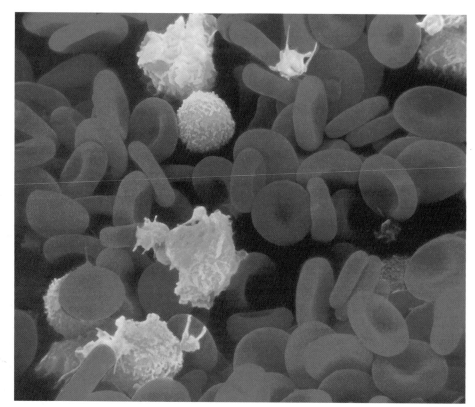

Figure 5.3 *Scanning electron micrograph of red and white blood cells. The red blood cells are thinner in the middle (biconcave). The white blood cells look yellow in this micrograph.*

Nerve cells are specialised to carry electrical impulses. They are very long so the impulse is carried over a large distance without interruption. The branched ends of a nerve cell allow many connections to other nerve cells so that the impulse can be co-ordinated.

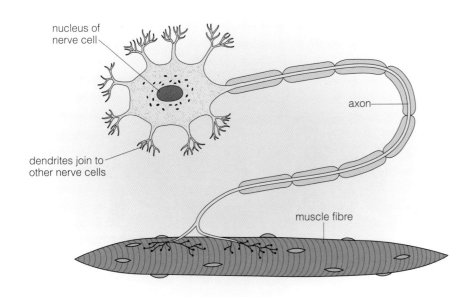

nucleus of nerve cell

axon

dendrites join to other nerve cells

muscle fibre

> An impulse travels along a nerve to the leg at 100 m/s. Those in the brain only travel at about 8 m/s.

Figure 5.4 *The nerve cell carries an impulse to make the muscle cells contract.*

The muscle cell is also long to help it contract further. It has proteins in the cytoplasm which can slide over each other so the cell contracts. There are many organelles to release the energy needed for contraction.

Plant cell specialisms

The **palisade** cells have many chloroplasts to capture light energy for the leaf to make the food for the plant (Figure 5.5). The cell wall and other parts of the cytoplasm are transparent to let the light through. The oblong shape allows many of the cells to pack closely together at the top of the leaf so that as much light as possible is trapped. Palisade cells use the light energy to turn carbon dioxide and water into glucose and oxygen.

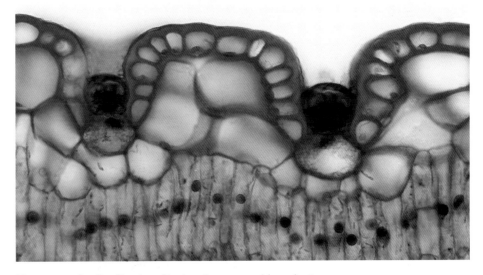

Figure 5.5 *Leaf palisade cells showing many chloroplasts.*

The surface area of a **root hair cell** is increased by the 'hair' so that more water can be absorbed into the root. There are no chloroplasts or storage structures so the cells are transparent and seem to lack structure. However, they have organelles to release energy so that some mineral salts can be actively absorbed into the cell from the soil.

?

4 Why do root hair cells not contain chloroplasts? *[Total 2]*

5 Explain how palisade cells are adapted for photosynthesis. *[Total 2]*

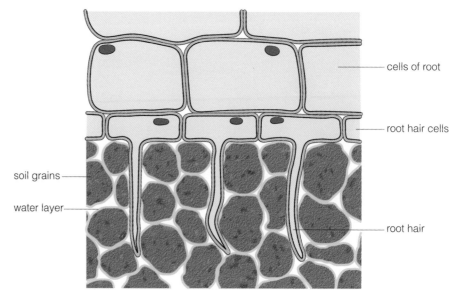

Figure 5.6 *Root hair cells have a large surface area for absorption.*

In plants, water is carried in long thin hollow tubes called **xylem vessels**. The vessels are formed from a column of cells but the end walls, cytoplasm and nucleus have all been destroyed. The water can flow freely from one 'cell' to the next.

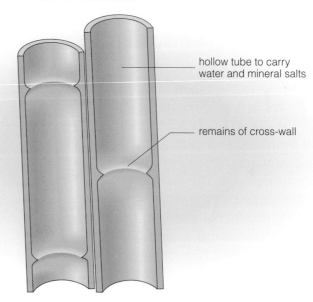

Figure 5.7 *Xylem vessels have no end walls, cytoplasm or nucleus.*

Summary

- An organism is made of organs, each having many tissues.
- The cells of most tissues in an organism are specialised.
- Specialisms allow each cell to carry out its function more efficiently.
- The structure of a cell indicates the type of function it does.

Questions

1 Copy and complete the following sentences.
Cells differ from each other so that they can do different _____. A _____ _____ cell has fine hairs (cilia) which are waved in a rhythm so that mucus can be moved. Sperm cells have a whip-like _____ to move them through a liquid. Red blood cells do not have a nucleus but the _____ has lots of haemoglobin to carry more oxygen. _____ cells are long to carry impulses quickly from one place to another. Plant cells like _____ hair cells have a long projection to increase the surface area for absorption of water. _____ cells are hollow tubes to let the water flow easily through them. All of these adaptations make the cells better at carrying out their function. *[Total 4]*

2 Explain, with as much detail as you can, how bacteria are moved out of the lungs. *[Total 3]*

3 How is a ciliated epithelial cell different from a squamous epithelial cell (lining cell of the cheek)? (Hint: See p14) *[Total 2]*

4 State similarities and differences between red blood cells and xylem vessels. *[Total 6]*

5 Describe how a palisade cell is adapted to make food for the plant. *[Total 3]*

6 What are the advantages of cells being specialised? *[Total 2]*

7 Suggest two reasons why there are more types of animal cell than plant cell. *[Total 2]*

8 The cell shown right is found in the intestines, where it helps absorb digested substances into the body.
a) What is the main visible specialisation for absorption of substances that is visible in this cell? *[1]*
b) Explain how the specialisation helps it perform its job. *[2]*
[Total 3]

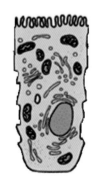

Transplants

A matter of life or death

Figure 6.1 *A human kidney being transplanted.*

Sometimes organs can stop working properly, either as a result of disease or injury. An organ transplant is one solution to this problem. It involves replacing the damaged organ with a healthier one from another person's body. The replacement organ (**donor organ**) may come from someone who has recently died, or in some cases it may come from a living donor.

When a person dies in an accident, many of their organs may still be in good condition and could be used to save someone else's life. This can only happen if they had previously expressed a wish to donate their organs after death. This can be done by joining the organ donor register. There are currently over 16 million people in the UK on this register – over a quarter of the population.

The biggest problem doctors face with transplantation is the lack of suitable organs. This means that many people may die while waiting for a suitable organ to become available. When an organ does become available, a decision has to be made as to who should receive it; this can be a very hard decision to make.

Once an organ has been transplanted, the recipient has to take drugs to stop their body from rejecting the donated organ. Rejection occurs when the immune system recognises the donated organ as being 'foreign', and then attacks it and destroys it. The drugs taken are called **immunosuppressants**, and they work by weakening the immune system. A side effect of taking these drugs is that a person will be more likely to fall ill from disease.

> **!**
> In 1967 the first human heart transplant was performed. Simpler transplants date back much earlier. The first successful **cornea** transplant dates back to 1905. A doctor called Eduard Zirm used corneas from the eyes of an 11-year old boy to restore the sight of a labourer who had been blinded by slaked lime (calcium hydroxide).

> **?**
> **1** What might be considered when deciding who should receive a donor organ? [Total 2]
> **2** Explain what an organ transplant is, using the term 'donor organ' in your answer. [Total 2]

Figure 6.2 *An athlete at the Transplant Games. All the athletes in these Games have had organ transplants.*

Difficult Decisions

When an organ becomes available for transplantation, several different organisations work together to decide who should receive the organ. Factors that are considered include the blood group, age, and size of potential recipients. When considering heart and liver transplants, the health of the potential recipients also needs to be considered; it may be more urgent for one person than another.

Some people argue that factors such as social worth should be taken into consideration; for example, should a donated organ be used to save the life of a young working man or an old retired man? Others point out that maybe someone who has caused damage to themselves through their own actions is not deserving of a transplant. An example of this would be an alcoholic receiving a new liver to replace their own diseased organ, caused by their own drinking.

In 2005 a French woman called Isabelle Dinoire became the first person in the world to undergo a partial facial transplant. Her pet Labrador had mauled her face, leaving her disfigured. Isabelle received a triangle of tissue containing a new nose and mouth from a female donor.

Figure 6.3 *Isabelle Dinoire after her partial face transplant.*

Questions

1 Kidney transplants as are much more common than heart transplants. Suggest reasons why this may be so.   *[Total 2]*

2 In 1954 the first kidney transplant between identical twins was performed in America. Richard Herrick received one of his brother Ronald's kidneys, and was soon back to good health. Despite not taking any immunosuppressant drugs, Richard's body did not reject the donated kidney. Suggest why not.

[Total 1]

3 Kieran is 18 years old and currently serving a 5-year prison sentence for manslaughter while drink driving. Alicia is 56 years old, has no close family, and works part-time in a garden centre. Both Kieran and Alicia are waiting for a liver transplant, without which they will probably die within the next year. A donor liver becomes available, and can be used to save the life of either Kieran or Alicia.

a) Suggest some reasons why Kieran should receive the new liver and Alicia should not.   *[3]*

a) Suggest some reasons why Alicia should receive the new liver and Kieran should not.   *[3]*

[Total 6]

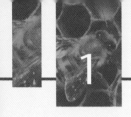
Microscopes and cells

A good scientist asks questions and makes observations. Sometimes the questions are too difficult to be answered by the equipment available at the time.

In 1665, Robert Hooke was trying to answer an intriguing question. What was living matter made up from? The development of microscopes to view living material started in 1608 when Zacharias Jansen developed a system of putting two lenses in sequence to give greater magnification than with a single lens. Unfortunately the quality of the lenses was poor and the image produced did not really help investigation of the minute world.

Galileo made improvements to microscope design (about 1610) and by 1660 simple microscopes were able to help Malpighi provide the evidence that blood went from arteries to veins through tiny vessels called capillaries. He had studied the lungs of a frog to come to this conclusion.

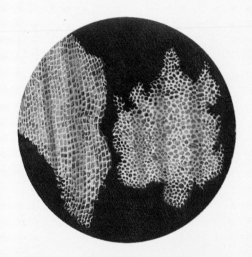

Figure 6.4 *Robert Hooke's drawing of cork cells.*

Five years later, when Charles II was king and England was suffering from the plague, Robert Hooke used a basic compound microscope of three lenses. He had to cut a very thin section of the soft cork tissue found under the bark of trees. The thin layer was put onto a black surface under the microscope and, with the light angled in the correct direction, he saw a series of pores like a honeycomb. The pores were not all the same size or shape. He interpreted them as boxes and called them 'cells'.

The amateur Dutch technologist Anton van Leeuwenhoek used a system of a single lens that gave a clearer image. He described what we now know as bacteria, protozoa, sperm and blood cells in about 1670.

The evidence of tiny units making up all organisms was not accepted until there was some way of showing they could reproduce.

More than one hundred years later Robert Brown (1773–1853) used a better series of lenses to identify a spot in all the cells of plants and animals. He called this the nucleus. Further studies by Matthias Schleiden (in 1838) and Theodor Schwann (in 1839) showed that the nucleus divided into two when more cells were produced. They put forward the idea that all tissues of plants and animals were made of cells.

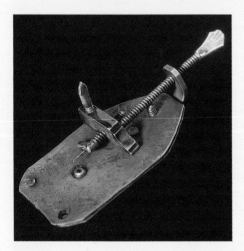

Figure 6.5 *Leeuwenhoek's microscope. The lens is mounted in a hole in the metal plate and the object moved by 2 screws next to the lens.*

Theodor Boveri (1887) went further by accurately describing coloured bodies (chromosomes) in the nucleus when the cell divided. Using sea urchin eggs and sperm he worked out the importance of the chromosomes to control the development of the cell and, from it, the whole organism.

The system for looking at small structures was now at its limit because it used light to see the objects. The smallest structure that could be looked at was about 0.0005 mm. Smaller parts of the cells were not seen until the development of the electron microscope.

In the 1930s various people, including James Hillier, developed the idea that electrons could be used instead of light in microscopes. Hillier managed a magnification of 7000 times with his electron microscope. Commercial electron microscopes were first made in Germany (Siemens in 1939). A detailed investigation of parts of cells needed thinner sections so different systems of preparing the tissues were also developed. It is now possible to see objects as small as 0.000 001 mm (1 nanometre). In the mid-1950s the structures inside cells were described for the first time e.g. membranes and ribosomes. Using knowledge of the structures, scientists started to understand the processes going on inside cells.

Three-dimensional images of the surfaces of structures can be seen using a scanning electron microscope. A scanning tunnelling electron microscope, developed in 1981 by Gerd Binnig and Heinrich Rohrer, is able to view the surface of molecules and atoms. This complements computer modelling of molecules to understand the interactions between them. Molecular biology is an active research field.

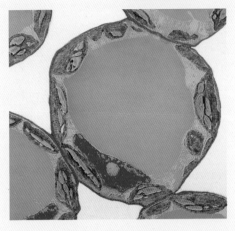

Figure 6.6 *Section through plant cell seen through an electron microscope. Note the cell wall (purple) around the cells, chloroplasts (green with pink starch grains) and permanent vacuole (blue). Magnification ×1000.*

Questions

1 What system of lenses gives a greater magnification than a simple hand lens?   *[Total 1]*

2 a) Who was the first person to see the tiny blood vessels called capillaries?   *[1]*
   b) What development enabled him to see capillaries?   *[1]*
   [Total 2]

3 What invention helped Robert Hooke describe cells?   *[Total 1]*

4 State four different types of cell that Leeuwenhoek described around 1670.   *[Total 4]*

5 How did the following scientists contribute to our ideas about cells:
   a) Robert Brown   *[2]*
   b) Schleiden and Schwann   *[2]*
   c) Theodor Boveri   *[2]*
   [Total 6]

6 a) What type of microscope gave a better magnification than a light microscope?   *[1]*
   b) How were tissues prepared so they could be seen by the microscope in part a)?   *[1]*
   [Total 2]

7 a) What type of microscope gave three-dimensional pictures of the surfaces of small objects?   *[1]*
   b) What other developments allowed the microscope in part a) to be useful?   *[1]*
   [Total 2]

8 Draw a time-line for the development of microscopes. Use your time-line to show when cells, named structures in cells and cell processes were discovered.   *[Total 8]*

End of section questions

1 Plants and animals carry out life processes in slightly different ways. Under two columns, 'plants' and 'animals', write the relevant statements. Each could apply to only one or to both.

use energy   reproduce   move from place to place   grow   make their own food   take in water   respond quickly   *[Total 10]*

2 Copy and complete Table 1.   *[Total 7]*

Organ system	Organs or tissues	Specialised cell type
	lungs	lining cells (epithelial)
breathing system	trachea	
	blood	red blood cell
reproductive system	ovary	
transport system		root hair cell
nutritional system	leaf	
	stomach	muscle cell

Table 1

3 Explain the differences between an organism, an organ system, an organ, a tissue and a cell.   *[Total 5]*

4 Draw labelled diagrams of a human cheek cell and a plant palisade cell.   *[Total 10]*

5 Match up the statement with the cell type. Write out the statement and cell type.   *[Total 10]*

Carries mucus and bacteria out of the lungs.	epithelial cell
Has a large store of food so it can divide and grow.	root hair cell
Is rectangular in shape and contains a large number of chloroplasts.	ciliated epithelium
Simple flattened cells on the surface of the skin.	white blood cell
Long and thin and can carry an electrical impulse.	bacterium
Is flexible and contains haemoglobin.	palisade cell
Carries water through a plant.	red blood cell
Can change shape to engulf a bacterium.	nerve cell
Does not contain a separate nucleus.	xylem vessel
Has a large surface area for absorption of minerals.	ovum cell

6 Figure 1 shows a fish and a seal. Suggest how the features labelled for each animal make it adapted for life in water.   *[Total 8]*

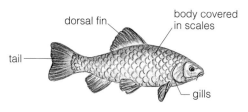
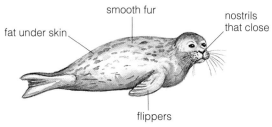

Figure 1

7 Suggest reasons why a plant does not need a skeleton to support it but an animal does.   *[Total 2]*

8 The amount of carbon dioxide in the air in a field of wheat changes during the day. The amount of water in the air was also recorded at the same time. The patterns are given in Figure 2.

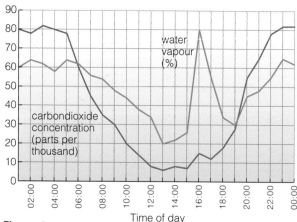

Figure 2

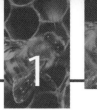

a) At what time of day does the amount of carbon dioxide start to decrease? [1]
b) What process speeds up at this time and why? [2]
c) What process returns the carbon dioxide to the air? [1]
d) Name two different groups of organisms that give out carbon dioxide. [2]
e) Suggest what may have caused the high water vapour level at 4 pm [1]
f) Describe how the pattern may be different in winter. [2]

[Total 9]

9 Tom tried to find out why different types of seaweed were found in different zones on the seashore. He said the zones depended on the time spent covered by sea water. He took some of the different seaweeds at four different zones, estimating the height above the low water mark.

He weighed the seaweeds then left them in the classroom in the same place for 24 hours and reweighed them. The results are given in Table 2.

Seaweed type	Height above low tide mark (m)	Initial mass (g)	Final mass (g)
A	1	100	60
A	3	120	73
B	3	120	84
C	5	100	80
D	5	120	106
D	8	80	72
E	8	80	78

Table 2

a) Find the difference in mass for each seaweed and height. What was the loss of mass due to? [8]
b) Which types of seaweed were sampled from two positions? [2]

c) Suggest a prediction that could be tested by sampling the same type of seaweed at different positions on the seashore. [2]
d) How could you make the loss of mass into a fair comparison between the types of seaweed? [1]
e) Plot a graph of average loss of mass against height above low water mark as a fair comparison. [8]
f) Describe the difference between the 'habitats' at the different heights above low water mark (the tidal range is 9 m). [3]
g) Suggest how the smaller loss of mass is an adaptation to the seaweed at the top of the shore. [2]

[Total 26]

10
R Find out what happens to organisms after they die.

11
R An *Amoeba* is a very small pond organism. Find out how it can carry out the seven life processes described in Topic 1.

12
R Find out how a type of animal or plant is able to live in its special habitat, e.g. how the blue whale breathes, feeds, moves, communicates, keeps warm and reproduces in the ocean.

13
R Find out about other materials that use holofibres. Why was it chosen for each purpose?

14
R Find out about the advances of xenotransplantation. Do you think it is right?

15
P What factors would affect the time of egg laying of blackbirds in a hedgerow?

16
P What factors would affect the growth of grass on the school playing field?

17
P How would you investigate the effect of wind on the distance a dandelion 'parachute' travels?

2.1 Making food from sunlight

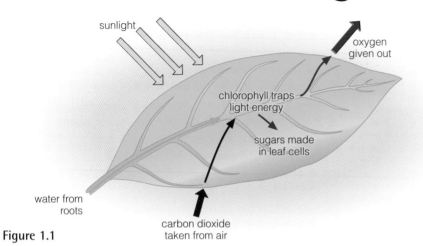

sunlight

oxygen
given out

chlorophyll traps
light energy

sugars made
in leaf cells

water from
roots

carbon dioxide
taken from air

Figure 1.1

How do plants make their own food? All they need are very simple substances and some energy. They use the substances produced to grow and to increase in mass.

Photosynthesis

The leaf is the organ where the plant makes food. The process is called **photosynthesis**. It uses light energy from the Sun to combine water with carbon dioxide (Figure 1.1). The products are oxygen and glucose (a type of sugar). Glucose is used by the plant to make every other substance the plant needs.

The equation for photosynthesis is:

$$\text{water} + \text{carbon dioxide} \xrightarrow[\text{chlorophyll}]{\text{light energy}} \text{glucose} + \text{oxygen}$$

> **!** 1 square metre of sweetcorn plants take in about 2.2 kg of carbon dioxide to produce 0.55 kg of corn in a season. 1 square metre of rainforest absorbs about 54 000 kJ of energy each year but a young pine forest in the UK absorbs only 31 000 kJ each year.

Figure 1.2 *Evidence that light is needed for photosynthesis. The leaf on the left is attached to a plant in light. The leaf on the right has been tested for starch. The blue-black colour shows that starch has been produced only where light shone on the leaf.*

> **!** Plants only use about 1% of the sunlight reaching the surface of the Earth.

Light shines onto the large upper surface of each leaf and travels through the transparent upper layers until it is trapped by the **chlorophyll** in the chloroplasts of the palisade cells. The chloroplast uses the light energy from the Sun to split water molecules into oxygen and hydrogen. The chloroplast then combines the hydrogen with carbon dioxide to form **sugars**. The first sugar formed is **glucose**. The glucose is then turned into **starch** to be stored for a short time by the leaf cells.

A leaf needs raw materials to start the process of photosynthesis and must be able to get rid of the products. The structures in a leaf are arranged so that carbon dioxide and water flow into the leaf and glucose and oxygen can leave easily. (Figure 1.3).

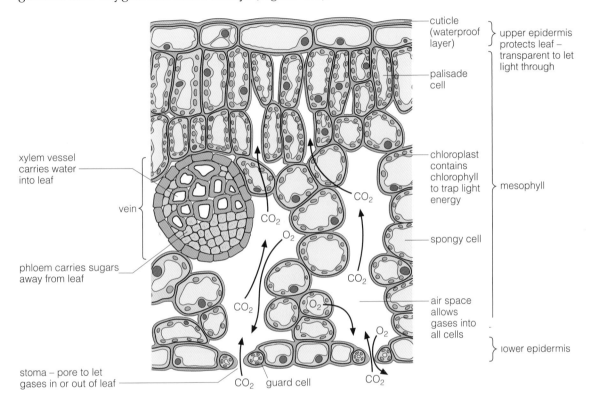

Figure 1.3 *A section through a leaf.*

On a bright summer's day bubbles can be seen coming from pondweed. The bubbles are oxygen because the pondweed is photosynthesising quickly. On a dull day fewer bubbles are seen. This shows that the amount of light alters the rate of photosynthesis. In the laboratory, you can investigate this observation using bench lamps, water and pondweed.

Use of food

Glucose is used by the plant as a supply of energy. The glucose is made into sucrose to be carried away from the leaf. It can be stored as starch for later use or converted into other substances like cellulose for the cell walls. Some of the glucose is combined with minerals (for example, nitrates taken in by the roots) to make proteins needed for growth. Even the chlorophyll used in the process of photosynthesis must be made by the plant from glucose and minerals (nitrogen and magnesium). Fats and oils found in seeds are also made from glucose.

All of the oxygen in the atmosphere has come from photosynthesis. The atmosphere was changed by a group of organisms called the blue-green bacteria. They were the first to use chlorophyll and released oxygen from water. This happened between 3000 million and 1200 million years ago!

Summary

- Plants get their energy from sunlight.
- Photosynthesis needs chlorophyll to trap light energy from the Sun.
- Photosynthesis combines water with carbon dioxide using light energy from the Sun.
- Glucose and oxygen are produced by photosynthesis.
- Glucose can be used to make starch, cellulose or other substances.

Questions

1 Copy and complete the following sentences.
Plants make their own food using _____
energy, carbon dioxide from the air and
_____ from the soil. The process is called
_____. _____ (e.g. glucose) is
produced and used to make all other substances the
plant needs. _____ is a waste product.
Leaves look _____ because they contain
chlorophyll. The _____ traps the light
energy. Most chlorophyll is in the _____
cells near the top surface of a leaf.   *[Total 4]*

2 Give two functions of the roots of a plant.   *[Total 2]*

3 List the raw materials and substances needed
for photosynthesis. In a second column state
where the plant gets the substance from.   *[Total 8]*

4 List the products of photosynthesis. In a second
column state where the substance goes to when
it moves out of the chloroplast.   *[Total 4]*

5 Name five substances that plants make from
the glucose produced in photosynthesis.   *[Total 5]*

6 A shoot of pondweed was placed in a boiling tube of
pond water. A bench lamp with a 60 W bulb shining on
the tube was placed 20 cm away. An oxygen probe was
put into the tube and the oxygen concentration
recorded by a data-logger. The oxygen concentration
was recorded after four minutes and again after a
further five minutes. The experiment was repeated with
the same pondweed but with the lamp 5 cm away from
the boiling tube. The results are given in Table 1.1.

Distance of lamp (cm)	Oxygen concentration after 4 min (% saturation)	Oxygen concentration after 9 min (% saturation)
20	60	65
5	64	84

Table 1.1

a) Work out the increase in oxygen percentage
per minute from the pondweed at 20 cm
and 5 cm lamp distances.   *[2]*

b) What is the effect of increasing the light
on oxygen production.   *[1]*

c) State the name of the process that
produces the oxygen.   *[1]*

d) Explain, in as much detail as you can, why the
amount of oxygen produced in this experiment
increased when the lamp was put closer to
the pondweed.   *[4]*

e) The lamp also gives off heat. Suggest how this
could affect the results.   *[2]*

[Total 10]

2.2 Gaining water and nutrients

Water is needed for life. How do animals and plants take in the water they need? Without enough water you feel thirsty and go for a drink. You swallow the water and it is absorbed into your blood from the digestive system. The water can then move to the tissues where it is needed and your thirst disappears.

Plants stay still so water is absorbed from the soil by the roots. It must then move through the plant into the stem and leaves to get to all the cells needing it. If the plant becomes short of water it wilts and may die.

Uptake of water

Water moves from the soil into the root hairs by **osmosis** (Figure 2.1). There is more water in the soil than in the root hair cells so the water moves through the partially **permeable cell membrane** into the root hair cell.

> Osmosis is the movement of water from an area of high water concentration to an area of lower water concentration through a partially permeable membrane.

The water will continue to move through the root cells, from cell to cell, until it reaches the **xylem vessels** in the middle of the root. It is then easy for the water to move through the hollow tubes of the xylem vessels, up the stem and into the veins of the leaf. The water moves to the leaf cells.

Water is used for photosynthesis, supporting the cells of the leaf or it evaporates into the air spaces and diffuses through the stomata into the air.

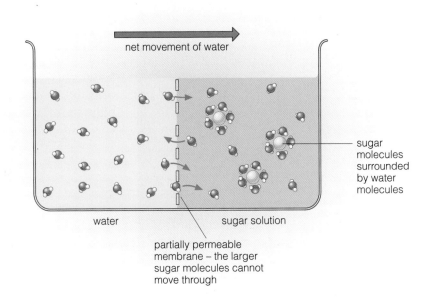

net movement of water

sugar molecules surrounded by water molecules

water

sugar solution

partially permeable membrane – the larger sugar molecules cannot move through

Figure 2.1 *There is a higher concentration of water molecules on the left of the membrane. Water moves by osmosis from a higher concentration of water to a lower concentration of water. The larger sugar particles cannot move through the membrane.*

The evaporation of water into the air means that there is less water in the leaf cells and xylem vessels. Water moving up the stem replaces this lost water. The water is pulled up the plant using the force from evaporation of the water.

The movement of water through the plant is called the **transpiration stream**. (Figure 2.2).

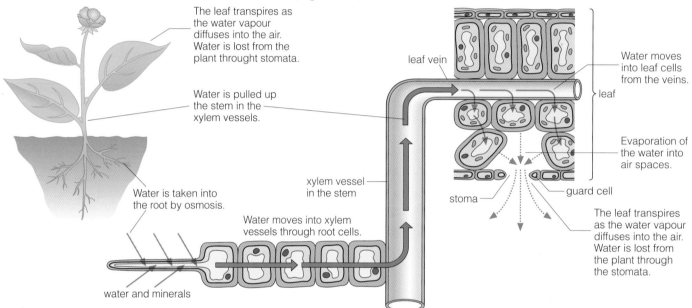

The leaf transpires as the water vapour diffuses into the air. Water is lost from the plant through stomata.

Water is pulled up the stem in the xylem vessels.

Water is taken into the root by osmosis.

Water moves into xylem vessels through root cells.

water and minerals

leaf vein

Water moves into leaf cells from the veins.

leaf

Evaporation of the water into air spaces.

xylem vessel in the stem

stoma

guard cell

The leaf transpires as the water vapour diffuses into the air. Water is lost from the plant through the stomata.

Figure 2.2 *The transpiration stream.*

Absorption of water into animal cells or into the blood also occurs by osmosis. The water moves from where there is a higher water concentration to where there is a lower water concentration e.g. from the intestines into the blood. The water enters the cytoplasm of the body cells that are short of water. Therefore the water is absorbed in the same way by plants and animals – by osmosis.

Figure 2.3 *The transpiration stream can even transport water to the top of a giant sequoia tree.*

What is water needed for?

Your body is about 70% water. If you weigh 50 kg then there is about 35 litres of water in your body. About 2.5 litres are found in the blood, so most is surrounding the cells as tissue fluid or in the cytoplasm of cells. The water is used in the following ways:

- As a solvent, to let all the other substances dissolve. These substances can then be carried in the water or move about by random motion of the molecules.
- As part of a chemical reaction. Water is often one of the reactants e.g. the breakdown of food in the intestine or in photosynthesis.
- As a coolant. Water forms part of sweat released onto the skin and is evaporated, so it takes away the heat with the vapour. Water also evaporates from plant leaves when the Sun shines on the leaf. The evaporation stops the leaf getting too hot. Most of the water absorbed by a plant is lost in this way. The loss of water is called transpiration.
- For support. Water, like other liquids, cannot be squashed into a smaller space. Plants fill up their cells so that there is a push against the cell wall. The cells become firm and cannot be squashed. The plant weight is then supported by these stiff cells. Some animals also use a similar system in their whole body to keep their shape, e.g. an earthworm.

> **!** If a red blood cell is put into water it will burst. The membrane is too weak to hold the cell together when it takes in the water.

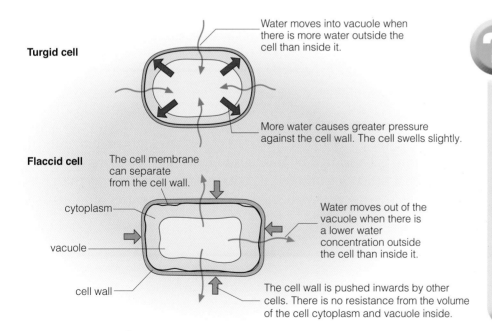

Turgid cell

Water moves into vacuole when there is more water outside the cell than inside it.

More water causes greater pressure against the cell wall. The cell swells slightly.

Flaccid cell

The cell membrane can separate from the cell wall.

cytoplasm

vacuole

cell wall

Water moves out of the vacuole when there is a lower water concentration outside the cell than inside it.

The cell wall is pushed inwards by other cells. There is no resistance from the volume of the cell cytoplasm and vacuole inside.

Figure 2.4 *Turgid and flaccid cells.*

> **?** **1** On a hot day, you might lose lots of water from your body through sweating. Suppose a 50 kg person were to lose 700 cm³ of water through sweating, during a period of exercise.
> a) What percentage of their total body mass does this sweating represent? [2]
> b) What percentage of their total body water does this represent? [2]
> [Total 4]

Uptake of mineral salts

Water moves into both plants and animals by osmosis. Do minerals enter both types of organism in the same way?

The minerals plants need must come from the soil and are absorbed along with the water. Plants need them in small or minute amounts compared to the amount of carbon dioxide and water used in photosynthesis. Animals also need the same minerals which must come from their food.

A mineral salt is soluble in water and the mineral particles can move about. They will always move from where there are more of them to where there are fewer of them. The concentration will eventually become equal in all places. This movement is called **diffusion**.

> Diffusion is the movement of particles from an area of high concentration to an area of lower concentration due to the random motion of the particles.

If a mineral salt is in a higher concentration in the soil than in the root then the mineral can diffuse into the root hair and so into the plant. However, many of the minerals are in short supply in the soil. The root hair cells use energy to absorb the mineral salt particles from the soil into the root. The partially permeable membrane makes sure that the mineral cannot leave the cell to return to the soil. The process of using energy to absorb a substance is called **active transport**.

> Active transport is the movement of particles against the concentration gradient, through a cell membrane, using energy.

> **!** Plant roots must be fussy. Some minerals are poisonous. Too much copper, lead or aluminium can kill a plant so these minerals must be kept out.

Plants need mineral salts like nitrates, phosphates, potassium and magnesium. Each is used by the cells to make new compounds which have special functions in the cell. Without the mineral salts the plants do not grow very well. Table 2.1 shows some uses of minerals salts in plants.

Mineral salt	Compound in plant	Use in the plant
nitrate	proteins	growth of new cells
phosphate	ATP	chemical energy in cells
potassium	enzyme activators	helps reactions of photosynthesis
magnesium	chlorophyll	traps light in photosynthesis

?

2 Sometimes plants may develop yellow patches on their leaves. This indicates that they are not getting enough of a particular mineral salt. Which salt do you think they are lacking? Explain your answer.   *[Total 3]*

Table 2.1 *Uses of mineral salts in plants.*

Animals also need mineral salts. They absorb them through the intestine. The lining of the intestine behaves like a selectively permeable membrane. The mineral salts can diffuse or be actively transported into the blood in just the same way as into the plant root.

Summary

- Water is absorbed into root hairs by osmosis.
- Water travels through the plant in xylem vessels.
- The flow of water through the plant is called the transpiration stream.
- Water evaporates from the leaves causing more water to be pulled up the stem.
- Animals absorb water from the intestine by osmosis into the blood.
- Mineral salts are absorbed by diffusion or active transport in both animals and plants.

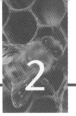
Questions

1   Copy and complete the following sentences.
Water is needed by plants and animals. Both types
of organism take in the water by _____.
The water helps to _____ the plant cells
and keep their shape. If too much _____ is
taken into animal cells they may burst. Water moves
through the plant using the _____ stream.
The water _____ through stomatal pores on
the leaves. _____ salts are needed by
animals and plants. Plants get their minerals from
the _____. Nitrates are important for
making _____.   *[Total 4]*

2   Explain how root hair cells increase the amount
of water absorbed by plants.   *[Total 2]*

3   a) Describe the route taken by a water molecule
from the soil, through a plant, to the air.   *[7]*
   b) What happens to most of the water absorbed
by a plant?   *[1]*
   c) Name the process by which water moves into
a root hair cell.   *[1]*
                                                [Total 9]

4   a) State four uses of water in plants.   *[4]*
   b) Why is each important to the plant?   *[4]*
                                                [Total 8]

5   Describe what happens to a whole plant
when it is short of water.   *[Total 2]*

6   Mineral salts are needed by animals and plants.
   a) Where do they come from in each case?   *[2]*
   b) Name two processes by which the mineral salts
enter the organisms.   *[2]*
   c) How do they get to the growing points at the top
of a plant?   *[1]*
                                                [Total 5]

7   What are the roles of each of the following mineral
salts in a plant:
   a) nitrates   *[2]*
   b) phosphates   *[2]*
   c) potassium   *[2]*
   d) magnesium?   *[2]*
                                                [Total 8]

8   Describe, with the aid of a diagram, how a
plant cell provides support to the plant.   *[Total 6]*

9   A potted plant was fully watered and placed on
a top pan balance. The mass was recorded for
10 hours. The results are given in Table 2.2.

Time (hr)	0	2	4	6	8	10
Mass of plant (including pot and soil) (g)	455	430	405	385	360	335

Table 2.2

   a) Work out the average rate of loss of mass. *[3]*
   b) Suggest why the mass was lost.   *[1]*
   c) What other factor must be known to compare
this rate of loss with another potted plant. *[2]*
   d) List factors that could affect the rate of the
loss of mass.   *[3]*
   e) Suggest a way to improve the experiment so
that all loss of mass must be due to loss from
the plant and not through the soil or pot.   *[2]*
   f) Suggest a prediction that could be tested
using this apparatus.   *[1]*
                                                [Total 12]

2.3 Human food and diet

Humans are typical animals. They move from place to place. If plants do not have to move why do humans bother?

Food

Food contains energy and substances that are needed by animals. The energy originally comes from plants trapping light energy from the Sun and adding it to carbon dioxide and water to make substances for their own growth (photosynthesis). Humans can then eat the plants to get the energy or they can eat other animals that have eaten the plants.

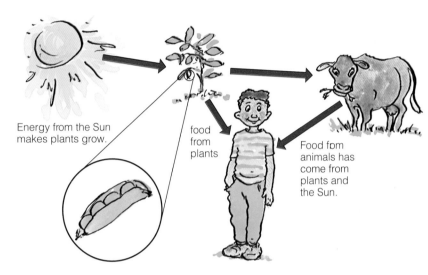

Energy from the Sun makes plants grow.

food from plants

Food from animals has come from plants and the Sun.

Figure 3.1 *Humans get energy from the Sun via other organisms.*

Food must be caught or gathered by animals. The animals must move to get the food.

There is an amazing range of foods that humans eat. They can be grouped in different ways. The Department of Health uses a system based on similar sources and structures of the foods. There is another system that colour codes foods as green, amber and red, but scientists group them according to the major nutrient type. There are seven nutrient groups; carbohydrates, fats, proteins, vitamins, minerals, fibre and water.

Figure 3.2 *A selection of different types of foods.*

Carbohydrates

Carbohydrates contain the elements carbon, hydrogen and oxygen. There is always twice as much hydrogen as there is oxygen (e.g. glucose $C_6H_{12}O_6$). Carbohydrates are used for energy storage or release of energy in cells.

There are two sub-groups of carbohydrates.

○ Simple carbohydrates (sugars) are sweet and dissolve easily. An example of a useful sugar in humans is **glucose**. The glucose is broken down in cells to release energy during respiration.

○ Complex carbohydrates (polysaccharides) are large molecules made of many glucose units. They are not sweet and are used to store energy. Humans store energy as a chemical called glycogen. The common carbohydrate stored in plants is starch which is in foods like potatoes and bread.

All carbohydrates can be broken down in respiration to release about 17 kJ/g.

?

1 Name the two different types of carbohydrates and give two examples of each type. *[Total 4]*

Nutrient group	Good sources	Uses
carbohydrates ○ sugars	sweets, cakes	provide instant energy
○ polysaccharides	bread, rice, cereals, pasta, potatoes	instant energy or energy storage (glycogen in humans)
fats	butter, cooking oil, cream, red meat	energy storage making cell membranes
proteins	meat, eggs, fish, nuts, peas	growth and repair (making new cells)
mineral salts ○ calcium	milk	bones and teeth
○ iron	red meat	red blood cells
○ sodium	salt and processed foods	water balance in cells
vitamins ○ A	fish oils, butter	aids night vision
○ B	liver, cereals, meat	chemical reactions in respiration
○ C	fresh fruit and vegetables	healthy skin and gums
○ D	dairy products, fatty fish	absorption and use of calcium for bones and teeth
fibre	cereals, vegetables, fruit	keeps food flowing smoothly in digestive system
water	drinks, liquid foods	dissolves chemicals in cells or tissue fluids.

Table 3.1 *Nutrients, sources and uses of foods.*

Fats

These also contain carbon, hydrogen and oxygen but there is very little oxygen compared to the amount of hydrogen (e.g. tristearin fat found in beef has the formula $C_{51}H_{104}O_6$). **Fats** do not dissolve in water and so have to be carried in the blood in a special way. They are combined with proteins (Figure 3.3). When broken down in respiration, fats give out twice as much energy as carbohydrates (34 kJ/g). Fats are made from two different parts – fatty acids and glycerol.

Fats can be taken into cells and broken down in respiration if energy is needed straight away or they can be stored in special cells under the skin. The fats form a concentrated energy store for the long term.

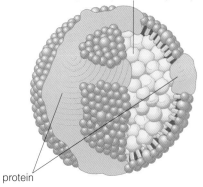

fat molecules in centre of globule protected by the protein

protein

Figure 3.3 *Fat combined with protein carried in the blood.*

Protein

Proteins are large molecules made up from chains of **amino acids**. Each amino acid contains the elements carbon, hydrogen, oxygen and nitrogen. Some amino acids also contain sulphur. Most amino acids can be made by our cells but some must come from our food. The amino acids which cannot be made by our bodies are called **essential amino acids**. Animal products like meat have more essential amino acids than plant products.

The protein in food is used by cells for growth and repair. This means that structures in new cells are made of proteins and the ability to carry out chemical reactions in the cells depends upon other proteins (enzymes).

Proteins can also be used for energy if the body is starving and no carbohydrate or fat is available. They are broken down into carbon dioxide, water and urea.

The chemical tests for the major nutrients in food are given in Table 3.2. In each test a small sample of food is ground up with a little water and put in a test tube.

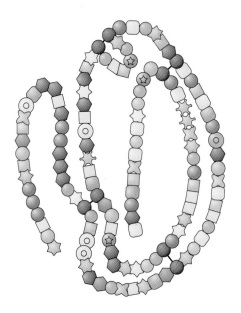

Figure 3.4 *A protein molecule. The different shapes represent the amino acids. A protein can be made from between 50 and 3000 amino acids joined in a long chain and folded up.*

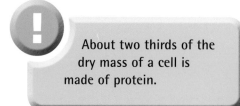

! About two thirds of the dry mass of a cell is made of protein.

Nutrient	Test name	Method	Result	Before	After
Sugar (except sucrose)	Benedicts' test	○ Dissolve food in 1 cm³ water. ○ Add 2 cm³ Benedicts' solution. ○ Boil using a water bath for 1 minute.	Blue solution becomes red.		
Starch	Iodine test	○ Add several drops of iodine solution.	Straw colour turns to blue-black.		
Fat	Emulsion test	○ Cut food into thin shavings without any water. ○ Add 5 cm³ of ethanol. ○ Shake well then leave to settle. ○ Half fill a second test tube with water. ○ Carefully add drops of the solution from the first test tube to the water.	Water becomes cloudy	dropping pipette / ethanol / food sample / water	ethanol / cloudy / water
Protein	Biuret test	○ Add 1 cm³ of dilute sodium hydroxide. ○ Add 3 drops of 1% copper sulphate solution. ○ Shake and watch	Pale blue colour turns to violet.	drops of copper sulpahte solution / sodium hydroxide	

Table 3.2 *Chemical tests for the major nutrients in food. Eye protection must be worn for each test.*

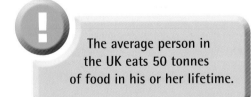

The average person in the UK eats 50 tonnes of food in his or her lifetime.

Mineral salts

These soluble substances are the same as the minerals needed by plants. Many foods contain different amounts of them but we usually need small amounts compared to the three major nutrient groups already described (see Table 3.1).

Calcium is needed for the structure of bones and teeth, iron for carrying oxygen in red blood cells, and sodium for keeping the correct concentration of substances in the cells by allowing water to move into or out of the cell. In addition, phosphorus is needed for energy release and potassium to help the chemical reactions in cells (respiration).

A deficiency of a mineral in the diet causes specific **symptoms** (signs) called a **deficiency disease** e.g. lack of iron causes anaemia and lack of calcium causes rickets. Too much of a mineral can also cause health problems.

Vitamins

The majority of this group of substances cannot be made in the body – they must be eaten in our food. Each vitamin has a special job to do in the body. Some of the vitamins and their jobs are described in Table 3.1. Without enough of each vitamin, deficiency diseases occur e.g. lack of vitamin C causes scurvy. The vitamins have been given letters but each does have a special name, e.g. vitamin C is called ascorbic acid. None of the vitamins provides energy.

Fibre

This is a group of substances that the body cannot digest. **Fibre** in the digestive system helps the movement of all the other substances along the canal. The fibre encourages the right types of bacteria to grow in the large intestine so that fewer poisons are produced from harmful bacteria. The waste food can be removed from the body easily because fibre provides the bigger bulk.

A large amount of fibre comes from plant cell walls. The cell walls contain cellulose that humans cannot break down. Therefore, plant matter is very important in a **balanced diet** to prevent diarrhoea or constipation and cancer of the colon.

Water

About 70% of your body mass is water.
Water is important for four reasons.

○ It dissolves most of the other substances in the body and allows the chemical reactions to go ahead.
○ It transports substances around the body.
○ Some reactions need water as a raw material. It is a **substrate** for the reaction.
○ Water is used to cool the body. It is lost by evaporation from sweat.

Water is lost from the body when you breathe out, through urine, faeces and through sweat. The diet must have sufficient water in it to make up for the loss.

Only humans, chimpanzees, fruit bats and guinea pigs cannot make vitamin C and need it in their diet.

Figure 3.5

?
2 a) Name two different vitamins. [1]
b) For each of the vitamins you named in part a) explain why they are important in a balanced diet. [2]
c) For each of the vitamins in part a) give two examples of foods they are found in. [2]
[Total 5]

!
If you lose more than 5% water then you become unconscious and more than 8% loss may cause death.

Balanced diets

A **balanced diet** has all of the nutrients required by the body to keep it healthy and in the correct amounts. An unbalanced diet can cause many different health problems including **malnourishment**.

People who take in too much energy, by eating either too much carbohydrate or fat, will become obese. The extra weight carried by the body means the heart must pump blood to more tissues. The extra pumping puts a strain on the heart. Obese people are more likely to suffer from many health problems including heart attacks. In Britain in 2007, it was estimated that about 24% of adults and 15.4% of 2–10 year olds were overweight. (Overweight is defined as 15% greater than the ideal mass for the height and build).

Too little food causes tiredness and wasting diseases which are most common in developing countries.

Eating most of the carbohydrate you need as sugar is bad for your teeth. Bacteria in your mouth use the sugar and produce acids, which rot the teeth. It is best to have a little sugar with meals instead of continuously eating sweets during the day.

!
Fluoride is added to drinking water to make teeth stronger.

?
3 a) Why should we be careful about the amount of sugar we eat? [2]
b) Why is too much fat in your diet a problem? [3]
[Total 5]

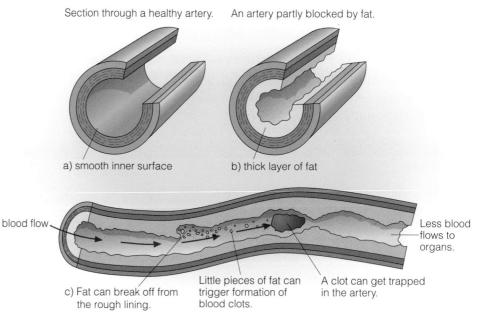

Section through a healthy artery.   An artery partly blocked by fat.

a) smooth inner surface   b) thick layer of fat

blood flow

Less blood flows to organs.

c) Fat can break off from the rough lining.   Little pieces of fat can trigger formation of blood clots.   A clot can get trapped in the artery.

Figure 3.6

If there is too much fat in the diet some is left in the blood vessels as it travels round. This narrows the vessels and causes a strain on the heart. The fatty deposit can trigger the formation of blood clots which can block narrow blood vessels. If a blood clot gets stuck in the brain, it causes a stroke. If it gets stuck in the blood vessels feeding the heart muscle with oxygen then a heart attack can occur.

Too much salt in food increases blood pressure which increases the chance of heart disease and strokes.

It is recommended that you should eat less processed food, e.g. sausages, beefburgers and crisps because they contain too much fat and salt. In food processing, most of the fibre is removed even from vegetables. Fresh fruit, pasta, wholemeal bread and white meats are recommended for supplying a balanced diet. Five servings of fruit or vegetables are recommended every day.

! Fish and plant oils are more easily carried in the blood than animals fats.

? 4 High blood pressure can be caused when blood volume increases too much. Suggest how too much salt might lead to an increase in blood pressure. (Hint: think about osmosis, and where water is found in the body.)

[Total 3]

Summary

- Carbohydrates, e.g. starch and sugar, give us energy.
- Fats give twice as much energy as carbohydrates.
- Fats and carbohydrates can be stored in the body.
- Too much fat in the diet leads to heart disease.
- Too much energy-rich food makes us overweight and this can also cause heart disease.
- Proteins are used for growth and repair of cells. They cannot be stored.
- Vitamins and minerals are needed to help special chemical reactions in the body.
- A balanced diet contains all the nutrients in the amounts needed by the body.
- Fibre helps the muscle contractions that move food through the gut.

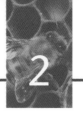

Questions

1 Copy and complete the following sentences.
Food is made up of many chemical _____.
A _____ diet contains all of the substances
needed by the body in the correct amounts.
_____ give the body energy when they are
broken down. Fats give twice as much energy as
_____. Proteins are needed for _____
and repair of tissues. _____ like calcium are
needed for special functions in the body. Calcium helps
to make _____ or teeth strong and hard. Most
_____ cannot be made in the body. If the body
is short of a vitamin a _____ disease occurs,
e.g. scurvy is a lack of vitamin C. Fibre is important to
help the food move along the gut and to stop
_____ of the colon. *[Total 5]*

2 Look at the list of foods below. Group them according
to the following categories. Each food should only be
put into one group for each exercise.
rice, bread, potatoes, chips, pasta, cereal, milk, eggs,
cheese, butter, museli, chocolate, crisps, chicken, bacon,
sausages, cooking oil, bananas, oranges, carrots, baked
beans, ice cream
   a) Department of Health groups (breads; fruit and
      vegetables; meat and fish; dairy products;
      manufactured foods with high salt or fat). *[2]*
   b) Groups found in a supermarket. *[2]*
   c) Healthy (green), satisfactory (amber) and
      unhealthy (red). *[2]*
                                    [Total 6]

3 a) How are fats carried in the human body? *[1]*
   b) Why is this necessary? *[1]*
                                    [Total 2]

4 Explain why all diets must contain some protein.
                                    [Total 2]

5 What is the difference between an essential and
non-essential amino acid? *[Total 2]*

6 Name types of food that contain:
   a) essential amino acids *[1]*
   b) non-essential amino acids. *[1]*
                                      [Total 2]

7 a) Where does fibre come from in our diet? *[1]*
   b) Why is fibre neccessary in our diet? *[1]*
                                    [Total 2]

8 a) What is water used for in the body? *[4]*
   b) Where does water come from in our diet? *[1]*
                                    [Total 5]

9 A beefburger contains 40 g of fat and 70 g of
carbohydrate. How much more energy does
the fat provide than the carbohydrate? *[Total 3]*

10 Describe how to carry out a chemical test
for sugars in some sweets. Explain what
you would see. *[Total 4]*

11 Megan wanted to find the energy content of some snack foods. She accurately weighed the snack food, placed it on a mounted needle, lit it and quickly held it under a boiling tube of water. The temperature increase of the water was recorded (Figure 3.7).

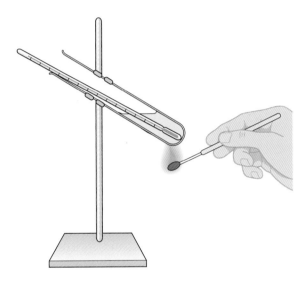

Figure 3.7

a) List the measurements needed for the experiment. [4]

b) The temperature increase worked out at an energy value for 100 g of 957 kJ. The packet information said it was 2257 kJ/100 g. Suggest four different reasons why her value was much less than the value on the packet. [4]

c) Suggest ways that the apparatus or method could be changed, still using school laboratory equipment, to improve the accuracy of the results. [3]

d) List the factors that must be kept the same to compare the energy content of several different snack foods. [4]

[Total 15]

2.4 Digestion in humans

How does the human body take in food and use it to grow? Food for humans comes from plants or other animals. The food is made from large molecules which cannot be absorbed into the blood. They must be broken down, absorbed and then changed into the form needed by our own bodies.

The digestive system

The organ system that has the job of taking in food and making it available for the rest of the body is the **digestive system**. It is a long tube running through the body from the mouth to the anus. Special substances called **enzymes** are released to break down the food. This process is called **digestion**. The digested food is then absorbed into the blood stream. Any food that cannot be digested is passed out of the anus, by a process called **egestion**.

The digestive system consists of many organs, each specialised for one function. The food passes through the organs in sequence so that it can be progressively broken down and then absorbed.

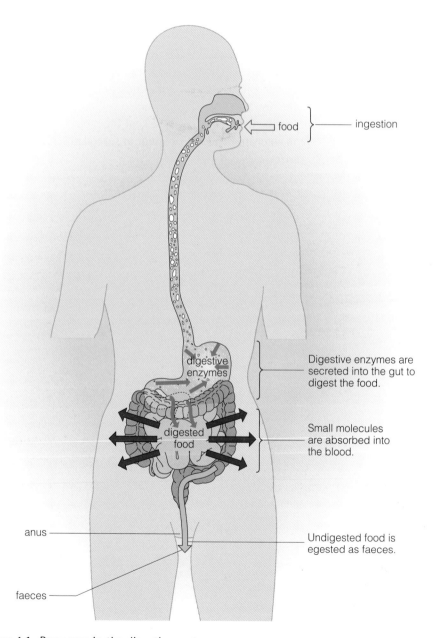

food — ingestion

Digestive enzymes are secreted into the gut to digest the food.

digestive enzymes

digested food

Small molecules are absorbed into the blood.

anus

Undigested food is egested as faeces.

faeces

Figure 4.1 *Processes in the digestive system*

The mouth and ingestion

Ingestion is the act of taking food into the mouth. It is chewed to break it down into smaller pieces and to mix it with **saliva**. The smaller pieces are easier to swallow and have a bigger surface area for enzymes to break down the food.

The saliva contains mucus which helps to lubricate the food. It also contains an enzyme which breaks down starch into simple sugar molecules (Figure 4.2).

Enzymes are special substances that speed up chemical reactions. They are proteins and each enzyme has a very specific shape. This special shape means that a **substrate molecule** can fit into the enzyme and be broken down in digestion. Anything that changes the shape of the enzyme, e.g. high temperatures, will mean that it does not work any more. Enzymes are used for many chemical reactions in the body. They are useful in digestion because they help to break down the food. The enzyme in your saliva is called **amylase** and it starts work on digesting food in your mouth.

1 What is the first stage in the digestion of your food? [Total 1]

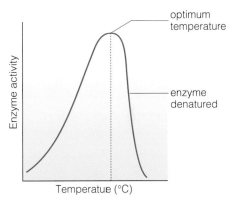

Figure 4.3 *Enzymes change shape if they are heated. This is called denaturing. The substrate molecule does not fit the active site any more.*

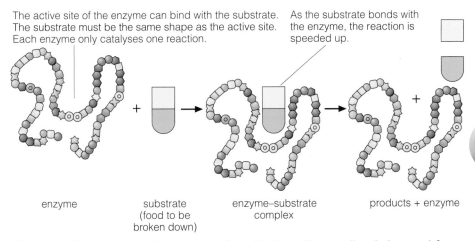

The active site of the enzyme can bind with the substrate. The substrate must be the same shape as the active site. Each enzyme only catalyses one reaction.

As the substrate bonds with the enzyme, the reaction is speeded up.

enzyme + substrate (food to be broken down) → enzyme–substrate complex → products + enzyme

Figure 4.2 *Enzyme action. Enzymes are found inside cells as well as being used for digestion. Enzymes can be re-used with new substrate molecules. They can build up molecules as well as break them down.*

Teeth are also important for digestion in the mouth. They are special structures which have a very hard coating on the surface. They grow from the jaw bones. Each type of tooth is adapted to its function in the mouth. The incisors at the front have a sharp edge for biting and the molars at the back have a broad surface with cusps to crush the food into small pieces.

The jaw muscles of a shark can exert a force of 600 N between the teeth – creating the greatest pressure ($30\,000$ N/cm^2) in the body.

Figure 4.4

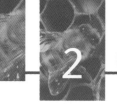

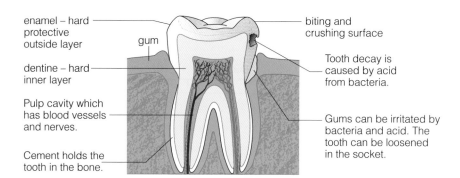

enamel – hard protective outside layer

gum

dentine – hard inner layer

Pulp cavity which has blood vessels and nerves.

Cement holds the tooth in the bone.

biting and crushing surface

Tooth decay is caused by acid from bacteria.

Gums can be irritated by bacteria and acid. The tooth can be loosened in the socket.

Figure 4.5 *Section through a molar tooth.*

Humans have two sets of teeth. In young children, the jaw grows but the teeth cannot. The second set grows larger than the first and there are 12 more teeth in total. If you look after your teeth, this makes sure you can chew your food for all of your life.

Food is swallowed by a special action that covers the windpipe when the food goes into the **oesophagus**. If food 'goes down the wrong way' i.e. goes towards the lungs, we cough to force the food back up.

The food travels down the oesophagus by **peristalsis** (Figure 4.6).

! Elephants have seven sets of teeth. Once the final set of teeth has worn out they die because they cannot chew vegetation any more.

muscle layers of intestine

A wave of contraction passes along the intestine pushing the food forward. The wave of contraction is called peristalsis.

Circular muscles behind the bolus contract.

bolus of food

Figure 4.6 *Food moves along the whole of the intestine by peristalsis.*

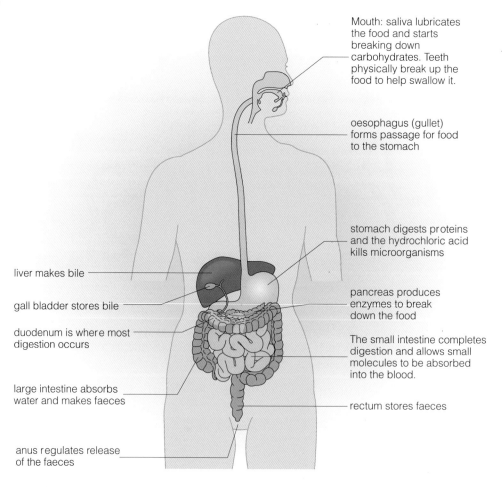

Mouth: saliva lubricates the food and starts breaking down carbohydrates. Teeth physically break up the food to help swallow it.

oesophagus (gullet) forms passage for food to the stomach

stomach digests proteins and the hydrochloric acid kills microorganisms

pancreas produces enzymes to break down the food

liver makes bile

gall bladder stores bile

duodenum is where most digestion occurs

The small intestine completes digestion and allows small molecules to be absorbed into the blood.

large intestine absorbs water and makes faeces

rectum stores faeces

anus regulates release of the faeces

Figure 4.7 *The digestive system.*

Digestion in the stomach and intestines

Food that has been swallowed enters the **stomach**. The stomach expands with the food eaten. Rings of muscle at the stomach entrance and exit control the direction and rate of flow of the food. A meal containing fat and protein remains longer in the stomach than a meal with only carbohydrates. The average time for food to stay in the stomach is about four hours.

The stomach walls are in constant motion. The churning of the stomach helps to physically break up the food and to mix it with the **gastric juice** produced by glands in the walls. The juice is mainly hydrochloric acid which kills most microorganisms in the food. An enzyme breaks down proteins into smaller molecules.

The acid mush is released from the stomach into the small intestine in small amounts. It is neutralised by alkaline secretions from the liver (**bile**) and **pancreas**. In the small intestine many different enzymes are used to break down the large molecules in foods (see Table 4.1). **Proteases** digest proteins, **lipases** break down fats and **carbohydrases** digest carbohydrates. Bile is not an enzyme but it contains substances that make the fats form tiny droplets in water. The fats can then be broken down more easily.

> ! Stress often causes too much acid to be made by the stomach. If any part of the stomach is inflamed then the acid and resistant bacteria further irritate the stomach lining. An ulcer is formed which can be very painful.

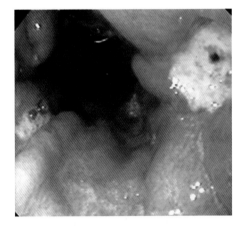

Figure 4.8 *An ulcer in the stomach.*

Area of alimentary canal	Enzyme	Gland producing enzyme	Food broken down	Products formed
mouth	amylase (carbohydrase)	salivary gland	starch	maltose
stomach	protease	gastric gland	protein	polypeptides
small intestine	amylase (carbohydrase)	pancreas	starch	maltose
small intestine	lipase	pancreas	fats	fatty acids and glycerol
small intestine	protease	pancreas and wall of small intestine	proteins and polypeptides	amino acids
small intestine	carbohydrases	wall of small intestine	milk and fruit sugars	simplest sugars, e.g. glucose

Table 4.1 *Digestion of foods by enzymes.*

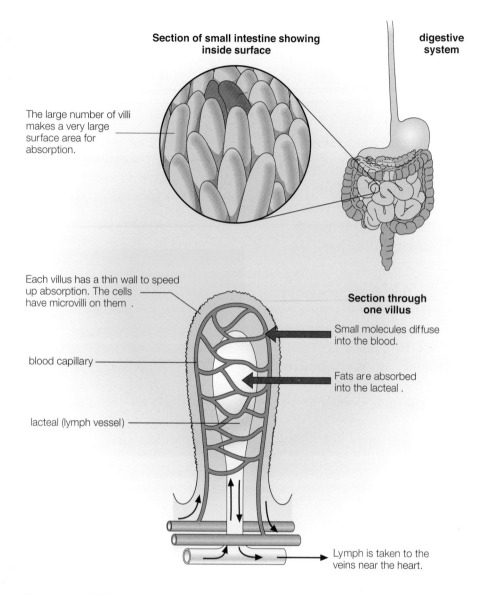

Section of small intestine showing inside surface

digestive system

The large number of villi makes a very large surface area for absorption.

Each villus has a thin wall to speed up absorption. The cells have microvilli on them .

Section through one villus

Small molecules diffuse into the blood.

blood capillary

Fats are absorbed into the lacteal .

lacteal (lymph vessel)

Lymph is taken to the veins near the heart.

Figure 4.9 *Villi have a large surface area for absorption of digested food.*

Absorption in the small intestine

The small intestine has a massive surface area (about $300\,m^2$) for absorption of the digested food molecules. The surface area is increased by the following:

○ It is long (approximately $7\,m$).
○ The absorbing surface (inside the tube) is folded so there is a larger surface.
○ On the folds are villi which stick up from the surface like many fingers.
○ Each villus has tiny projections called microvilli.

The soluble food is absorbed into the blood by diffusion. However, if some substances are in short supply, the lining cells of the villi can use energy to help absorb them quickly. The blood goes to the liver and any poisons that have been absorbed with the digested food can be destroyed.

The large intestine

This is the area where most water is absorbed into the blood. Some of the bacteria in the large intestine can use the remains of the food to make some vitamins the body needs. These are absorbed with the water. The remainder of the undigested food needs the fibre to help it move smoothly through the large intestine.

The faeces are stored in the last part of the large intestine and must be removed from the body regularly. This process is called egestion.

Egestion means getting rid of undigested food that has not been absorbed into the cells of the body. Egestion should not be confused with excretion which means getting rid of waste substances from within the cells of the body e.g carbon dioxide and urea.

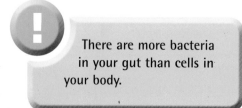

There are more bacteria in your gut than cells in your body.

Summary

- Digestion breaks down large food substances into small, soluble molecules for absorption into the blood.
- Enzymes speed up chemical reactions including the breakdown of substances.
- Enzymes are specific for each reaction. Carbohydrases break down carbohydrates, proteases break down protein and lipases break down fats.
- The small intestine completes digestion and absorbs the soluble molecules.
- The food moves along the digestive system by peristalsis.

Questions

1 Copy and complete the following sentences.
Food must be made soluble for it to be
_____ into the blood. It is broken down
by _____ into simple chemicals. Each
_____ has an active site which is a special
shape for the reacting substance.
The stomach is acidic to _____
microorganisms in the food. The acid is _____
by pancreatic juice and bile in the small intestine. The
bile breaks up fats into tiny droplets for the
_____ enzyme to digest. The digested food is
_____ into the blood in the small intestine.
Undigested food is _____.   [Total 4]

2 Name the four processes that occur along
the length of the digestive system.   [Total 4]

3 Describe how food is pushed through
the digestive system.   [Total 3]

4 Give three ways that the surface area
of the small intestine is increased.   [Total 3]

5 2 cm² of boiled egg white (containing undigested
protein) is put into a series of test tubes labelled A,
B, C and D. Substances are added to the tubes as
shown in Table 4.2. The tubes were placed in a beaker
of warm water (37 °C) and the time required for the
liquid to become clear was recorded.

Tube	A	B	C	D
Substances added	1 cm³ water, 1 cm³ protease	1 cm³ acid, 1 cm³ water	1 cm³ acid, 1 cm³ protease	1 cm³ acid, 1 cm³ boiled protease
Time for solution to be clear (min)	15	still cloudy after 30 min	2	20

Table 4.2

a) List the reactions in order, fastest first.   [1]
b) Suggest why the solutions became clear.   [2]
c) i) What was the effect of the acid on the
       speed of the reaction?
   ii) State the tubes you compared to give your
       answer to part i).
   iii) Explain your answer to part i).   [3]
d) Suggest why boiling the protease slowed
   down the reaction.   [2]
e) What is the purpose of tube B in the
   experiment?   [2]
                                                  [Total 10]

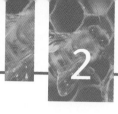

Vitamin deficiencies

The thought that a disease could be caused by something missing from the diet must have occurred to many people. The ancient Greek physician Hippocrates recommended eating 'raw liver' as a cure for night-blindness. Folklore (or traditional remedies) used many different foods for curing illnesses.

The captain's log from Ferdinand Magellan's voyage around the world (1519–1522) gave detailed descriptions of scurvy in the crew and officers.

> '... we sailed the space of three months and 20 days, without tasting any fresh provisions. The biscuit we were eating. ... it was nothing but dust, and worms which had consumed the substance; ... we were obliged to subsist on saw-dust, and even mice were sought after with such avidity that they sold for half a ducat a piece.
>
> Nor was this all, our greatest misfortune was being attacked by a malady in which the gums swelled so as to hide the teeth, as well in the upper as the lower jaw, whence those affected thus were incapable of chewing their food.'

As the disease got worse the men became very tired and could not do any work. Many ships were wrecked because the crew were too tired to sail. Some captains thought that the sailors were simply lazy.

Sir Richard Hawkins found that oranges and lemons were 'a certain remedie for this infirmite' on his expedition around the world which began in 1593. Other sailors also purchased lemons before long journeys but they were difficult to keep fresh.

James Lind, a British naval doctor, carried out a careful scientific study in 1747 to find the cure for scurvy. He found that the only treatment which prevented scurvy was to eat oranges and lemons. In 1753, he published *A treatise on the scurvy*. It described that within a week of eating two oranges and one lemon each day, signs of scurvy disappeared from the sailors. Captain Cook put this knowledge to good effect in his voyages around the world in the 1770s. Captain Cook introduced raisins and sauerkraut as well as citrus fruits and he never missed an opportunity to take on board fresh fruit and vegetables.

In 1795, lemon juice was made compulsory for Royal Navy crews. Sixty years later the merchant seamen were required to take lemon juice. The sailors became known as 'limeys' because when they docked in America, the Americans thought they were drinking lime juice after the long sea passage. However, lime juice is not as effective as lemon juice in preventing scurvy.

Figure 5.1 *James Lind.*

Despite this evidence nobody knew what was in the fruit that prevented the disease. The cure was associated with sharp tastes (acids) and many were tried – even sulphuric acid! It was not until 1928 that the active ingredient of the fruit juice was found. It was first manufactured in 1933 and it is called vitamin C (ascorbic acid). The RDA (recommended daily amount) is 0.04 g, a tiny amount compared to carbohydrates but enough to help form the substances needed in the cells of the skin, blood vessels and bones.

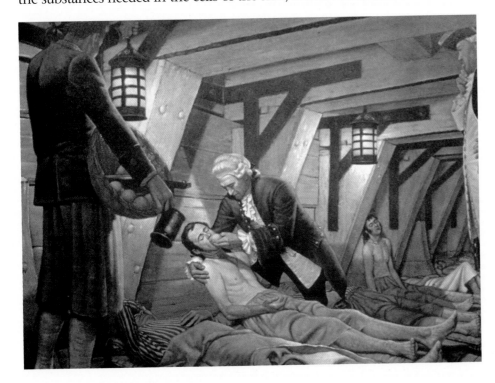

Figure 5.2 *A sailor being treated for scurvy.*

Questions

1 a) Why do you think that sailors often suffered from malnutrition? *[2]*
b) What are the signs of scurvy? *[3]*
[Total 5]

2 a) What is the chemical name for vitamin C? *[1]*
b) What foods can it be found in? *[1]*
[Total 2]

3 a) Name the person who recommended eating fresh fruit to stop scurvy. *[1]*
b) What was his job in the navy? *[1]*

c) How did he share his cure for scurvy with others? *[1]*
[Total 3]

4 a) What is meant by the RDA? *[1]*
b) What is the RDA for vitamin C? *[1]*
[Total 2]

5 What did Captain Cook do to stop his sailors getting scurvy on his voyages? *[Total 2]*

6 a) Who called the English sailors 'Limeys'? *[1]*
b) Why were they given this name? *[1]*
[Total 2]

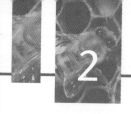

Eating to excess

Too much of a good thing?

In developed countries the vast majority of the population have access to more than enough food to meet their body's demands. As a result, deficiency diseases are uncommon. However, a different problem exists; a combination of too much food and too little exercise can result in **obesity**.

When someone exceeds their recommended **body mass**, we say they are **overweight**. If someone is very overweight, we use the term obese to describe their condition. One way to determine whether someone is overweight is to calculate their **body mass index (BMI)**.

$$BMI = \frac{\text{body mass (kg)}}{(\text{height (m)})^2}$$

A BMI of 20–25 is considered normal, whereas a BMI of 25–30 counts as overweight. Obesity is defined as having a BMI of greater than 30 (and 40 or higher is morbidly obese). In 2007, 24% of adults and 16% of children in the UK were obese. Table 5.1 (below) shows how the levels of obesity in children aged 11–15 have changed since 1996.

Figure 5.3 *Obesity is becoming increasingly common.*

?

1 Nikolay Valuev is a rather large Russian boxer. He stands 2.13 m tall, and he has a body mass of 151 kg. Calculate his BMI. *[Total 2]*

Year	1996	1998	2000	2002	2004	2006
Percentage of obese 11–15 year olds	14.3	16.9	18.5	19.5	25.4	17.4

Table 5.1 *Obesity in 11–15 year olds.*

A new epidemic: globesity

The increase in obesity rates is a global phenomenon, and doctors are worried because of the health problems that being obese can cause. Being obese greatly increases your chance of developing many diseases, including diabetes, cardiovascular disease (disease of the heart and blood vessels) and some forms of cancer. Many obese people also become depressed or suffer from low self-esteem.

?

2 What advice would you give an obese person who wants to lose weight? *[Total 2]*

Figure 5.4 *Nikolay Valuev.*

Atherosclerosis

One common form of cardiovascular disease is atherosclerosis, otherwise known as hardening of the arteries. In this condition, fatty deposits build up inside arteries, making them less flexible and too narrow. This makes it harder for blood to flow through them. When the arteries that supply blood to the heart are affected in this way, the heart muscle may not get enough oxygen for respiration. This can result in a chest pain called **angina**.

Cholesterol – good or bad?

Cholesterol is needed by our bodies for many important things, including making hormones, but too much can result in atherosclerosis. Lots of people have to take medication to lower their blood cholesterol. A group of chemicals called **statins** are some of the most widely used medicines available today, with over 3 million people in the UK taking them. Testing the effects of statins took many years as the diseases they help to prevent take a long time to develop. This meant scientists had to be very patient when waiting to see if these new drugs worked or not.

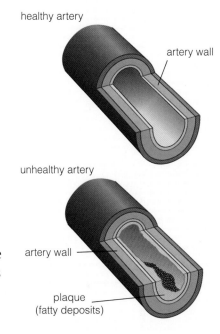

Figure 5.5 *An unhealthy artery compared to a healthy artery.*

In some countries obesity is a rare problem. In Japan for example, it only affects about 5% of adults. The levels are surprisingly high in other countries though, with over 30% of adults in the US being obese.

Questions

1 BMI values are not always good indicators of obesity. For example, athletes with lots of muscle may be classed as obese by their BMI, even though they are clearly not. Why do you think this is? *[Total 2]*

2 Suggest two reasons for the difference in obesity rates in Japan and the US. *[Total 2]*

3 Look at the data in Table 5.1.
   a) Draw a bar chart of the data. *[2]*
   b) Describe the change the chart shows. *[2]*
   c) Suggest reasons for the change you have described. *[3]*
   [Total 7]

4 Imagine you are a scientist who wants to see whether a new drug can lower cholesterol. Why do you think it might be difficult to find out whether it works? *[Total 2]*

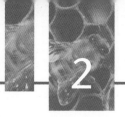
Enzymes

Enzymes in action

The properties of enzymes make them very useful in many areas of industry, and they may also be used in various ways in the home. Their ability to speed up very specific reactions under low temperatures and pressures means they can save a lot of time, energy and money.

Cheese production

Humans have been making cheese for thousands of years. The methods used have changed a great deal, but they have always relied on the action of enzymes in one way or another. Enzymes from the stomach lining of slaughtered calves or pigs were very widely used during the twentieth century, but technological advances have meant that microbes are now the main source of enzymes for use in cheese manufacture. Microbes can be grown in large vessels, and the enzymes they produce can be extracted from the liquid in which the microbes grow.

Medical uses

One of the symptoms of diabetes is the presence of glucose in urine. This can happen when blood glucose levels are too high for the kidneys to cope with. Doctors use strips called Clinistix™ to test urine for glucose, as it is an easy and quick way to tell if someone might have diabetes. Clinistix™ contain two enzymes and a substance that changes colour. The strips work in the following way:

a The stick is dipped into a urine sample.
b If there is any glucose in the sample, the first enzyme in the strip acts on it, producing a new chemical.
c The second enzyme in the strip then catalyses a reaction between this new chemical and the colour-changing substance in the strip.
d The resulting colour can be compared to a chart, from which the urine glucose level can be read off.

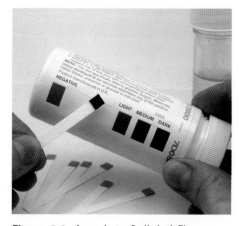

Figure 5.6 *A packet of clinistix*™.

> **!** In the 1980s, scientists discovered that some molecules of a substance called ribonucleic acid (RNA) could act as catalysts, just like enzymes. These catalytic RNA molecules are referred to as 'ribozymes'.

> **?** 1 Which groups of people do you think would object to eating cheese produced using enzymes from animal sources? *[Total 2]*

> **?** 2 What are the advantages of testing urine instead of blood for glucose? *[Total 2]*

Enzymes at home

Washing powders are big business. Biological powders contain enzymes that can digest substances that stain our clothes. The advantage of using biological washing powders is that they work much better than non-biological powders at low temperatures.

Biological washing powders usually contain one or more of the following types of enzymes:

○ proteases – which break down protein-based stains
○ amylases – which break down starchy material
○ lipases – which break down fatty or oily deposits.

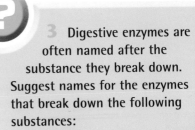

3 Digestive enzymes are often named after the substance they break down. Suggest names for the enzymes that break down the following substances:
   a) cellulose   [1]
   b) DNA   [1]
   c) lactose.   [1]
                  [Total 2]

The microorganism *Thermus aquaticus* grows in hot springs, at temperatures in excess of 70 °C – hot enough to hard-boil an egg. Its enzymes are very stable and do not denature at these temperatures.

Figure 5.7 *Enzymes are used in biological washing powder.*

Questions

1 Suggest why enzymes are useful in industry.
                          [Total 3]

2 Explain how glucose is detected by a Clinistix™.
                          [Total 4]

3 Enzymes can act as catalysts as they have very specific 3-dimensional shapes. Suggest why enzymes might stop working at high temperatures.   [Total 2]

4 Which type(s) of enzyme might be needed to break down each of the following stains?
   a) mashed potato   [1]
   b) blood   [1]
   c) butter   [1]
                          [Total 3]

End of section questions

1 Grass does not grow very well in the shade of large trees because it is in competition. Give three reasons why the grass only grows slowly. *[Total 3]*

2 The leaf is sometimes compared with a factory. Describe what you have to put into a leaf and what you get out. *[Total 5]*

3 Compare the different structures and functions of palisade cells and xylem vessels. *[Total 6]*

4 Describe two ways that small soluble substances can be absorbed into the blood. *[Total 4]*

5 Match the labels on Figure 1 with their name and function from the following list. Identify the part using the letter. *[Total 20]*

Name	Function
stomach	produces the enzyme amylase to start the digestion of starch
small intestine	produces bile to break down the fats in the diet
salivary gland	absorbs water from undigested remains of the food
gall bladder	crush the food into small manageable lumps
anus	produces acid to kill micro-organisms
liver	
pancreas	where faeces leaves the body
large intestine (colon)	temporary store of bile
teeth	has large surface area for absorption into the blood
rectum	produces enzymes to digest starch, protein and fat

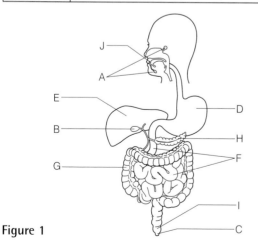

Figure 1

6 Frederick Gowland-Hopkins investigated the need for vitamins in the early twentieth century. He did the following experiment. Young rats were fed on a diet of pure milk protein, starch, sugar, lard and mineral salts for 18 days. A control group was fed on the same amount of each but each day 3 cm^3 of milk was added. The mass of the rats was recorded. The two groups were then fed on the opposite diet for a further 30 days. The results are shown in Figure 2.

a) What was in the milk that helped the growth of the rats? *[1]*

b) Which of the group of substances in part a) is most likely to be responsible for the difference in growth? *[1]*

c) State a conclusion for the experiment. *[1]*

d) Suggest why the without milk treatment was swapped between groups after 18 days. *[2]*

e) Suggest other factors that Gowland-Hopkins would need to keep the same between the two groups of rats. *[3]*

[Total 8]

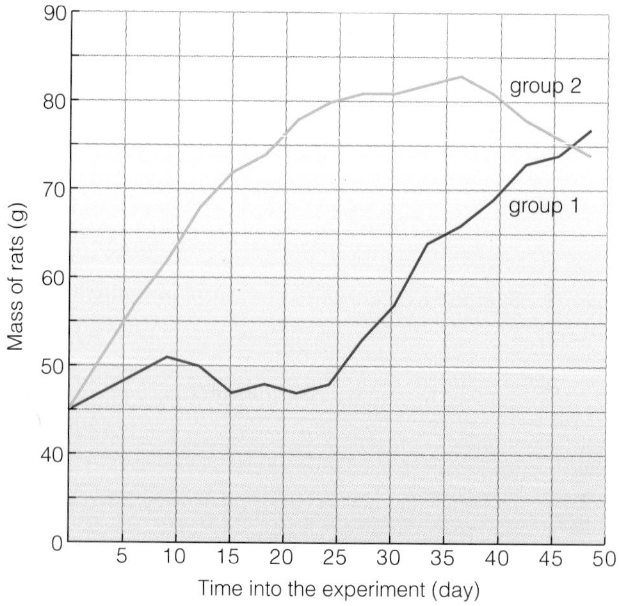

Figure 2

7 A trailing nasturtium plant was seen to be growing in bright sunshine but parts of the same stem was also entwined in a hedge. The light level was recorded for each of the leaves in the different positions. The leaves were taken and samples of each cut with a cork borer. 3 cm² was taken from each leaf and the amount of starch in each sample found. The leaf discs were crushed in a mortar and pestle, 5 cm³ of iodine solution added, the mixture filtered and the filtrate put into a colorimeter. The absorbance of the blue-black colour was measured. The results are shown in Table 1.

Light (lux)	3000	2500	2400	1500	900	850	750
Absorbance (%)	80	83	76	55	24	20	22

Table 1

   a) Plot the data on graph paper using suitable axes. [8]
   b) Explain why the leaf samples were ground in a mortar and pestle. [2]
   c) Why was iodine solution used? [1]
   d) What did the blue-black colour show? [1]
   e) Make a conclusion from the data. [1]
   f) Suggest how might this not be a fair test? [2]
                                             [Total 15]

8 Describe why we have different shapes of teeth.
                                             [Total 2]

9 a) What causes tooth decay? [3]
   b) How can we prevent tooth decay? [3]
                                             [Total 6]

10 Name two substances found in saliva and state what their functions are. [Total 4]

11 R Find out what good sources of protein are available to:
   a) a vegetarian
   b) a vegan.

12 R Find out the nutrients in a range of different foods. Use this information to help you plan a menu for a day. Make sure there is the RDA for each nutrient in your menu.

13 R Try to find out where a plant stores the products of photosynthesis. What types of chemicals are produced.

14 R Find out the menus available for the International Space Station from the NASA web site.

15 P How would you investigate the prediction that more light produces more bubbles from a piece of pondweed?

16 P How could you investigate the prediction that 40 °C is the best temperature for the protease enzyme pepsin to digest egg white?

3.1 Respiration

Oxygen and energy-rich substances like glucose are taken into the body but how does the cell get the energy it needs to work?

Use of energy

One of the characteristics of living organisms is **respiration**, the release of chemical energy in cells. Cells use the energy for all their reactions and processes. These processes include:

- movement – muscle contraction.
- making new substances from small molecules, e.g. proteins from amino acids.
- growth and repair – putting together substances to make new cells or to replace old cells.
- active transport – moving substances through a cell membrane against a concentration gradient.
- nerve impulses – energy is needed for nerve cells to pass impulses along their length.
- heat – to keep mammals and birds at a constant body temperature.

Plants also need energy for all the processes listed above, except for movement and nervous impulses.

Respiration

All organisms must have a source of energy. Animals eat food containing energy-rich substances like fat and starch. The substances are broken down by the digestive system into smaller molecules such as glucose. The digested molecules are absorbed into cells. Respiration takes place in the cytoplasm of cells. In the cytoplasm glucose is broken down to give carbon dioxide and water. This process also releases energy.

Plants get their energy from light. Most of the light energy is transferred to the energy-rich substances of glucose and starch. These substances are broken down and are used to release energy when the plant needs it. Plants need energy as much as animals do. Plants and animals need to release energy for cell reactions. The process of respiration occurs all the time in plants, just as it does in animals.

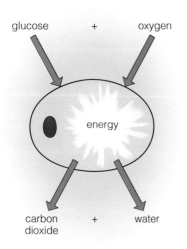

Figure 1.1 *Respiration.*

The reactions inside the cells need **enzymes** to carry them out. The enzymes help to control when the energy is released. If a cell does not need much energy, the enzymes are stopped from working.

Aerobic respiration

Aerobic respiration means the release of energy using oxygen. Oxygen is carried by the blood in animals and diffuses into cells. Glucose also travels to the cells in the blood. In plants the sugars are carried in phloem tissue. The phloem is found in the veins of the leaves and stem. Oxygen diffuses to all of the cells from the surface of the plant.

In the cytoplasm of cells there are specialised **organelles** called **mitochondria** which contain the enzymes needed for respiration. Oxygen diffuses into the mitochondria and is used to react with glucose to produce carbon dioxide and water. The chemical energy is transferred to a substance called ATP (adenosine triphosphate). Each molecule of ATP has a small amount of energy. The ATP can move around the cell to take the small packets of energy to all the reactions that need it. The word equation for aerobic respiration is:

glucose + oxygen → carbon dioxide + water + (energy)

When the glucose molecules are broken down inside a cell, some of the chemical energy cannot be transferred into ATP. About 60% of the energy is given off as heat. This is why your muscles get warm when they are working hard. All organisms give off heat to the environment.

Anaerobic respiration

Anaerobic respiration is the release of energy *without* oxygen. If a person runs very quickly then breathing might not bring in enough oxygen. The person still needs to move so the muscle cells short cut the respiration process. The glucose is only partly broken down. This happens very quickly but only a little of the energy can be transferred to the ATP. Most of the energy is left in the remaining substance which is called lactic acid.

?

1 In Section 1.5 you saw many different types of specialised cells. Which of them do you think have many mitochondria?

[Total 3]

!

You can test for carbon dioxide from respiration using limewater. If it becomes cloudy, then there was carbon dioxide in the air that was bubbled through it.

The word equation for anaerobic respiration in a muscle is:

$$\text{glucose} \rightarrow \text{lactic acid} + (\text{some energy})$$

There is enough energy released for the muscle to keep on working without oxygen. However, lactic acid is a poison and makes the muscle get tired. Too much lactic acid causes cramp and so it must be removed as soon as possible. The muscle cells need extra oxygen after the runner has stopped to turn the lactic acid into carbon dioxide and water. This extra oxygen is called the **oxygen debt**. It is why runners pant at the end of a sprint race.

In plants and microorganisms a different temporary substance is released instead of lactic acid. It is alcohol which is slightly less toxic (poisonous). Some types of yeast can stand up to 14% alcohol in their cells. The word equation for anaerobic respiration in plants and yeast is:

$$\text{glucose} \rightarrow \text{alcohol} + \text{carbon dioxide} + (\text{some energy})$$

The alcohol is usually excreted from the plant or yeast cells and they lose the energy in the molecules.

Humans have made use of this process of anaerobic respiration. It is called **fermentation**. One type of fungus called yeast is used to produce the alcoholic drinks wine and beer. Yeast is also used to make bread. Bread rises because the yeast gives off carbon dioxide both in aerobic and anaerobic respiration. The gas gets trapped in the sticky doughand forms bubbles. The bread becomes light and airy.

Figure 1.2 *Fermentation of hops and malted barley makes beer.*

Figure 1.3 *Yeast ferments sugar in bread.*

Summary

- Respiration is the release of energy in cells.
- Aerobic respiration uses oxygen and produces carbon dioxide and water.
- Anaerobic respiration releases less energy than aerobic respiration.
- Lactic acid causes tiredness and cramp in muscles.
- Fermentation is used in the food industry to produce wine, beer and bread.

Questions

1 Copy and complete the following sentences.
Respiration is the _____ of energy in cells.
Glucose is broken down into carbon dioxide and
_____ with the released energy able to be
used by the cell. Aerobic _____ releases
more energy for the cell than anaerobic respiration.
Lactic acid causes cramp. Alcoholic drinks are made
by a _____ reaction. *[Total 2]*

2 Write the word equation for aerobic respiration.
[Total 2]

3 Copy and complete Table 1.1. *[Total 4]*

	Aerobic respiration	Anaerobic respiration in humans
substrates	glucose oxygen	_____
products	_____ _____ ATP	lactic acid ATP
amount of energy released	high	_____

Table 1.1

4 a) Explain why a runner must respire anaerobically
after a while. *[1]*
  b) Explain what happens during anaerobic
respiration. *[2]*
  c) Why does the body need to remove lactic acid? *[1]*
  d) Explain what oxygen debt is. *[2]*
[Total 6]

5 Why does beer production give off bubbles
during fermentation? *[Total 1]*

6 The amount of respiration in seeds was measured in an
experiment. Some germinating seeds were put into a test
tube with some soda lime to absorb the carbon dioxide.

A manometer was attached and the position of the
dye measured at the start and after 10 minutes. The
apparatus is shown in Figure 1.5 and the results in
Table 1.2. A second tube containing sterilised, dead
seeds was also set up and the results recorded.
  a) By how much does the volume of the gases in
the respiration chamber of tube A decrease
in the 10 minutes? *[1]*
  b) Explain why the volume of gas decreased. *[2]*
  c) Give a conclusion about germinating seeds. *[1]*
  d) Suggest why the volume of gas increased in
tube B. *[1]*
  e) Suggest a change in the apparatus to make sure
that tube B stayed at a constant volume. *[1]*
[Total 6]

Figure 1.5 *A respirometer.*

	Tube A: germinating seeds	Tube B: sterilised, dead seeds
mass of seeds (g)	25	25
initial position of dye (mm³)	20	20
position of dye after 10 min (mm³)	5	22

Table 1.2

3.2 Breathing

You need to breathe to get oxygen. Oxygen is needed to release energy from food but how does breathing happen? Breathing can be divided into two parts. **Ventilation** is getting the air into and out of the lungs and **gas exchange** is getting the gases to move into or out of the blood. Gas exchange is a two-way process: waste gases are removed and oxygen is absorbed.

Ventilation in humans involves the movement of air through the nose or mouth, down the windpipe and into the lungs (inhaling). When you inhale the **diaphragm** contracts and flattens. The **rib muscles** move the ribs outwards and upwards. When the diaphragm and rib muscles contract, the volume in the chest increases so the air pressure in the lungs goes down. It goes below the atmospheric air pressure. Air rushes from the higher pressure outside the mouth into the area of lower pressure inside the lungs.

Figure 2.1 *Breathing system and lungs.*

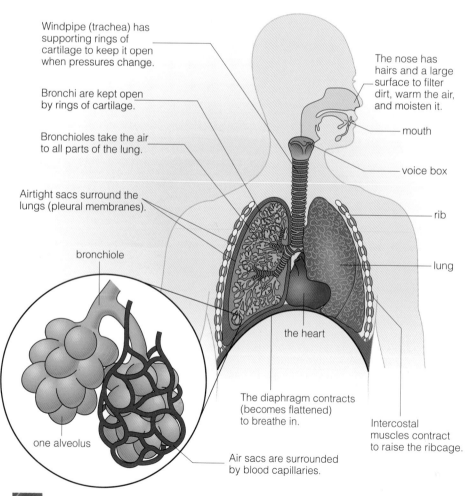

Windpipe (trachea) has supporting rings of cartilage to keep it open when pressures change.

Bronchi are kept open by rings of cartilage.

Bronchioles take the air to all parts of the lung.

Airtight sacs surround the lungs (pleural membranes).

bronchiole

one alveolus

Air sacs are surrounded by blood capillaries.

The diaphragm contracts (becomes flattened) to breathe in.

the heart

Intercostal muscles contract to raise the ribcage.

The nose has hairs and a large surface to filter dirt, warm the air, and moisten it.

mouth

voice box

rib

lung

To get the air out of the lungs again (exhaling), both the rib and diaphragm muscles relax. The ribs move down and in. The diaphragm returns to a dome shape making the volume of the chest smaller. This makes the air pressure in the lungs higher. The air is pushed out of the lungs.

The tissues of the lungs are elastic and recoil after being stretched like an elastic band. The elastic recoil helps the exhalation of the air. The lungs naturally return to the smaller, deflated, state.

In the lungs, gases can **diffuse** between the air and the blood. This gas exchange depends on the concentrations of each gas in the **alveoli** of the lungs and the concentration in the blood. The gases always move from where there is more of it (higher concentration) to where there is less (lower concentration). Table 2.1 shows typical concentrations of the gases. The difference in concentrations means that oxygen diffuses from the alveoli into the blood and carbon dioxide diffuses from the blood into the alveoli. This movement of the gases is called gas exchange. The changed air is then exhaled by the process of ventilation (breathing out).

Gas	Air entering lungs (%)	Blood entering lungs (% of saturation)
oxygen	20	10.6
carbon dioxide	0.03	58.0

Table 2.1 *Composition of gases in alveoli and blood.*

The diffusion depends on three factors.

- Large surface area. The larger the surface area, the more gas can diffuse. Breathing in deeper lets the air get to more alveoli and therefore more oxygen can diffuse into the blood.
- Short distance. The walls of the alveoli and capillaries (tiny blood vessels) must be very thin and close together so diffusion can happen as quickly as possible. The lining cells of the alveoli and capillaries are flattened like cheek cells but are even thinner (about 0.001 mm).
- Diffusion gradient. Diffusion happens faster when there is a bigger difference in concentrations. Breathing replenishes the oxygen in the alveoli and the blood flow takes the oxygenated blood away. This maintains a large difference in concentration between the gases in the alveoli and in the blood.

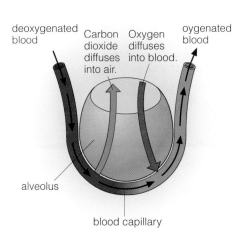

deoxygenated blood

Carbon dioxide diffuses into air.

Oxygen diffuses into blood.

oygenated blood

alveolus

blood capillary

Figure 2.2 *Alveolus and blood capillary showing diffusion of gases.*

The breathing system is designed to make sure the gases are exchanged at the rate they are needed. If more oxygen is needed by muscles because we are exercising, then the ventilation (breathing) rate goes up to increase the gas exchange. If the person rests then the breathing rate slows down.

> **!** Opera singers or anyone who trains their voice, can delicately control the flow of air to produce long notes from the voice box. The muscles between each rib and the stomach muscles give small contractions needed for the control.

> **?** 1 What is the difference between ventilation and gas exchange? [Total 2]

> **!** The muscles controlling breathing are under automatic as well as conscious control. This means that you will always breathe even if you are asleep.

Smoking

Breathing in substances other than fresh air causes harm to the breathing system. Smoke from tobacco causes many problems.

The smoke contains particles that irritate the lungs as well as thousands of different chemicals. The medical effects of the smoke are shown in Figure 2.3. The nicotine in cigarettes is addictive. Smokers cannot get as much oxygen into the blood or remove as much carbon dioxide. They cannot be as active as if they could if they did not smoke.

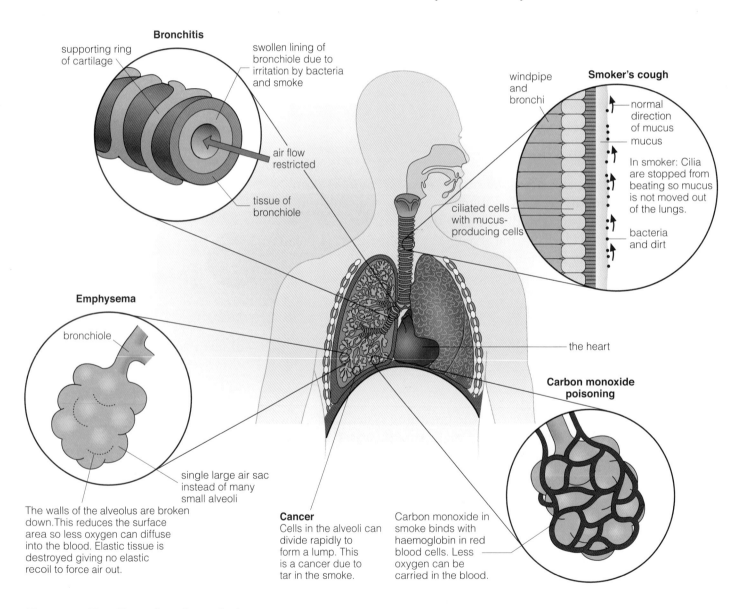

Figure 2.3 *The effects of smoke on the lungs.*

Asthma

Asthma develops when the bronchial tubes become swollen or inflamed. The muscles around the tubes contract to make the tubes narrow or the tubes are partly blocked by mucus. The narrowing of the tubes causes wheezy breathing.

The tubes usually narrow because of an allergy to house dust including house mite faeces. The faeces irritate the lining cells of the bronchi. The body reacts by getting a type of white blood cell to destroy the lining cells. The lining becomes swollen. Mucus, produced by the lining cells, becomes thicker and is not removed from the lungs. The mucus starts to block the airways.

The drugs in inhalers make the muscles around the bronchi relax so that the tubes open and it is easier to breathe. They do not cure the disease.

Gas exchange in plants

Plants also need to exchange gases. They need oxygen for respiration in the same way as animals but they also need carbon dioxide for photosynthesis.

Plants exchange the gases in their leaves. The air outside the leaf is free to move into the air spaces inside the leaf, through **stomata**. When the plant is photosynthesising, the carbon dioxide diffuses into the **mesophyll** leaf cells and oxygen diffuses out. In respiration the oxygen diffuses into the cells and carbon dioxide diffuses out. We notice this most when the plant is not photosynthesising i.e. when it is dark.

Figure 2.4 *The inhaler puts a very fine spray of a chemical around the air tubes inside the lungs, to make the muscles relax. This relieves the patient of the immediate problem and makes breathing easier.*

! Asthma is not a recent disease. The word asthma comes from the Greek (ασθμα) meaning 'short drawn breath'.

	Light (daytime)	Dark (night-time)
process	more photosynthesis than respiration	respiration only
oxygen	moves out of plant	moves into plant
carbon dioxide	moves into plant	moves out of plant

Table 2.2 *Gas exchange in plants.*

The leaf has similar adaptations to human lungs as there is a large surface area for diffusion inside the leaf and a short distance for the gases to move.

In a plant, the stem uses very little energy and so does not need much oxygen. The roots, buds and flowers have their own stomata to allow the gases to get to the cells. If the soil is full of water, all the air is pushed out. The roots of the plant cannot get oxygen for respiration. They cannot control the movement of the mineral salts into the plant and the plant may die.

Plants like the common rush (*Juncus squarrosus*) which live in boggy ground survive because they have special star shaped cells in the middle of the stem and root to keep the cells apart. This allows the air to move down to the roots from inside the plants. The oxygen is used by the root cells.

air space to take air into roots

Figure 2.5 *Common rush grows well in waterlogged ground.*

Summary

- Breathing is separated into ventilation and gas exchange.
- Air is moved into the lungs by contraction of diaphragm and rib muscles.
- Lung tissue is elastic to allow stretching and recoil for breathing out.
- Air moves through the nose or mouth, windpipe, bronchus, bronchiole, and into the alveoli.
- Diffusion of gases is made quicker by a large surface area, short distance and steeper diffusion gradient.
- Ciliated cells remove the mucus and trapped dirt or bacteria out of the bronchi and windpipe.
- Smoking causes heart disease, cancer, bronchitis and emphysema.
- Asthma is due to the narrowing of the air passages.
- Gases diffuse into and out of plant leaves through stomata.
- Carbon dioxide diffuses into the leaf in bright light and out of the leaf in darkness.

Questions

1 Copy and complete the following sentences.
The movement of air into and out of the lungs is called _____. The air movement is caused by pressure differences between the _____ in the lungs and the atmosphere. The _____ and rib muscles cause the ventilation. Oxygen diffuses into the blood and carbon dioxide _____ out. The alveoli in the lungs have very _____ walls to allow quick diffusion. The _____ carries the oxygen to all parts of the body. *[Total 3]*

2 Explain briefly why you need to breathe. *[Total 1]*

3 Briefly explain what is meant by:
a) ventilation *[1]*
b) gas exchange. *[1]*
[Total 2]

4 What is the difference between inhalation and exhalation? *[Total 2]*

5 Describe how the structure of the lungs makes gas exchange quick and efficient. *[Total 3]*

6 A smoker's cough is a deep clearing cough usually in the morning when the person first wakes up. It is caused because the cilia have worked and cleared some of the mucus with particles nearer to the throat. A cough clears some of the mucus. Use information about smoke to explain why the person stops coughing later in the day. *[Total 2]*

7 Explain why it is hard to breathe out during an asthma attack. *[Total 2]*

8 Match up the two halves of the sentence. Write out each full sentence. *[Total 4]*

Oxygen diffuses into the blood	in the blood.
Carbon dioxide is carried to the lungs	when there is a higher concentration in the lungs and a lower concentration in the blood.
In the dark, carbon dioxide	diffuses into a leaf.
When a plant photosynthesises the carbon dioxide	diffuses out of a leaf.

9 The gas contents of air and blood were measured to find out which gases were being used by the student. The results are shown in Table 2.3.
a) Which air sample contains the most oxygen? *[1]*
b) Which blood sample contains the most oxygen? *[1]*
c) Give a conclusion about the movement of oxygen. *[1]*
d) Which air sample contains the most carbon dioxide? *[1]*
e) Which blood sample contains the most carbon dioxide? *[1]*
f) Give a conclusion about the movement of carbon dioxide. *[1]*
g) Suggest why the nitrogen concentration remained the same for both the air and the blood. *[1]*
[Total 7]

Gas	Inhaled air (%)	Exhaled air (%)	Blood entering lungs (cm³ per 100 cm³)	Blood leaving lungs (cm³ per 100 cm³)
oxygen	21	16	10	19
carbon dioxide	0.03	4	58	50
nitrogen	79	79	0.9	0.9

Table 2.3

3.3 Blood and circulation

What is special about blood and the **circulatory system** of animals? Animals need to move about and must be a compact shape. However, exchanges with the environment need a large surface area. This conflict has been answered with the circulatory system. For example, an animal can take in oxygen through the lungs and get rid of carbon dioxide. The oxygen is transported quickly to the tissues by the circulatory system.

Circulation

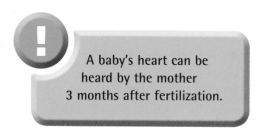

A baby's heart can be heard by the mother 3 months after fertilization.

The transport system develops very early in the embryo and is essential to make sure all the developing cells, tissues and organs get all the substances they need. Waste substances are also taken away from the cells.

The transport system consists of a pump (**the heart**), tubes to direct the flow (the **blood vessels**) and the **blood** as the carrying substance.

The circulatory system in humans is very efficient at taking oxygen to all of the organs and at removing waste carbon dioxide. Blood leaving the heart going towards the body will go to only one of the many organs. It is then returned to the heart and then the lungs for exchange of gases. The blood will always be carrying a large amount of oxygen to any organ and be able to remove the carbon dioxide quickly.

Before the blood goes to any organ, it is pumped by the heart so that it is always at high pressure. This means it always travels quickly to the organs and delivers the oxygen needed for respiration.

How quickly oxygen is delivered and carbon dioxide removed is important when we are exercising. The faster the delivery of oxygen, the more aerobic respiration can occur and the less tired we will be.

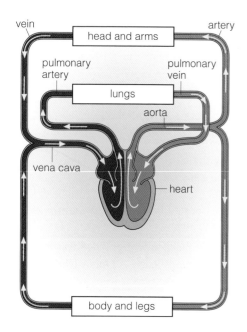

Figure 3.1 *The human double circulatory system.*

The heart

The heart works as two pumps. One pump pushes the blood towards the lungs and the other pushes blood to all other organs of the body. Both pumps work at the same time and push out the same volume of blood. The pump on the left side pushes blood to the body organs. It has a thicker wall of muscle because it must push the blood to more organs and this needs a greater force.

The blood flows into the heart at the top. It enters the very elastic, thin-walled chambers (the **atria**) and goes through open valves into the main pumping chambers called the **ventricles**. To push the blood out of the heart the thick walled ventricles contract strongly. The valves separating the chambers are automatically shut by the increasing pressure in the ventricles so that blood can not go back into the top chambers (atria). Blood rushes out through arteries to the body organs or to the lungs.

The **valves** in the heart make sure that the flow of blood does not go backwards. Sometimes the valves fail and a heart murmur can be heard through a stethoscope. Artificial valves have been made and implanted into the human heart. These have helped patients survive for many years.

The muscle of the heart is very special because it has its own rhythm of contraction. All of the atrial muscle contracts at the same time, just before all of the ventricular muscle contracts. The rhythm is set by a patch of cells in the wall of the right atrium (natural **pacemaker**). The overall rate is changed on demand by a nervous connection to the brain. More carbon dioxide in the blood causes the pacemaker to speed up it's rhythm.

Blood vessels

The blood is carried in continuous tubes of different sizes called blood vessels. They carry the blood to each organ in the body and take it back to the heart. In each organ blood vessels allow substances to move into and out of cells. Oxygen and glucose diffuse out to cells and carbon dioxide diffuses back into the blood. The direction of flow is kept up by the pumping of the heart. On the return journey valves are present in the veins to make sure blood does not flow back but continues towards the heart.

The blood leaves the heart through **arteries**. The arteries carry blood to an organ and then divide up into smaller arterioles and then into **capillaries**. Capillaries are the smallest blood vessels. They have very thin walls and allow exchange of soluble substances with the cells. The **veins** take the blood back to the heart.

The thickness of the blood vessel walls depends on the pressure of the blood in the vessel. Table 3.1 shows the differences between the types of blood vessel.

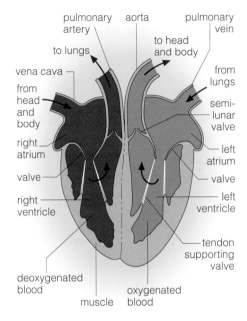

Figure 3.2 *Section through the heart. In the body the pump to the lungs is on the right side and the pump to the body is on the left side. The diagram appears the wrong way round because the view of the section is to the persons front.*

A human heart beats about 42 million times in a year.

The heart pacemaker starts its rhythm 6 weeks after fertilisation of the ovum.

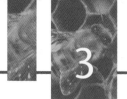

Arteries	Capillaries	Veins
carry blood away from heart	carry blood through organs and tissues	carry blood towards heart
blood at high pressure	blood at low pressure	blood at lowest pressure
no valves	no valves	valves to stop blood flowing back
thick muscular walls	very thin walls for escape of fluids	thinner walls with less muscle
no substances leave or enter vessel	exchange of substances with tissues	no substances leave or enter vessel
pulse created by heart pumping and contraction of wall muscle	no pulse	no pulse
strong walls	delicate and easily broken	flexible and squashed easily so blood pushed further along vessel

Table 3.1 *Differences between types of blood vessel.*

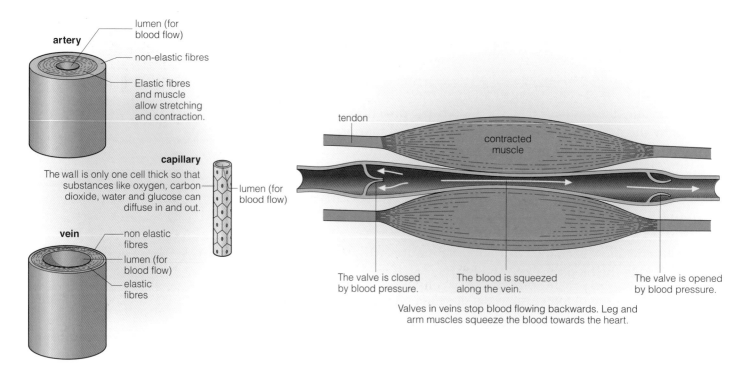

Figure 3.3 *Blood vessels.*

Figure 3.4 *Longitudinal section of vein.*

Blood

There are about 5 litres of blood in an average adult person and it makes one complete circuit of the body about once a minute, i.e. two passes through the heart, one through the lungs and once to one of the organs.

Blood is about 50% water and 50% cells by volume. Most of the cells are red because they contain the substance **haemoglobin**. These **red blood cells** are specialised: their function is to carry oxygen from the lungs to the tissues. They do not have a nucleus so the cell can contain more haemoglobin. Each blood cell is made in the bone marrow and only lasts for about four months as it travels round the body. Worn out or damaged red cells are destroyed by the liver. If the haemoglobin has been poisoned by carbon monoxide the whole red blood cell is destroyed. People who smoke have fewer working red blood cells to carry the oxygen because of the carbon monoxide they inhale.

White blood cells have the task of fighting disease. There are about 500 times fewer white blood cells than red blood cells. White blood cells are divided into different types, each with a special function. For example, the **phagocytes** can engulf a bacterium by moving around it and enclosing it. The phagocyte then digests the bacterium inside the cell. If many phagocytes have gone to one point in the skin to get rid of invading bacteria they form the white pus that you see in spots.

Other white blood cells called lymphocytes produce antibodies which are released into the blood plasma. Antibodies are substances which are specially produced to destroy just one type of invader. They help the body to kill a bacterium or a virus. If that type of bacterium invades the body again the same antibody can be produced more rapidly than before. The person is then immune to the bacterium.

Small fragments of cells, called **platelets**, help the blood to clot. Clotting is very important to stop bleeding and prevent microorganisms entering the body.

The liquid part of the blood is called **plasma**. It is water with many substances dissolved in it making it a pale yellow colour. Plasma carries small molecules such as glucose, amino acids and vitamins from the diet as well as hormones and heat. It is very important for the muscles and nerve cells to be given glucose as well as oxygen, so that they have a steady supply of energy. The waste products carbon dioxide and urea (from waste protein) are also carried in the plasma.

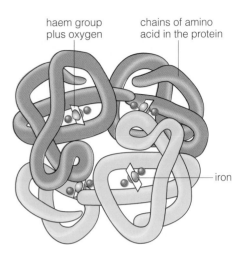

haem group plus oxygen
chains of amino acid in the protein
iron

Figure 3.5 *Haemoglobin molecule showing the need for iron and the carriage of oxygen. Haemoglobin is a type of protein.*

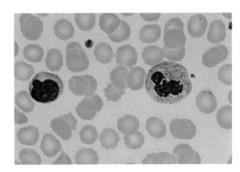

Figure 3.6 *Red and white blood cells. The red cells are thinner in the centre so have a lighter colour there. They do not have a nucleus. The white cells have a nucleus which has been stained to show up in the photograph.*

Figure 3.7 *The heart during an operation. The blood vessels feeding the heart muscle itself can be seen. These are the ones that can be blocked in a heart attack.*

Health problems of the heart and blood vessels

Heart attacks are caused by a blockage in a coronary artery (the blood vessels going to the muscular wall of the heart). The heart muscle does not get enough oxygen or glucose. That part of the heart muscle stops working so the whole heart cannot beat properly. The blockage can be caused by a blood clot getting stuck in a narrowed artery.

Nicotine from cigarette smoke makes the blood more likely to form clots. Too much fat in the diet causes a type of fat called cholesterol to be left on the inside of the arteries (atheroma). This makes them narrower and so a blood clot is more likely to get trapped.

A first aider will give cardiac compressions to the chest to squash the heart and so make the blood move around the body.

High salt in the diet causes blood pressure to increase. The higher blood pressure causes more fluid to be pushed out of the capillaries. The person is often heavier than necessary due to the extra fluid carried.

Angina is the first sign of heart disease with several of the arteries becoming narrower. A sharp pain develops in the left arm and the heart and the person gets tired much more quickly than they should.

A **stroke** happens when there is a blood clot in the blood vessels of the brain. The person becomes confused and usually becomes unconscious. Permanent damage to the brain can occur but a person can completely recover from the first stroke.

Summary

- The circulatory system carries substances around the body and helps to fight against disease.
- Humans have a double circulatory system, one to the lungs and one to the body.
- The heart acts as a pump for the blood to carry oxygen, nutrients, waste substances and hormones.
- Arteries carry blood away from the heart and veins carry blood towards the heart.
- Capillaries are found in the tissues, are very narrow and allow exchange of substances.
- Haemoglobin in red blood cells carries the oxygen.
- Blood platelets help clot the blood.
- White blood cells fight disease.
- Heart attacks occur when the heart stops pumping.
- Strokes occur due to a blood clot in the brain.

Questions

1 Copy and complete the following sentences.
Blood is pumped by the _____ The blood leaves the heart through _____. It goes to the _____ of the body where exchange of substances can occur. The _____ blood vessels are called capillaries. They have very thin walls to let the substances _____ in or out. The blood returns to the _____ in veins. Oxygen is carried in _____ blood cells by haemoglobin. A person with a high fat diet is likely to have _____ arteries. A blood _____ is more likely to form and get stuck at the narrowed point. If it happens in the _____ muscle the person may have a heart attack. *[Total 5]*

2 a) How many chambers does the human heart have? *[1]*
b) Name the two types of chambers. *[2]*
[Total 3]

3 a) What makes the valves in the heart shut? *[1]*
b) Why do they need to do this? *[1]*
[Total 2]

4 Explain why the left side of the heart has thicker muscle than the right side. *[Total 1]*

5 Explain what is meant by 'double circulation'. *[Total 2]*

6 a) Where are red blood cells made? *[1]*
b) What substance can poison red blood cells? *[1]*
[Total 2]

7 Copy and complete Table 3.2. *[Total 5]*

Artery	Capillary	Vein
carries blood from the heart	blood flows from arteries to veins	
very thick wall consisting of muscle		thinner wall with no muscle
	blood flows slowly	blood flows slowly
can feel pulse	no pulse	
no valves		valves to stop blood flowing back

Table 3.2

8 Describe the flow of blood from a leg muscle to the heart and lungs and back to the muscle listing each organ the blood travels through and what happens at each place. *[Total 8]*

9 a) What type of cell helps to form blood clots? *[1]*
b) Why is blood clotting important? *[2]*
[Total 3]

10 Explain the following conditions:
a) a heart attack *[3]*
b) a stroke *[2]*
c) atheroma. *[2]*
[Total 7]

11 What makes the human circulatory system so efficient at carrying oxygen to the tissues? *[Total 3]*

3 Releasing energy

Athletics and training

Figure 4.1 *Sprinters can allow anaerobic respiration to be their main source of energy.*

When an athlete runs, the small amount of energy stored as ATP in their muscles is used up quickly. More energy must be released by respiration. The available stores of oxygen and energy rich compounds in the muscles start to be used up. New supplies must be taken to the muscles by the blood. If the muscles need more energy than can be released with the supply of oxygen, then anaerobic respiration occurs.

The amount of carbohydrate (energy supply) stored in the muscles can be increased if the athlete trains until exhausted and eats a high carbohydrate diet. The muscle gets better at absorbing glucose and converting it into the storage carbohydrate, glycogen. The glycogen can be used to supply energy because it is broken down into glucose and used in respiration. The person does not get as tired as quickly and can carry on at higher speeds for longer. Taking sports drinks with glucose in them can help to increase performance. As well as the extra energy it gives them the water in the drink also stops athletes getting dehydrated and they can keep on cooling the body by sweating. Too much fat in the diet stops the muscle cells taking up glucose from the blood and makes the cells slower to release energy needed.

Exercising muscles helps them to grow. Eating the RDA (recommended daily amount) of protein is enough for the muscles to grow and be stronger. Some athletes eat high-protein diets to increase their muscle growth.

If not enough oxygen is provided during exercise, anaerobic respiration occurs until the muscles poison themselves with lactic acid (see pages 63–64). Short duration, 'explosive' events can allow anaerobic respiration to be the main source of energy. A top class sprinter running a 100 m race may not breathe at all during the race (Table 4.1).

Table 4.1 *Summary of approximate oxygen needs of winning athletes in different kinds of events.*

Event	Total energy expended (kJ)	Oxygen needed (dm^3)	Oxygen breathed in (dm^3)	Oxygen debt (dm^3)	% of energy from aerobic respiration	% of energy from anaerobic respiration
100 m	200	10	0–0.5	9.5–10	0–5	95–100
1500 m	720	36	19	17	55	45
42 186 m (marathon)	14 000	700	685	15	98	2

However, a person running a marathon can't allow anaerobic respiration to be the main source of energy. Marathon runners train so they do not build up any lactic acid until the last moments of the race. Their speed is limited by the ability of the circulatory system to get oxygen to the muscles and release energy (see Table 4.1). The last lap of a race or last few minutes is when the marathon runner can run faster.

Training for athletics can help the body do the following:

- increase glucose uptake into muscle cells from the blood
- increase the storage of glycogen (carbohydrate energy) in the muscle cells
- increase tolerance of the muscles to lactic acid – they can carry on working with more lactic acid in them
- increase the strength of the heart muscle and skeletal muscles
- increase the volume of blood that can be pumped out of the heart at one beat (stroke volume)
- increase the number of red blood cells in the blood
- increase the depth and rate of breathing for more gas exchange.

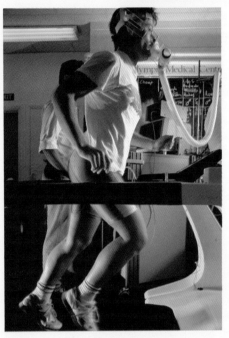

Figure 4.2 *Marathon runners must train in a very different way to sprinters.*

Questions

1 a) Sprinters eat high-protein diets. Explain why. *[1]*
  b) Suggest why a high-protein diet does not improve performance for marathon runners. *[2]*
    [Total 3]

2 Explain how the following allow a better performance by athletes:
  a) greater number of red blood cells *[2]*
  b) greater store of glycogen in the muscles *[1]*
  c) increased tolerance of muscles to lactic acid *[1]*
  d) taking in liquids during a marathon race. *[1]*
    [Total 5]

3 Which type of athletic race receives the greatest proportion of energy from:
  a) anaerobic respiration *[1]*
  b) aerobic respiration? *[1]*
    [Total 2]

4 According to Table 4.1, 1500 m runners show the highest oxygen debt.
  a) How does an oxygen debt form? *[1]*
  b) Suggest why 1500 m runners develop a greater oxygen debt than marathon runners. *[2]*
    [Total 3]

5 a) What is meant by the term 'stroke volume'? *[1]*
  b) Suggest how increasing the stroke volume helps athletes. *[1]*
    [Total 2]

6 Suggest a training regime for a long-distance runner in order for him or her to improve his or her performance. *[Total 4]*

3 Releasing energy

Ideas about blood circulation

Ideas in science develop over long periods of time. Careful observation and investigations are needed and many scientists are often involved. However, William Harvey is always associated with the 'discovery' of circulation of the blood.

During the Roman Empire the philosopher Galen (born about AD 130) was the first to describe the organs of the body. He thought that the liver was the centre of the circulatory system and that the heart regulated the flow and cooled the blood by the chest movements. He wrote, 'Smoky vapours from the heart were given out'. Galen believed that blood passed from the right side to the left side of the heart through invisible pores in the dividing wall.

Religious beliefs stopped further observations until the Renaissance period when a Belgian scientist called Andreas Vesalius (1514–1563) made careful observations. Vesalius said that the blood could not pass from the right to the left side of the heart but he did not provide another idea. He still thought that Galen's idea about the importance of the liver in the flow of blood was correct. Vesalius lost his job at the University of Padua (Italy) because of his ideas.

In 1553, a Spanish theologian and physician called Servetus wrote a book that included the idea that the blood must go through the lungs to get from the right to the left side of the heart. He died at the stake because he preached ideas which did not agree with the teachings of the Catholic Church.

Gerolamo Fabrizio d'Aquapendente (called Fabricius) (1533–1619) also worked at Padua and described the operation of valves in veins to show one-way flow. However, he got the direction wrong believing the blood flowed away from the heart in the veins. Fabricius was one of the tutors for the Englishman William Harvey (1578–1657) who is credited with the discovery of the circulatory system.

Harvey was the first to collect all the observations together and add his own evidence. His work *Exercitatio anatomica de motu cordis et sanguinus in animalibus* (anatomical study concerning the heart and blood in animals) was published in 1628. He described the heart as a pump. The chambers were filled during the resting phase and then the muscles contracted to force the blood out. The blood flowed from the left ventricle, through the aorta to the different organs of the body. Somehow it then got to the veins where it returned to the heart.

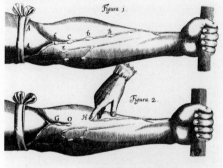
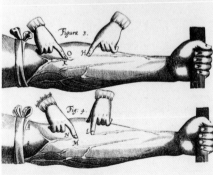

Figure 4.3 *Diagram from Harvey's book. It shows valves in the veins only allowing blood to flow back up the arm.*

The valves and direction of flow were correctly observed and the evidence of swelling of the veins by the valves was described (Figure 4.3).

Harvey described the return of the blood to the right side of the heart followed by movement to the lungs where it was turned into arterial blood. By this he meant oxygenated. It was not until later that John Mayow (1643–1679), who was born in Cornwall, carried out a simple experiment to show the oxygenation of blood. He passed air through venous blood. It became bright red like arterial blood. This confirmed Harvey's idea of the connections in the lungs. The idea that oxygen was needed by the body and carried in the blood was not realised until a century later, after the work of Priestley and Lavoisier, who discovered the element.

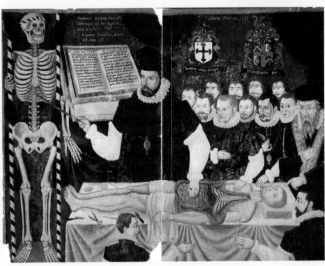

Figure 4.4 *Teaching anatomy.*

In 1660, Marcello Malphighi managed to see minute vessels with blood flowing through them (capillaries). He used a simple microscope and the wing of a bat to see the tiny vessels in the thin membrane of the wing. This completed the evidence needed for Harvey's ideas about the circulation of blood.

Questions

1
a) What did Galen think was the centre of the circulatory system? [1]
b) What role did Galen find for the heart? [1]
c) How did Galen think the blood got from the right side of the heart to the left? [1]
[Total 3]

2
a) What was the difference between Galen's and Vesalius' ideas? [1]
b) What were the similarities between their ideas? [1]
[Total 2]

3
a) How did Servetus suggest that the blood could get from the right to the left side of the heart? [1]
b) How did Servetus share his ideas with others? [1]
c) How might he share his ideas with others today? [2]
[Total 4]

4
a) How did Harvey describe the heart? [1]
b) What did Harvey consider to be the role of:
i) the aorta (and other arteries)
ii) the veins? [2]
c) What did Harvey think was the function of the valves in the veins? [1]
d) How did John Mayow build on Harvey's ideas? [2]
[Total 6]

5
a) Which type of blood vessel was the last to be discovered? Suggest why it was last. [2]
b) What needed to be invented before this blood vessel was discovered? [1]
[Total 3]

6 Suggest a reason why some scientists do not want to publish their results. [Total 1]

End of section questions

1 Which of the following cell types would have more mitochondria. State a reason for the answer.

Human cheek cell   Muscle cell
Ciliated cell   Fat storage cell   *[Total 2]*

2 Copy and complete the table to explain the differences between aerobic and anaerobic respiration in animals.

Feature	Aerobic respiration	Anaerobic respiration
gases used		
substances used		
gases produced		
other substances produced		
amount of energy released		

Table 1 *[Total 10]*

3 Make a table to compare features of lungs and leaves for gas exchange. *[Total 8]*

4 Explain how the following conditions make it more difficult to breathe:
a) emphysema   *[2]*
b) asthma   *[2]*
    [Total 4]

5 a) What is the commonest cause of asthma?   *[1]*
b) Treatment using the muscle relaxant in blue inhalers does not cure asthma. Explain the difference between stopping the signs of the asthma attack and curing the disease.   *[2]*
    [Total 3]

6 a) What is diffusion?   *[1]*
b) Describe how the diffusion gradient for oxygen from the alveolus to the blood is maintained.   *[2]*
    [Total 3]

7 Ben investigated his breathing rate during exercise. He used an exercise machine for 5 minutes and breath sensors. The results are recorded below.

Exercise rate	Volume of air per breath (cm^3)	Breaths per minute
at rest	400	20
during running	800	45
after running for 5 min	1000	32

Table 2

a) What is the total volume of air breathed in per minute:
  i) at rest
  ii) during running
  ii) after running for 5 min?   *[3]*
b) The difference in amount of oxygen between the air breathed in and out is 4%. Calculate how much oxygen is diffused into the blood per minute:
  i) at rest
  ii) during running
  iii) after running.   *[3]*
c) Ben felt tired after running. What type of respiration was occurring in their muscles towards the end of running?   *[1]*
d) Why is the amount of oxygen diffusing into the blood greater after running than at rest?   *[2]*
e) List five different uses of the energy released when Ben was at rest. For each one suggest how it allows the person to survive.   *[10]*
    [Total 19]

8 Draw a sketch diagram of the double circulation system of humans labelling the 'body', heart and lungs. On it colour the oxygenated blood bright red and the deoxygenated blood dark red. Label the arteries and veins.   *[Total 10]*

9 Make a table to show the different parts of the blood, the special features of each part and the function that each part does. *[Total 12]*

10 Copy and complete the table below.

Substance carried in plasma	Organ or tissue where substance enters the blood plasma	Organ or tissue where substance leaves the blood plasma
oxygen		all tissues
	all tissues	lungs
glucose		all tissues
	lymphocytes	all tissues

Table 3   *[Total 4]*

11 a) Give two examples of foods produced using anaerobic respiration. *[2]*
b) Explain how anaerobic respiration is used in the production of each food from part a). *[4]*
[Total 6]

12 Explain why the following features are needed for efficient gas exchange:
a) rings of cartilage surrounding the windpipe and bronchi *[1]*
b) very thin lining cells of the alveolus *[1]*
c) chest cavity made air-tight by a pair of pleural membranes *[1]*
d) air moves into the lungs when the space in the chest gets bigger *[1]*
e) elastic air sacs *[1]*
[Total 5]

13 R Find out why it is more difficult to breathe (ventilate the lungs) at high altitude (e.g. walking in the Himalayas) than at sea level.

14 R Find out how the oxygen is carried to the cells in insects and simple animals like sea anemones.

15 R Find out how whales are able to hold their breath for up to 112 minutes during a single dive.

16 R a) Find out the name of some illnesses related to smoking.
b) Find out how many people in the UK die each year from smoking-related illness. Also find out what the estimated cost of treating smoking diseases is.

17 R A man has a heart attack. A first-aider gives 'cardiac pulmonary resuscitation' (cardiac compression). How does the first-aider do the CPR and how could it save the man's life?

18 P Bread rises because of the respiration of yeast. What factors would affect the amount that bread might rise?

19 P How would you investigate the effect of increasing sugar concentration on the speed of respiration of a suspension of yeast?

20 P How would you investigate the effect of increasing rate of exercise on the breathing rate? [Write your answer as a series of bullet point statements. Include the terms dependent and independent variables.]

4.1 Skeletons and movement

Why do you have a skeleton? Animals have a skeleton to support their bodies, and muscles that help them to move. Movement requires energy. Muscles use energy in the body to produce movement.

Skeleton

A skeleton provides support and protection. Animals like jellyfish and earthworms do not have a bony skeleton. However, jellyfish are supported by water around them. Earthworms are supported by water inside their bodies: this is called a hydrostatic skeleton. Animals with backbones are called **vertebrates** and have internal skeletons called **endoskeletons**. Animals like lobsters and insects, which are **invertebrates**, do not have a backbone. However, they have a tough outside (external skeleton), which is called an **exoskeleton**.

Exoskeletons provide good overall protection. The skeleton is like an armoured overcoat but as the animal grows, it needs to replace its exoskeleton. It sheds its tough protective outer skeleton, and a new larger skeleton takes its place. However, the new skeleton is soft to start with. During the shedding of the old skeleton and the hardening of the new one, the animal is extremely vulnerable to predators, because it has no protection.

The human **skeleton** is sometimes referred to as a framework. Without a skeleton we would be shapeless blobs. A skeleton has many similarities to the frame of a bicycle:

- both must be strong and light for easy movement.
- they are both structures made up of many parts.
- bones and bicycle frames tend to be tubes, which carry loads and transfer forces efficiently.

Bones

There are 206 bones in the human skeleton. Some of the bones are hollow in the middle and contain a substance called **marrow**. This makes them extremely light and strong. The total weight of an adult skeleton is approximately 9 kg. Bone is a mixture of living tissue and non-living material. The living tissues contain cells and collagen fibres. The collagen allows the bones to be flexible. The non-living part of bone is made up of mineral salts such as calcium phosphate.

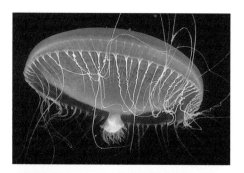

Figure 1.1 *Jellyfish have no skeleton. Locusts have an exoskeleton that they must shed as they grow.*

! The backbone (vertebral column) is not the longest bone in the body. The backbone is actually 33 small bones joined. They protect the spinal cord. The longest bone in the skeleton is found in the thigh and the smallest is found in the ear.

The calcium phosphate makes the bone hard. Without it the bone would be flexible like the cartilage found in the ear or in the end of the nose.

Bone growth occurs in children and adolescents. Growth takes place at the ends of the bones. If there is a shortage of calcium during a child's life then the bones remain soft and can become deformed. This is called **rickets**. In later life, adults whose bones lack calcium can develop brittle bones which break easily.

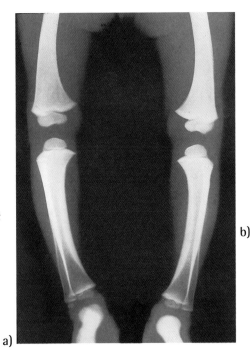

a)

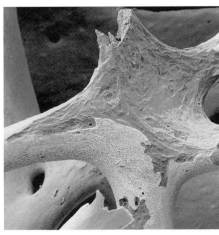

b)

Figure 1.2 a) *X-rays of bones of a child with rickets* b) *Brittle bones in an adult.*

Although bone is a strong material it can be broken. Breaks are repaired by the bone cells producing more collagen fibres and releasing more calcium phosphate. However, bone can also be strengthened during exercise. This is because extra fibres and calcium salts are added to the parts of the bone where most stress takes place.

The bones of the skeleton have four main functions:

⦿ They provide *support*, which allows the body to stand upright.
⦿ They give *protection* to many organs. For example the bones of the skull are joined together to make a strong box to protect the brain, and the ribs form a cage that protects the lungs and heart.
⦿ Together with muscle they can produce *movement*.
⦿ *Blood cells* are made in the bone marrow.

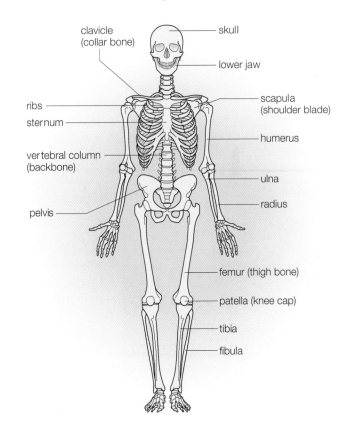

Figure 1.3

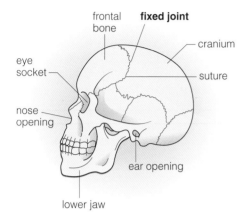

Figure 1.4 *Fixed joints in the skull.*

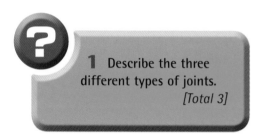

1 Describe the three different types of joints.
[Total 3]

Figure 1.5 *Hinge and ball and socket joints.*

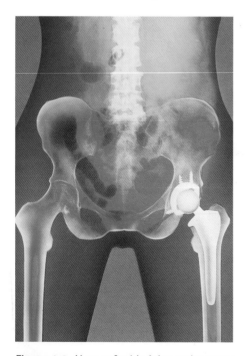

Figure 1.6 *X-ray of a hip joint replacement.*

Joints

Different parts of the body need to move in different ways. A **joint** is a place where two bones meet. There are three types of joint:

- **Fixed joint:** bones meet but there is no movement. The bones of the skull demonstrate this.
- **Hinge joint:** the bones here move in only one direction, a good example is the knee joint.
- **Ball and socket joint:** the bones can swivel and move in any direction. One bone of the joint has a round end that fits into a round hole in the other bone, as in our shoulders and hips.

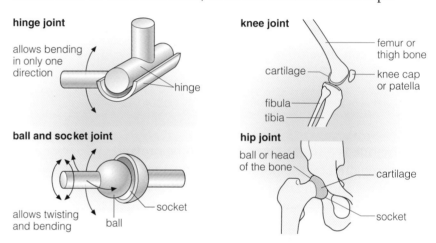

The skull protects the brain and has joints. The bones grow joints where they meet. In a fetus the skull bones are not joined (fused). This is because during birth the bones of the skull move so that the head of the baby can be squashed and pass through the mother's pelvis. Once born, the baby has a hole in its skull called the **fontanelle**, or soft spot. The joints of the skull close up slowly to allow brain growth.

The joints that allow movement do so because the bones can slide against each other. The surface of the bones at the joints is covered in a tough, smooth substance called **cartilage**. This protects the bones so that they do not wear away. The cartilage also acts like a shock absorber. The joints are lubricated with a liquid called **synovial fluid**. The whole joint is wrapped by a **ligament** which is a flexible, elastic material.

Exercising regularly helps to keep joints working smoothly. As people get older the lubricating fluid in the joints may dry up. This may result in them suffering with diseases such as arthritis or rheumatism. The cartilage gets so worn down that the end of the bone cannot move freely and rubs together. The diseased joints become swollen and painful. Doctors are able to replace some diseased joints.

Movement

The bones of a skeleton cannot move on their own. The movement of joints is controlled by **muscles**. These are attached to the bones and can pull the bones into different positions.

Muscle is tissue that can contract and makes up part of the body. It is attached to bones by cords called **tendons**, which do not stretch. A muscle works by shortening and pulling. When this happens a muscle gets shorter. We can actually see our muscles working. As a muscle works it gets shorter or **contracts**. It becomes hard, looks fatter and bulges out more. A muscle can **relax** and stop pulling, but it cannot stretch and push on the bones to get the joint back to its original position. The bone must be pulled by another muscle. Muscles always work in pairs. Wherever there is one muscle there is another to work against it. This arrangement is known as an **antagonistic pair**.

The arrangement of the bones in a bird's wing is similar to the bones of a human arm. The bird's wing is moved by muscles. The flight muscles are large and powerful and are attached to the breast bone. There are two flight muscles. One pulls the wing up and the other pulls it down. The most powerful muscles are the ones that pull the wings down. Bird bones are extremely light.

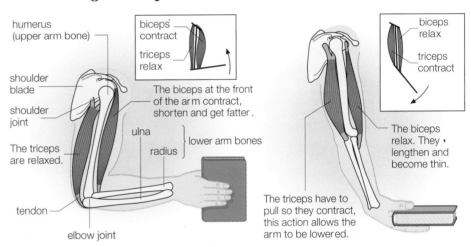

Figure 1.7 *The contraction of one muscle causes the opposite effect in its paired muscle.*

Summary

- An external skeleton provides protection and support, but it must be shed so that growth can occur.
- The major functions of the internal skeleton are to support and protect vital organs and aid movement.
- All moveable joints of the body have cartilage to protect the bones and synovial fluid to lubricate them.
- The bones of a joint are held together by ligaments.
- Muscles are attached to bones by tendons.
- Bones move because muscles contract and pull on the tendons.
- Muscles always work in pairs.

Questions

1 Copy and complete the following sentences.
The human _____ contains 206 bones. Many of the tissues of the body are soft and need strong _____ to give them support. The skull, ribcage and pelvis are where bones surround and _____ organs. _____ are attached to bones and can pull, which results in _____. Bones are linked by different types of _____. Joints are protected from wear and tear by _____ at the ends of bones and _____ fluid in between them.   *[Total 4]*

2 a) Explain why some of the bones of the skeleton are hollow.   *[1]*
b) What properties does this give bones?   *[2]*
[Total 3]

3 What are the three main functions of the skeleton?   *[Total 3]*

4 The skull that protects the brain has joints. State two reasons why this is so.   *[Total 2]*

5 Osteoporosis is a condition which affects one in three women and one in twelve men over the age of 60. Their bones become thin and brittle. What measures could people take to stop this condition arising?
[Total 2]

6 Copy and complete Table 1.1.   *[Total 7]*

Part of body	Type of joint
knee	
hip	
elbow	
shoulder	
ankle	
finger	
top of skull	

Table 1.1

7 Footballers often damage their joints. They may tear a ligament in the ankle or damage the cartilage in their knee.
a) Explain simply why these accidents happen. *[1]*
b) Why does damaging cartilage make it painful to move the joint?   *[2]*
c) What properties do ligaments have?   *[2]*
d) Suggest how the properties of ligaments help them in their function.   *[2]*
[Total 7]

8 a) What is muscle?   *[1]*
b) Where are the biceps and triceps?   *[1]*
c) Explain why muscles work in pairs.   *[2]*
d) What are tendons?   *[1]*
[Total 5]

9 As well as calcium phosphate, bone contains calcium carbonate. Hydrochloric acid will remove the calcium carbonate by dissolving it. Describe what you think would happen to bone if it were treated with hydrochloric acid for 24 hours.
[Total 2]

10 Some animals have an exoskeleton.
a) Describe what an exoskeleton is.   *[2]*
b) What disadvantage is there in having an exoskeleton when growing?   *[2]*
[Total 4]

4.2 Responses and behaviour

How do living things respond to changes in their environment? **Stimuli** are changes in the environment, which cause a response (or a reaction). A stimulus can be large or small and may come in different forms. Your alarm clock in the morning is a stimulus. In plants, light is an important stimulus. The responses in plants are slow because they are controlled by chemicals. Animals respond more quickly and their behaviour is coordinated by the nervous system. The main function of the nervous system is to carry messages called **impulses** to and from parts of the body.

The nervous system

The nervous system is made up of two parts – **the central nervous system** (CNS) and the **peripheral nervous system** (PNS). The brain and spinal cord form the CNS which interprets and coordinates the information. The PNS has nerves and **receptors**. Receptors are cells or modified nerve endings that can respond to a stimulus. The receptors detect stimuli and send electrical impulses to the CNS. The five sense organs (eyes, skin, ears, nose and tongue) are important **receptor organs** of the nervous system. The nervous system contains many nerve cells called **neurones**.

There are two examples of neurone.

- Sensory neurones carry impulses from a receptor to the CNS.
- Motor neurones carry impulses from the CNS to a muscle or a gland. These cause a response in the body, for example a muscle will contract and move a limb.

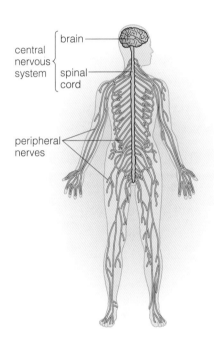

Figure 2.1 *The nervous system.*

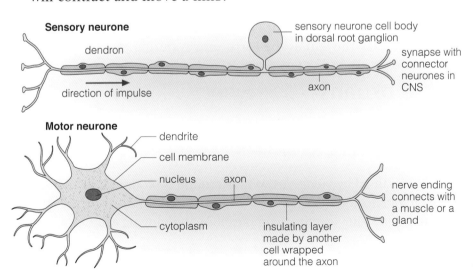

Figure 2.2 *Types of nerve cells.*

Nerve cells are made up of a **cell body** that contains the nucleus and a long fibre called an **axon** (Figure 2.2). The position of the cell body is different in sensory neurones and motor neurones. The **dendrites** at the ends of the nerve cell body are very important. These interconnect with other neurones so that nerve impulses can pass from one neurone to another, but only in one direction.

Neurones do not touch each other. **Synapses** are junctions in-between neurones. The synapses pass information between neurones. Substances are released from the end of a neurone. These substances diffuse across the gap between the two neurones and then set up an impulse in the next neurone. Substances like alcohol reduce the speed of the substances crossing the gap. This slows down the body's reactions.

> ❗ People who suffer with the disease multiple sclerosis eventually lose the use of their muscles. The disease causes the cells around the axon to break down, which stops nerve impulses from reaching the muscles.

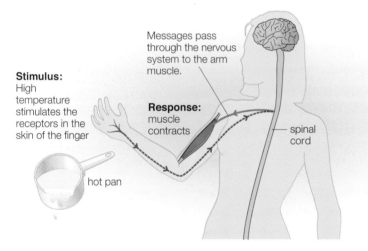

Stimulus:
High temperature stimulates the receptors in the skin of the finger

Messages pass through the nervous system to the arm muscle.

Response: muscle contracts

spinal cord

hot pan

Figure 2.3 *A reflex arc.*

Reflex actions

A rapid automatic response to a stimulus is called a **reflex action**. When you move your hand away from a hot object you are responding to a heat stimulus. The impulses are sent from the hand to the spinal cord then to the muscle, which moves the hand. The impulses take the shortest possible route which is called a **reflex arc**. There are different types of reflexes, e.g. blinking or coughing if food goes down the wrong way. Most reflexes all protect the body from harm.

Plants do not have reflexes but do respond to stimuli such as light. Sunflowers track the Sun as the Earth moves during the day.

Sense organs

The ear

Our ears help us to hear and to balance.

Sounds are caused by vibrations. When a sound is produced the molecules in the air vibrate and the sound moves one place to another by the molecules squeezing together (compression) and moving apart.

Figure 2.4 *Sunflowers point towards the sun all day.*

The ear is very sensitive. When taking off in aeroplanes, our ears sometimes hurt. This is due to a change in air pressure, which makes the eardrum bulge outwards. When we swallow or yawn the eardrum moves back to its original position. Loud noises can cause damage to the nerves in the ear and even a blocked ear channel can result in a temporary loss of hearing or deafness.

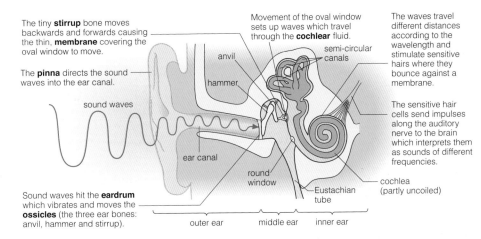

The tiny **stirrup** bone moves backwards and forwards causing the thin, **membrane** covering the oval window to move.

The **pinna** directs the sound waves into the ear canal.

sound waves

Sound waves hit the **eardrum** which vibrates and moves the **ossicles** (the three ear bones: anvil, hammer and stirrup).

Movement of the oval window sets up waves which travel through the **cochlear** fluid.

anvil

hammer

ear canal

round window

Eustachian tube

semi-circular canals

The waves travel different distances according to the wavelength and stimulate sensitive hairs where they bounce against a membrane.

The sensitive hair cells send impulses along the auditory nerve to the brain which interprets them as sounds of different frequencies.

cochlea (partly uncoiled)

outer ear   middle ear   inner ear

Figure 2.5 *Inside the ear.*

When we move our head the fluid in the **semi-circular canals** moves. Each canal has a small chamber called the **ampulla** at one end that is lined with sensitive hair cells. These hair cells are connected to a nerve, which sends information to the brain about the person's state of balance or movement. The reason we feel dizzy after spinning around, is because fluid in the semi-circular canal continues to move even when we have stopped. The brain is confused, because although the body is stationary, conflicting messages are still being sent from the ear.

! Ballet dancers can stop themselves from getting dizzy when spinning. They turn their heads in a series of jerks so that it does not spin with the rest of their body.

The eye

The structure of the eye is very complex. The eye senses light and enables us to see (Figure 2.6). The image that is formed on the retina is upside-down because light travels in straight lines. The brain then processes the information so that the image is interpreted as being the correct way up.

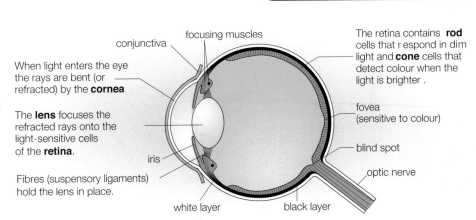

conjunctiva

focusing muscles

When light enters the eye the rays are bent (or refracted) by the **cornea**

The **lens** focuses the refracted rays onto the light-sensitive cells of the **retina**.

iris

Fibres (suspensory ligaments) hold the lens in place.

white layer

black layer

The retina contains **rod** cells that r espond in dim light and **cone** cells that detect colour when the light is brighter .

fovea (sensitive to colour)

blind spot

optic nerve

Figure 2.6 *The eye*

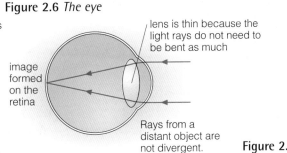

lens is thick to focus rays onto the retina

image formed on the retina

Rays from a near object are diverging as they enter the eye.

lens is thin because the light rays do not need to be bent as much

image formed on the retina

Rays from a distant object are not divergent.

Figure 2.7 *Focusing light*

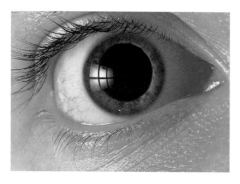

Figure 2.8 *Pupils in dim and bright light.*

The coloured part of the eye, the **iris**, is made of muscle tissue. The muscle fibres contract and control the size of the **pupil**, which regulates the amount of light that enters the eye. The brighter the light the smaller the pupil gets. Too much bright light can cause damage to the sensitive retina.

The **lens** can change thickness. It is thicker for focusing when reading a book and thinner when looking at a distant object. Some peoples' eyes cannot focus properly, and their vision is corrected with spectacles or contact lenses.

The tongue and nose

The tongue is covered with many bumps called **taste buds**. Taste buds contain sensory cells that are sensitive to certain substances. The tongue is sensitive to four stimuli in dissolved substances: sweet, sour, bitter and salt. The saliva in the mouth acts as a solvent. These four stimuli are detected at different parts of the tongue.

Inside the roof of the nose are sensory cells to detect smells. Smells are substances in the air that dissolve in the moist lining of the nose. They stimulate the chemical sensory cells that then send impulses to the brain. The sensory cells are very sensitive.

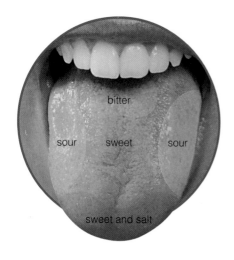

Figure 2.9

Skin

The skin is made up of layers with sensory cells called receptors underneath the top layer of the skin. These receptors are **nerve endings**. When the receptors are stimulated, impulses are sent to the brain. The skin is sensitive to four stimuli: pain, temperature, touch and pressure.

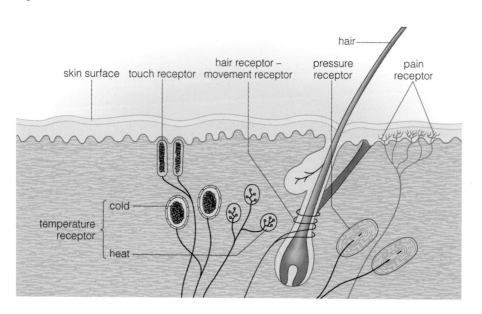

Figure 2.10 *Section through the skin.*

Summary

- The central nervous system consists of the brain, spinal cord and nerves.
- Reflexes are rapid automatic responses, which protect the body.
- The ear detects sounds and converts them into electrical signals.
- Light enters the eye through an adjustable opening called the pupil.
- The lens changes thickness to focus the light onto the retina.
- The nose and tongue both have sensory cells that are used to detect dissolved substances.
- Sensory nerve endings in the skin detect temperature and touch.

Questions

1 Copy and complete the following sentences. The control centres of the CNS are the _____ and the _____ _____. Messages are carried to and from the CNS to different parts of the body by _____. Cells making up the brain, spinal cord and nerves are called _____. The body responds to different stimuli. A quick response is called a _____ action. There are five sense organs: ear, eye, _____, _____, and _____, which help the body interpret _____.

[Total 5]

2 a) What are stimuli? [1]

b) Why do animals respond faster than plants? [2]

[Total 3]

3 How do the central and the peripheral nervous systems differ? List the main parts of each one. [Total 2]

4 a) Explain how neurones are similar to other animal cells. [3]

b) Explain how neurones are different to other animal cells and how these adaptations help them to carry out their function. [4]

[Total 7]

5 a) Explain why reflexes are important. [1]

b) Give one example or a reflex. [1]

[Total 2]

6 Suggest why your ears pop when you go on vertical drop rides at theme parks. [Total 2]

7 The eye is often compared to a camera. Use Figure 2.11 to explain why. [Total 3]

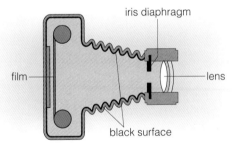

iris diaphragm

film

lens

black surface

Figure 2.11

8 Copy and complete Table 2.1 indicating which sensor would detect the different substance. [Total 6]

Food	Sensory taste cells
lemon juice	
coffee	
chocolate	
sherbet	
crisps	
lime jelly	

4.3 Hormones

Hormones are blamed for making teenagers moody! What are hormones? **Hormones** are substances that help us control our bodies.

We have two control systems, the nervous system and hormonal system. Responses controlled by the nervous system are fast and are over quickly, e.g. muscle contraction. The responses that are controlled by hormones are slow but may last for a longer time. Plants also have a hormonal system, and plant growth is controlled by plant growth substances.

Hormones in animals

Hormones are soluble substances made by a number of glands that make up the **endocrine** system. An endocrine gland makes hormones and releases (or secretes) them directly into the bloodstream. Endocrine glands have a good blood capillary network inside. Hormones help us control organs inside our bodies and carry messages throughout the body. Not all organs in the body will respond to a certain hormone. Hormones affect specific organs called target organs. Most endocrine glands are controlled by the **pituitary gland**, which is at the base of the brain.

For the body to work properly, it needs to have the correct amount of each hormone. The pituitary gland is known as the master gland because it produces many hormones, which control and coordinate other hormones.

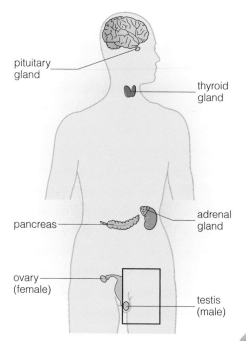

Figure 3.1 *The main hormone - producing glands in the body.*

?

1 Suggest why endocrine glands have a good capilliary network inside. *[Total 2]*

! Some tall people have grown more than usual because they have too much growth hormone. Others are small because they have too little growth hormone.

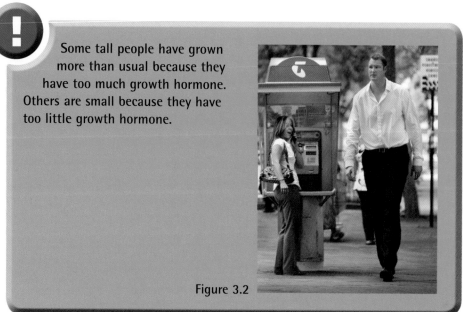

Figure 3.2

Specific examples of hormones

The **thyroid** gland is found in the neck, and secretes the hormone **thyroxine**. Thyroxine controls the body's **metabolism** and growth. Metabolism is the release of energy carried out inside cells. A person who secretes a lot of thyroxine becomes thin, excitable and over-active. A person with low levels of thyroxine secretion puts on weight as the metabolic rate slows down, and he or she becomes sluggish.

The **pancreas** secretes the hormone **insulin**, which controls the body's blood sugar levels. Insulin production is increased if there is too much sugar (glucose) in the blood. The insulin makes the liver take in the glucose and store it. (It is stored in the form of glycogen, which is a large molecule made of lots of small glucose molecules joined together.) This makes glucose levels fall back to normal. Most people have the correct blood sugar levels. People who suffer from the disease **diabetes** can't control the level of sugar in their blood because they do not make enough insulin. Symptoms of diabetes include being very thirsty and not having very much energy. Diabetics can control their condition with regular injections of insulin and careful eating.

Preparing for action

The adrenal glands secrete the hormone **adrenaline**. Adrenaline prepares the body for action and causes an immediate response in the body. The adrenal glands only make a very small amount of adrenaline, but it has an instant and dramatic affect on the body. The rate and force of the heart beat increase, breathing rate increases and blood is directed away from the stomach towards the muscles. The effect is a rush of extra energy that helps to *fight* the stressful situation or *flee* and run away from it. Adrenaline is an unusual hormone because it acts very quickly but its effects do not last.

Hormones and the control of sexual development

The **testes** secrete the male sex hormone **testosterone**. Testosterone causes sexual development in males, e.g. production of sperm and the deepening of the voice. **Oestrogen** is the hormone that causes sexual development in females, e.g. the development of breasts and the widening of hips. The female sex hormones are secreted from the **ovaries**. The female sex hormones are also responsible for controlling the menstrual cycle.

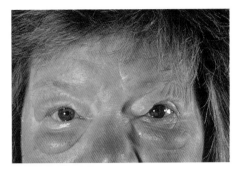

Figure 3.3 *Low levels of thyroxine secretion causes a low metabolic rate resulting in puffiness around the eyes.*

Figure 3.4 *Adrenaline in action.*

> **!** Hormones can be used in the treatment of diseases. Corticosteroids, which are made from cortisone (a hormone), are used to treat rheumatoid arthritis. The chemicals are made into a cream that can be rubbed on painful joints to reduce swelling.

Hormones in plants

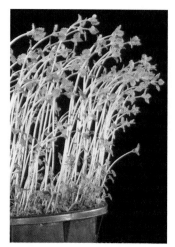

Plants are sensitive to different stimuli: light, moisture, gravity and touch. They do not respond to the stimuli by moving muscles, but by growing in a certain direction. The growing responses are called **tropisms**. Tropisms are controlled by plant growth substances. The main substances that control growth in plants are called **auxins**. Plant hormones are also known as plant growth substances.

Figure 3.5 *Plants grow towards the light.*

Tropisms

There are two main growth responses in plants. The response to light is called **phototropism**, and the response to gravity is called **geotropism**. Hormones are not spread evenly in the plant. Hormones are produced in the growing tips of shoots and transported in the phloem.

Auxin in shoots causes the cells to lengthen and grow. Auxin collects on the shaded side of the shoot. The cells therefore elongate. Light from one direction makes the shoot curve and grow towards the light. This is called **positive phototropism**. Roots grow in the direction of gravity (this is called positive geotropism), and are attracted to water in the soil.

> **!** Seedless grapes are produced with the help of hormones. The hormones allow the fruit to grow without fertilisation so there are no pips.

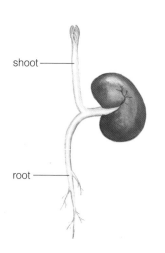

Figure 3.6 *A germinating seedling.*

shoot

root

> **!** Gardeners use hormone-rooting powder to encourage the growth of roots in stem cuttings.

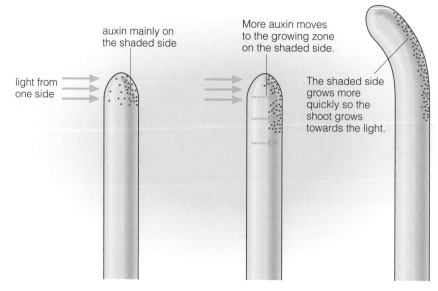

light from one side

auxin mainly on the shaded side

More auxin moves to the growing zone on the shaded side.

The shaded side grows more quickly so the shoot grows towards the light.

Figure 3.7 *Response of shoots to light.*

Summary

- Hormones are substances that control changes in the body.
- Hormones are transported in animals as a solution in the blood plasma.
- Examples of hormones in animals include insulin, adrenaline, testosterone, progesterone and oestrogen.
- Auxins are a group of plant hormones.
- The movement of shoots in the response to light is called phototropism.
- The movement of roots in the response to gravity is called geotropism.

Questions

1 Copy and complete the following sentences. Hormones are _____, which are released by different glands. The glands make up the _____ system. Hormones act more slowly than the _____ system. _____ control responses in plants. Plant shoots grow towards _____ and the roots grow towards moisture and in the direction of _____. *[Total 3]*

2 a) What are hormones? *[2]*
b) Explain how hormones enter the blood. *[2]*
[Total 4]

3 The nervous system and the hormonal system control the sending of messages in the body differently. Describe two of these differences. *[Total 4]*

4 Harry and Stephen have just finished running, and both have a high sugar sports drink. Table 3.1 shows their blood glucose levels.
a) Plot a graph to show the changes for the two boys. *[5]*
b) Which boy has diabetes? *[1]*
c) Explain your answer *[1]*
[Total 7]

Time after drinking sports drink (min)	Blood glucose level (mg per 100 cm³ blood)	
	Harry	Stephen
0	74	80
15	85	90
30	110	125
45	140	170
60	115	190
75	90	210
90	80	210
105	84	200
120	85	180
135	74	145

Table 3.1

5 Explain the role of auxin in plant growth. *[Total 2]*

6 Show with the use of diagrams the effect that gravity and light have on plants. *[Total 4]*

4 Controlling life

Anatomy and dissection

The dissection of human bodies is nothing new in science; over two thousand years ago Greek physicians were learning about the workings of the body through careful dissection of dead bodies. In some countries though, this was illegal and scientists wanting to learn about anatomy had to resort to dissecting other animals instead. Dissection of humans is now widely used, and is an important part of training to become a doctor. Some people choose to donate their bodies to science after death, so that medical students can learn human anatomy.

Dissection and the law

In Britain, changes in the law during the eighteenth century made it possible for researchers to use the bodies of executed murderers. As the number of medical schools increased over the years, the demand for bodies grew and grew, and supply could not meet demand. This led to a black market in dead bodies and body parts, and grave robbing became common.

The law changed again in 1832, with the Anatomy Act being passed. This gave physicians and surgeons access to any unclaimed corpses, which usually meant the bodies of the poor who had died in government workhouses, or of prisoners who had died while imprisoned. It also became possible for people to donate their body to science, though this was uncommon, and relatives of the deceased could overrule the decision if they wanted to.

Dissection and technology

The Visible Human Project® was completed in 1994. It was an effort to make detailed images of human anatomy available for study. The images were produced by taking thin slices through a frozen corpse, all the way from head to toe, and then photographing them. Computer software can recombine the images to produce a three-dimensional body that can be explored and manipulated. The male body that was used came from a murderer who had been executed by lethal injection.

?

1 Suggest why the dissection of human bodies was illegal in many countries.   [Total 2]

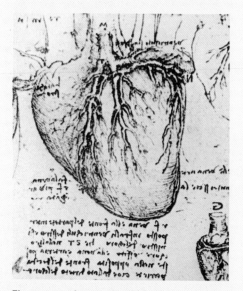

Figure 4.1 *Leonardo di Vinci produced many detailed drawings based on dissections.*

!

William Burke was a grave robber who turned to murder to obtain bodies for dissection. He was eventually caught and executed by hanging. His body was then publicly dissected in front of a crowd of 20 000 people. His skin was used to make several items, including a wallet which is on display in the Anatomy Museum of the Royal College of Surgeons in Edinburgh.

He agreed to donate his body to science but did not know that it would be used for the project. Some people felt that it was unethical to use his body for the project.

Dissection for display

In the late 1970s a special technique for preserving bodies was developed by Professor Gunther von Hagens. His method involved replacing the fluids in a dead body with chemicals that set hard and prevented the body from decomposing. He called this technique 'plastination'.

Plastinated bodies are rigid and can be positioned and cut in ways that enable particular parts of the body to be seen. Professor Gunther von Hagens uses carefully prepared specimens in exhibitions that he puts on around the world. These exhibitions began in 1995 and have grown in size and popularity ever since. It seems that the public are just as interested in dissection as scientists, as over 26 million people worldwide have visited one of these exhibitions. His exhibitions are always controversial and many people believe that they should be banned. They have not been though, as he is not breaking any laws.

?

2 Why do you think some people felt it was unethical to use the murderer's body for the Visible Human Project®?
[Total 2]

Figure 4.2 *Professor Gunther von Hagens and one of his plastinated bodies.*

Questions

1 In some medical schools dissection of human bodies is not as commonplace as it used to be because of technological advances. How has technology reduced the need for dissection? [Total 2]

2 In American schools, the dissection of a fetal pig is often used to teach students about anatomy.
a) Suggest two reasons why some people think that dissecting a fetal pig is a good thing. [2]
b) Suggest two reasons why some people think that dissecting a fetal pig is a bad thing. [2]
[Total 4]

3 What do you think prompted the government to pass the Anatomy Act in 1832? [Total 2]

4 Some people think that Professor Gunther von Hagens' exhibitions should be banned. Imagine that you are Professor von Hagens. Write a letter explaining why you think you should be allowed to continue putting on your exhibitions. [Total 3]

4 Controlling life

Senses

Supermarkets and senses

Large supermarkets are carefully designed. The designers want the customers to stay in the store for as long as possible and they want to encourage the customers to buy as much as possible. The store designers try to stimulate all the senses.

- Melodic music is played in the background. This is not too loud as it would be regarded as a nuisance by many customers. The music is seldom from current pop charts as the store has customers with a range of musical preferences. The music is designed to help relax the customer.
- Low-level lighting is used in the main part of the store. Fluorescent lighting is used for the signs of the different sections within the store such as the bakery. The main lighting is designed to be soothing, without glare.
- Many supermarkets now have in-store bakeries and coffee shops. The aroma from the bakery is piped back into the store. This has the effect of making people feel hungry. They may buy more than they need or they may stop in the coffee shop for refreshments.
- Samples of products are often available. Tasting the produce has the effect of encouraging customers to buy a new product.
- Colourful signs may be used to draw attention to particular products or special offers, increasing the chance of customers buying items they wouldn't normally consider.

> **!** A study in the 1980s showed that customers spent more money when shopping if the background music had a slow tempo. Shoppers walked around more slowly and were more likely to see items that they wanted to buy!

> **?** **1** Imagine you are designing a television advert to increase sales of a new brand of crisps. What would you include in the advert and why? *[Total 4]*

Bionic body parts

Many people across the world are deaf or blind, either because they were born that way or because of accident or disease. Advances in modern medicine have led to the development of implants that can restore hearing to some people who have become deaf. These are called cochlear implants. They detect sound and convert it into electrical signals that are sent to the brain.

Restoring vision in the blind is a harder task, as the sensitive structures in the eye are much more complex than those in the ear.

> **?** **2** Builders often take special precautions to reduce the chance of being accidentally blinded or deafened when using certain tools or machinery. What sort of precautions might they take? *[Total 2]*

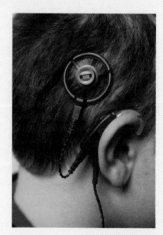

Figure 4.3 *This boy has a cochlear implant fitted.*

Scientists are working hard to build an 'artificial retina' that could be implanted into the eye. Prototype versions have already been built and are being tested in the USA.

Biological wiring

When we look at how many nerve fibres connect to the brain from each sense organ, it is not surprising that deafness is easier to treat than blindness. There are around 30 000 connections between each ear and the brain, compared to over 1 000 000 connections between each eye and the brain.

The surgery involved in connecting manmade components to the body is very complicated, as well as being very expensive. The components, surgery and **rehabilitation** involved in one cochlear implant cost around £30,000 for the first year. It is not always possible to treat deafness with an implant; for some people it may be the connections between the ear and the brain that do not work, rather than a problem with the parts of the ear which detect sound.

Figure 4.4 *A prototype artificial retina.*

Many bats hunt by producing loud calls and then listening for the echoes (echolocation). They can tell how big their prey is, how far away it is and how fast it is moving all from the reflected sound!

Questions

1 Describe how each of the following is using senses to try and increase sales in a supermarket:
   a) playing slow music in the background   [1]
   b) having an in-store bakery   [1]
   c) providing samples of products for people to try [1]
   d) using large, colourful signs.   [1]
                                    [Total 4]

2 Table 4.1 shows the number of sensory neurones (a type of nerve cell) responsible for the sense of smell in three different animals:

Animal	Number of sensory neurones
human	12 000 000
rabbit	100 000 000
dog	1 000 000 000

Table 4.1
   a) Use the data in the table to suggest which animal has the best sense of smell.   [1]

   b) How many times more sensory neurones does a rabbit have for smell compared to a human?   [2]
   c) Why do you think a good sense of smell is more important for some animals than others?   [2]
                                    [Total 6]

3 In the late eighteenth century an Italian scientist called Lazzaro Spallanzani discovered that bats could fly in the dark because of their hearing rather than their eyesight. One of his experiments involved blinding bats with a red hot needle.
   a) Under what circumstances do you think that experimentation on animals is right?   [2]
   b) Under what circumstances do you think it is wrong?   [2]
                                    [Total 4]

4 Make of list of similarities and differences between the human eye and a camera.   [Total 4]

4   Controlling life

Figure 4.5 *Seedlings growing towards a source of light.*

?

1 Why is it important for plants to grow where there is plenty of light?

[Total 1]

!

A group of plant hormones called jasmonates are currently being tested for use in treating cancer. In trials they have been shown to target and kill cancerous cells while leaving healthy cells relatively untouched.

?

2 Other than by applying gibberellins to his trees, how else might a farmer try to ensure a big crop of apples? *[Total 2]*

Plant hormones

When a plant grows, it is important that it doesn't get too spindly and that it doesn't produce fruit until its flowers have been pollinated. Plants also need to ensure that their leaves grow towards the light and that their roots grow down into the soil where there is water. All of these things and more are controlled by plant growth substances, which are usually referred to as 'plant hormones'.

Good crop, bad crop

Sometimes apple trees develop the curious habit of producing a huge crop one year, followed by little or no fruit the following year. This is called biennial bearing. The alternation of 'good crop, bad crop' is controlled by hormones and is bad news for a farmer who needs produce to sell every year.

Trying to stop biennial bearing can be very difficult. One option is to cut off branches or flowers at the beginning of a good year to try to even things out. This doesn't always work very well. An alternative method of controlling the fruit production of a tree is to use plant hormones called gibberellins. Carefully determined doses of these hormones can improve the size of the crop much more effectively than the older methods.

Dangerous doses

Different types of plants can respond very differently to a dose of a plant hormone. One example of this is how plants respond to a group of hormones called auxins. Grasses do very little when a large dose of auxins are applied, whereas broad-leaved plants (such as dandelions and plantains) are much more sensitive and are killed. This means that auxins can be used as selective weedkillers, e.g. to help clear a lawn of unwanted weeds.

Figure 4.6 *A lawn is the perfect place for weeds to grow. Selective weedkillers can be used to keep the grass weed-free..*

Need for seed?

Most people don't like finding seeds in the fruit they eat. Fruit develops from flowers which have been pollinated. After pollination of a flower has occurred, seeds start to develop and release hormones which stimulate the growth of the fruit that will surround the seed. Artificial hormones can be used to 'trick' a plant into reacting as if it has been pollinated even when this has not happened. This results in the plant growing fruit which contains no seeds. This technique is often used to produce seedless grapes.

! Charles Darwin is most famous for his work on natural selection and evolution, but he also carried out some of the earliest experiments into plant responses. No one knew about plant hormones at the time, but Darwin correctly predicted their existence years before they were isolated and identified. He based his conclusions on the results of several cleverly designed experiments.

Questions

1 What would you say to a farmer to convince him to use plant hormones to prevent biennial bearing instead of older techniques? *[Total 2]*

2 Briefly describe an application for each of the following types of plant hormones:
a) gibberellins *[1]*
b) jasmonates *[1]*
c) auxins. *[1]*
[Total 3]

3 Some plant responses are not controlled by hormones. Specialised hinged leaves on the Venus fly trap snap shut to trap insects, and the sensitive plant (*Mimosa pudica*) droops its leaves to stop insects from eating it. Suggest a reason why controlling these responses using hormones would not be suitable. *[Total 2]*

End of section questions

1 Why is it important that a good diet contains calcium? *[Total 2]*

2 a) Why do muscles work in pairs? *[1]*
b) Explain why muscles pull but do not push. *[2]*
[Total 3]

3 Using the diagram of the skeleton on page 85 match the bones listed with the correct region of the body. *[Total 7]*

Bones:
ribs, humerus, tibia, skull, pelvis, vertebrae, fibula

Regions:
neck, arm, hips, leg, head, chest

4 Explain why it is mainly elderly people who undergo hip replacement operations. *[Total 3]*

5 a) Organs (excluding bones and muscles) account for 20 % of the body's weight, muscles account for 45% of the weight. Calculate the mass of your skeleton. *[1]*
b) What percentage of your total body mass is your skeleton? *[2]*
[Total 3]

6 a) Why is it important to be able to detect changes in the environment? *[1]*
b) Name the type of response used when a person lets go of a hot saucepan handle. *[1]*
c) Explain each of the steps in this response. *[2]*
[Total 4]

7 a) Explain how the ears can help you balance. *[2]*
b) List three activities that might confuse your sense of balance. *[3]*
[Total 5]

8 a) Suggest reasons to explain why the brain is surrounded by bone. *[1]*
b) Explain how hinge joints move. Give an example of this type of joint. *[2]*
c) Explain how ball and socket joints work. Give an example of this type of joint. *[2]*
[Total 5]

9 Why is it important that reflex actions are fast? *[Total 1]*

10 a) Why are the three small bones of the ear important? *[2]*
b) What jobs are done by the eardrum, oval window and the fluid in the cochlea? *[3]*
[Total 5]

11 a) What is a receptor? *[1]*
b) What do receptors do? *[1]*
[Total 2]

12 Explain how we hear sounds. *[Total 6]*

13 a) Explain how we see things. *[4]*
b) Explain why animals that come out at night have lots of rods in their retina. *[1]*
[Total 5]

14 Suggest what the effect of using growth hormone on meat cattle might be. *[Total 1]*

15 a) Name the two hormones involved in the control of sexual development. *[2]*
b) Explain the role of the two hormones in part a). *[5]*
[Total 7]

16 a) Where are hormones made? [1]
   b) If you were being chased by a dog which hormone would your body be releasing? [1]
   [Total 2]

17 a) What is insulin? [1]
   b) What effect does insulin have on the body? [3]
   [Total 4]

18 Outline the different sensations detected by sensory receptors as you take off your shoes and clothes and get into a hot bath. [Total 2]

19 a) Suggest the effect eating two chocolate bars might have on a diabetic. [1]
   b) Explain how the body would try to correct the situation. [1]
   c) What would the diabetic person need to do? [1]
   [Total 3]

20 R Find out how physiotherapists deal with sports injuries.

21 R Find out about different bone fractures and how they are treated.

22 R Find out what effect different drugs have on the nervous system e.g. cannabis, ecstasy, heroin. Include long term and short term effects in your research.

23 R Find out what research was carried out by Dutch scientist, Fritz Went.

24 R Find out about the following diseases of the nervous system: multiple sclerosis, Parkinson's disease and Altzheimer's.

25 R Find out about Darwin's experiments on plant responses.

26 P Investigate how sensitive different parts of the body are to stimuli.

27 P Investigate your reaction times. Are your reactions quicker with your left or right hand?

28 P Investigate the effect of light on young seedlings.

29 P Investigate the detection of different flavours when blindfolded.

5.1 Reproduction in plants

How are new plants formed? New plants can grow in several ways: from seeds (**sexual reproduction**) or by producing things such as bulbs or tubers (**asexual reproduction**).

Structure of a flowering plant

There are four main organs of a flowering plant.

- The flower contains the reproductive organs.
- The leaves use light energy, carbon dioxide and water to make food by photosynthesis.
- The stem provides support and a transport system for water and minerals to the leaves and flowers. It also transports food from the leaves to the roots and flowers.
- The roots anchor the plant to the ground and absorb water and minerals.

Sexual reproduction

Flowers contain a plant's reproductive organs. Most plants contain both male and female parts. However, some plants have only male sex organs while others contain only female sex organs. The organs may even be separate on the same plant, e.g. hazel.

Sexual reproduction needs special sex cells called **gametes**. The advantage of sexual reproduction is that it leads to genetic variation. If a species is varied it is more likely to be able to adapt to any changes in its surroundings.

In a flowering plant the flower develops on the **receptacle**. The buds of the flower are protected by **sepals**. Sepals are small leaves. The **petals** of many flowers are brightly coloured and highly scented which attracts insects. Inside the flower there are pin-like structures called **stamens**. The top of the stamen produces pollen cells, which contain the male sex cells. The club-like structure is the **stigma**. In the base of the stigma is the **ovary** which contains ovules. Each ovule contains a female sex cell. The carpel is made up of the stigma, style and ovary. When the tip of the stigma is sticky it indicates that the carpel is ripe and ready to receive grains of pollen.

Flowers differ in external colour, size and shape. However they all have a similar internal structure. Some have carpels with one ovule, others have rows of ovules.

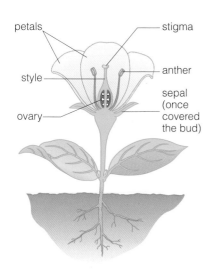

petals — stigma
style — anther
ovary — sepal (once covered the bud)

Figure 1.1 *Flowering plant.*

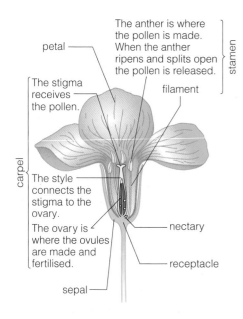

petal
The anther is where the pollen is made. When the anther ripens and splits open the pollen is released.
stamen
filament
The stigma receives the pollen.
carpel
The style connects the stigma to the ovary.
The ovary is where the ovules are made and fertilised.
nectary
sepal
receptacle

Figure 1.2 *The structure of the flower.*

joined petals   no sepals   lots of flowers

Figure 1.3 *Different external structures.*

Pollination

Pollination is the transfer of pollen from anthers to stigmas. This must occur before a male sex cell can fuse with a female sex cell. There are a number of ways pollination can happen.

Self-pollination is when pollen is transferred from an anther to the stigma of the same flower or of another flower on the same plant.

Cross-pollination is when pollen is transferred from a flower on one plant to flowers on a different plant of the same species. There are different ways that this can happen.

> **!** Many plants are unable to self-pollinate. In a number of plants the pollen and ova ripen at different times, so preventing self-pollination.

Wind pollination happens as wind blows pollen from anthers of one plant to the stigmas of others. Plants that are wind pollinated are not usually brightly coloured, for example grasses. They do, however, have long filaments with anthers that hang down in the wind. They produce millions of pollen grains. The pollen is very light: some grains even have small air sacs to help them stay in the air longer.

Figure 1.4 *Wind pollinated plant.*

Figure 1.5 *Insect pollinated plant.*

Insect pollination happens when insects like bees carry pollen on their bodies as they move from flower to flower. The insects are attracted to the plants because the plants produce a sugary liquid called **nectar** which the insects like. The flowers of plants that are insect-pollinated tend to be brightly coloured, which makes it easy for the insects to find them. The pollen of these types of plant have large pollen grains and is a good food supply for the insects. Some pollen grains have spikes, which stick to the hair of insects.

> **!** Pollen carried by the wind can irritate people who are sensitive to it. This pollen is responsible for hay fever. In fact, hay fever derives its name from the fact that grasses (hay) are wind-pollinated plants.

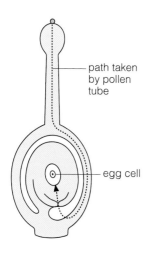

path taken by pollen tube

egg cell

Figure 1.6 *Fertilisation in a plant.*

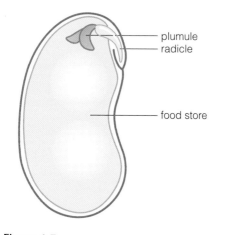

plumule
radicle

food store

Figure 1.7

Fertilisation

Fertilisation is the fusion of the male sex cell with the female sex cell. Together they produce a single cell that can grow into a new plant. When a pollen grain lands on the ripe stigma, it grows a long **pollen tube** down through the style to the ovary. The male nucleus travels down the tube until it reaches an ovule inside the ovary. The male nucleus from the pollen grain **fertilises** the female sex cell in the ovule.

After fertilisation the ovule develops into a seed which begins to grow. The petals and stamens of the flower fall away. The ovary is left and this swells to form the fruit as the seeds grow.

Seeds and fruit

After fertilisation the fertilised ovule divides into many cells to form a seed. The seed develops a thick tough outer coat for protection. The seed then grows in two parts:

- the embryo – this contains a **plumule** which grows into the shoot and the **radicle** which becomes the root.
- the food store – cells packed with starch or oil. The food store may be part of the embryo.

When the seed germinates, the embryo must have a source of food. The food store in the seed provides nutrients for growth until the seedling photosynthesises and can make its own food. This food store also provides food for many animals. We eat many foods that are seeds, e.g. wheat flour for bread, rice, beans and corn on the cob.

We usually think of fruits in terms of apples and pears, but a complete ovary after fertilisation is a **fruit**.

Figure 1.8 *An ovary is a structure packed with fertile seeds. The ovary wall grows and develops as the seed grows. When a fruit is cut open seeds can be seen inside.*

Dispersal

There is increased chance of survival for new plants if the seeds are scattered or **dispersed** as far as possible from the parent plant. The seed cannot grow and develop in shadow or overcrowded conditions. It is also better for the species if the seedlings start to grow in new places. There are many different ways that seeds and fruits can be dispersed.

- **Wind dispersal.** This happens to plants such as the poppy whose seeds are light and are simply blown and spread by the wind. Sycamore seeds have wings, which allow them to move through the air, far away from the parent. In other plants such as the dandelion, little hairs attached to the ovary help carry the fruits through the air.

- **Animal dispersal.** There are two methods. When fruits are eaten by animals, the seeds in the fruit pass through the animal and are egested in their droppings. Some fruits have hooks that cling to the fur of animals and are dispersed as the animals move around.

Figure 1.9 *Seeds dispersed by the wind.*

Figure 1.10 *These fruits have hooks.*

- **Water dispersal.** This happens to plants which grow near the water. The seeds contain air spaces that help them to float, and they are carried away on currents.

- **Self-dispersal.** This happens when the fruit walls of some plants simply dry out and burst. The split ovary scatters all its seeds explosively.

> **?**
> **1** Why do you think plants relying on wind dispersal tend to produce many more seeds than those that rely on animal dispersal?
> [Total 2]

Figure 1.11 *Water dispersal.*

Figure 1.12 *Self-dispersal.*

Germination

When a seed starts to grow this is called **germination**. Seeds will only germinate if conditions are right. Three conditions are needed for germination: water, warmth and oxygen. As seeds germinate, a radicle (root) grows downward and a plumule (shoot) grows upwards towards the light. Seeds have their own food store but they are quickly used up. Once the plant emerges into the light the leaves of the seedling open out and begin to make chlorophyll. The new plant can then make its own food by photosynthesis.

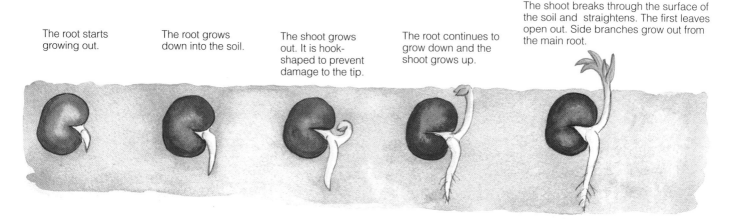

The root starts growing out.

The root grows down into the soil.

The shoot grows out. It is hook-shaped to prevent damage to the tip.

The root continues to grow down and the shoot grows up.

The shoot breaks through the surface of the soil and straightens. The first leaves open out. Side branches grow out from the main root.

Figure 1.13 *Germination of a seed.*

Asexual reproduction

Asexual reproduction is reproduction with only one parent. The offspring produced are genetically identical to their parent. The advantages of asexual reproduction are:

- many offspring can be produced quickly
- favourable conditions are maximised efficiently.

The main disadvantage of asexual reproduction is that the offspring are more likely to be killed by outbreaks of disease. They do not have the genetic variation needed to fight diseases.

Some new plants can be produced without seeds. Asexual reproduction in plants is also called **vegetative reproduction**. There are two main ways that this can happen.

- Bulbs and tubers – these are the swollen roots or stems of plants which if planted grow into new plants. Potatoes are tubers, and onions are bulbs.

Figure 1.14 *Potato tubers.*

Runners – these are side branches of some plants that grow along the surface of the soil. Roots grow down from buds on the runners. These develop into new plants. Strawberry plants reproduce in this way.

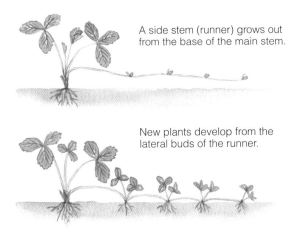

A side stem (runner) grows out from the base of the main stem.

New plants develop from the lateral buds of the runner.

Figure 1.15 *Strawberry runners.*

There are many different ways that plants can be reproduced artificially.

Cuttings – this method involves cutting a small piece of the stem which has leaves, away from a plant. The cutting is then placed in water until roots develop. Once the roots have developed the plant is placed in soil and develops into a new plant. To speed up the process hormone rooting powder can be used on the end of the cutting and the cutting can be put straight into the soil.

Grafts – this method involves making a cut into the stem of a tree. A small stem from another tree which has buds is fitted into the cut.

Figure 1.16 *A plant cutting that has started to develop roots.*

2 What are the advantages and disadvantages of plants producing runners to reproduce? [Total 3]

Figure 1.17 *Bitumen is applied to this grafted apple tree to prevent drying out.*

● Cloning – this involves taking small pieces of a plant and placing them in a sterile nutrient solution where the cells can multiply. Separate cells are then taken out, placed into different sterile nutrient solutions with plant growth substances and allowed to develop to form many embryos. Each embryo then develops into a new plant. This procedure is also called **tissue culture**.

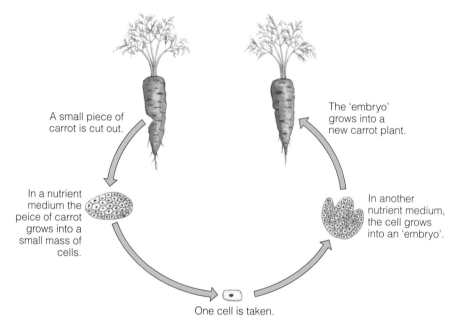

A small piece of carrot is cut out.

In a nutrient medium the peice of carrot grows into a small mass of cells.

One cell is taken.

In another nutrient medium, the cell grows into an 'embryo'.

The 'embryo' grows into a new carrot plant.

Figure 1.18 *Cloning.*

Summary

- ● Flowering plants reproduce by sexual reproduction.
- ● Male sex cells are contained in pollen grains and female sex cells are contained in ovules.
- ● Flowers may be pollinated by insects or wind.
- ● Pollination is the transfer of pollen from anthers to stigmas.
- ● Fertilisation involves the fusing together of the male and female sex cells.
- ● The swollen ovary of a plant becomes a fruit.
- ● Seeds may be dispersed by wind, water, animals or by the fruit.
- ● Three conditions are needed for germination: water, warmth and oxygen.
- ● Asexual reproduction needs only one parent.

Questions

1 Copy and complete the following sentences.
There are four main parts in a flowering plant
_____, _____, _____,
and _____. Sexual _____ is where
a _____ gamete joins with a _____
gamete. The male sex cell is in the _____
and the female sex cell is in the _____.
_____ reproduction requires only
one parent plant. *[Total 5]*

2 a) Which part of the plant prevents it from being
blown over? *[1]*
b) Where is water absorbed in a plant? *[1]*
c) What part of the plant transports water to the
leaves and food to the roots? *[1]*
d) Which part of the plant carries out
photosynthesis? *[1]*
[Total 4]

3 a) What is the function of a flower? *[1]*
b) Explain what gametes are. *[1]*
c) List and give the functions of the female
parts of a flower. *[3]*
d) List and give the functions of the male
parts of a flower. *[2]*
[Total 7]

4 a) What is pollination? *[1]*
b) What are the different types of pollination? *[4]*
c) What is fertilisation? *[1]*
d) Explain the difference between pollination
and fertilisation. *[3]*
[Total 9]

5 a) What do the ovules become after
fertilisation? *[1]*
b) Name the parts of a seed and their functions. *[6]*
[Total 7]

6 In an experiment broad beans were grown in jars
(Figure 1.19). The data collected are given in Table 1.1.
a) Draw a graph of this data (include a key). *[6]*
b) Describe what the results show. *[3]*
[Total 9]

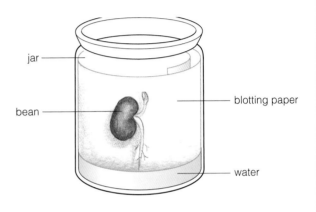

Figure 1.19

Day	Length of radicle (mm)	Length of plumule (mm)	Total length of seedling (mm)
1	0	0	0
2	1	0	1
3	2	0	2
6	3	1	4
18	12	6	18

Table 1.1

7 a) What is dispersal? *[1]*
b) Outline the two possible roles that animals
play in dispersal. *[2]*
c) Name the possible adaptations seeds may have
to help their dispersal by the wind. *[3]*
[Total 6]

8 Why is it important that seeds grow away from
their parent plant? *[Total 3]*

5.2 Reproduction in animals

How do humans reproduce? Humans reproduce through sexual reproduction. A human fetus develops for nine months in the mother's uterus before being born.

Making cells

There are two ways by which new cells can be made. The first way is called **mitosis**, which happens when organisms are growing or replacing old or damaged cells. This can also happen during asexual reproduction. **Asexual reproduction** is a special type of reproduction that involves only one parent. In some forms of asexual reproduction the organism splits into two. Organisms such as yeast reproduce by dividing into two in this way. This is known as budding. (Yeast is a fungus and not an animal.) Each new cell that is produced is called a daughter cell. The new cells have exactly the same genetic code as the parent.

During mitosis the nucleus of the cell divides, so that the daughter cells have an identical set of genes to the parent cell. Genes are carried in the nucleus on long strands called chromosomes. Nearly all the cells in humans have 46 chromosomes in the nucleus. The new cells formed from mitosis are **clones**, exact replicas of the parent cell.

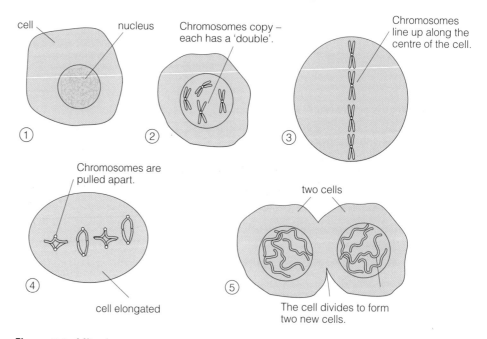

Figure 2.1 *Mitosis.*

Meiosis is the other way in which new cells can be made. Meiosis results in gametes having half the number of chromosomes as the parent cell. Meiosis happens in the production of sex cells. Sex cells are called **gametes**. After meiosis, a human sex cell contains 23 chromosomes rather than 46. Fertilisation involves the nucleus of a female sex cell fusing with the nucleus of a male sex cell giving the fertilised egg 46 chromosomes again.

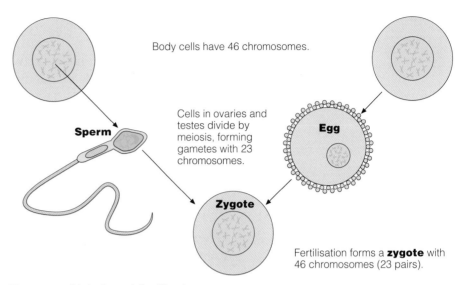

Body cells have 46 chromosomes.

Cells in ovaries and testes divide by meiosis, forming gametes with 23 chromosomes.

Fertilisation forms a **zygote** with 46 chromosomes (23 pairs).

Figure 2.2 *Meiosis and fertilisation.*

Sex cells

There are two types of sex cell in humans: the female egg cell is called the **ovum**, and the male cell is called the **sperm**. Both of these cells are specially adapted to their functions. The female cell has large food reserves in the cytoplasm and so is big and round. The male cell has a long tail and streamlined body because it needs to swim. The sperm cell also has substances called enzymes in the 'head' to help it digest away the membrane of the ovum as it makes its way through. During fertilisation each sex cell has a nucleus containing 23 chromosomes.

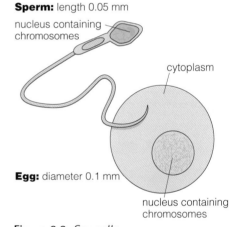

Sperm: length 0.05 mm

nucleus containing chromosomes

cytoplasm

Egg: diameter 0.1 mm

nucleus containing chromosomes

Figure 2.3 *Sex cells*

Male reproductive system

Sperm, the male sex cells, are made in the **testes**. The testes hang outside the body in a bag called the **scrotum**. The testes are not inside the body because body temperature is too high for sperm production. Each testis is connected to the **penis** by a tube called the **sperm duct**. Before sperm leave the body they are mixed with a liquid which comes from two small glands called seminal vesicles. Together sperm and the liquid are called **semen**. The penis has a tube running through it called the **urethra**. Semen and urine from the bladder both leave the penis through the urethra. The urethra can carry either semen or urine but not both at the same time.

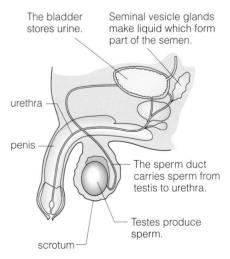

The bladder stores urine.

Seminal vesicle glands make liquid which form part of the semen.

urethra

penis

The sperm duct carries sperm from testis to urethra.

Testes produce sperm.

scrotum

Figure 2.4 *Male reproductive system.*

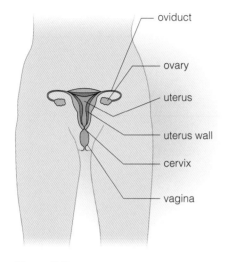

Figure 2.5

Female reproductive organs

The ova (egg cells) are made in two **ovaries**. These are found inside the abdomen on either side of the uterus. They are connected to the uterus by tubes called **oviducts**. The ends of the oviducts have funnels, which catch the ova as they are released from the ovaries. An oviduct carries the ovum from the ovary to the **uterus**. The uterus is like a bag with a thick muscular wall where a fertilised egg cell can grow and develop. It takes between four and five days for the ovum to reach the uterus from the ovary. The uterus connects to the outside of the body by a muscular tube called the **vagina**. The neck of the uterus is called the **cervix**.

When a man and woman have sex the penis is inserted into the vagina. Sperm may be released at the neck of the uterus.

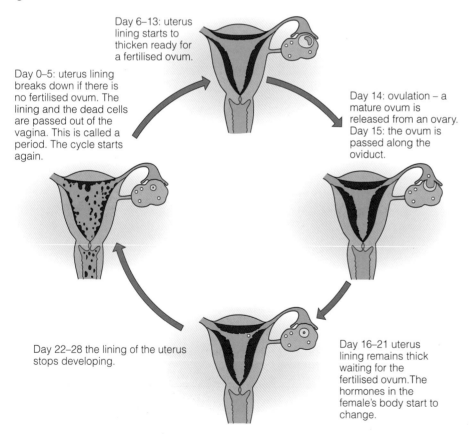

Day 6–13: uterus lining starts to thicken ready for a fertilised ovum.

Day 0–5: uterus lining breaks down if there is no fertilised ovum. The lining and the dead cells are passed out of the vagina. This is called a period. The cycle starts again.

Day 14: ovulation – a mature ovum is released from an ovary. Day 15: the ovum is passed along the oviduct.

Day 22–28 the lining of the uterus stops developing.

Day 16–21 uterus lining remains thick waiting for the fertilised ovum.The hormones in the female's body start to change.

Figure 2.6 *Menstrual cycle.*

Menstruation

A girl who has reached puberty releases an ovum from one of her ovaries every 28 days. This is called **ovulation**. Close to the time of ovulation the uterus must prepare itself for the ovum. The lining of the uterus thickens as a network of blood capillaries grows in it. If the ovum is fertilised by a sperm it develops into a baby. If the ovum remains unfertilised, it dies and the lining of the uterus then breaks up. The lining and the dead ovum pass out of the body through the vagina. This is called a **period** or **menstruation**. A period may last between three and seven days. Women use sanitary protection to absorb the blood which is lost.

The menstrual cycle can vary in lengths of time for different women. It can also be painful for some females because the muscles in the uterus wall contract. This may result in cramps and cause stomach and back pains. Occasionally water collects in body tissues which makes them swell up, resulting in swelling of the ankles and fingers.

After menstruation the uterus grows a fresh lining for each new ovum. The cycle of making a new lining and a new ovum is called the **menstrual cycle**. If an ovum is fertilised on day 14 then the lining of the uterus remains, and the placenta develops, partly from the fertilised egg and partly from the mother, to feed and protect the developing embryo. The lining of the uterus does not break down this time.

Fertilisation

Sexual intercourse involves a man inserting his penis into the woman's vagina. Before this can be done blood pressure in the tissue stiffens the penis. This is called an **erection**. It happens whenever a man becomes sexually aroused. Once the penis is inside the vagina, sperm may be released. The release of sperm is called **ejaculation**. The sperm are mixed with a small amount of fluid and squeezed along the sperm duct into the urethra. They are released as semen out of the end of the penis and deposited at the neck of the uterus, the cervix. From here the sperm swim through the uterus and up into the oviducts. This takes about 48 hours. Once in the oviduct they may meet an ovum. Only one sperm can fertilise the ovum.

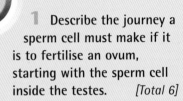

1 Describe the journey a sperm cell must make if it is to fertilise an ovum, starting with the sperm cell inside the testes. [Total 6]

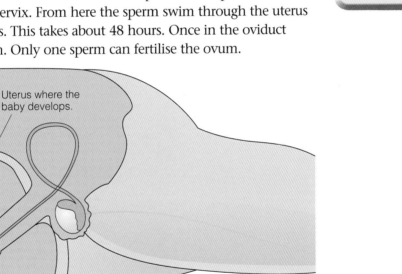

Oviduct: ovum is carried to uterus.

Uterus where the baby develops.

Ovary where ova are produced.

Uterus wall is thick and muscular.

The cervix is the neck of uterus where sperm are placed.

Figure 2.7 *Sexual intercourse.*

Ova (plural of ovum) are much larger than sperm. More than 300 million sperm enter a female during sexual intercourse. Approximately 100 of them reach the ovum but only one occasionally gets in.

When one sperm enters the ovum the surface membranes of the ovum change to stop any more sperm getting into it. After the sperm enters the ovum, the nucleus of the sperm (which contains genetic material) fuses with the nucleus of the ovum. The fusion of the two gametes is called **fertilisation**. A fertilised ovum contains two sets of genetic material. One set comes from each parent so that the new individual will have characteristics from both of the parents and will be unique.

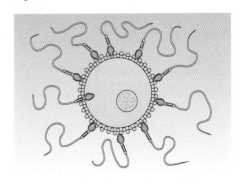

Figure 2.8 *Sperm grouped around an ovum.*

117

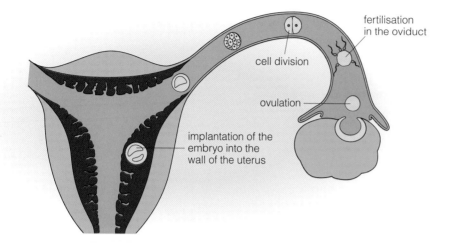

Figure 2.9 *The journey of the ball of cells to the uterus.*

Pregnancy

The newly fertilised ovum then begins to divide by mitosis and moves down the oviduct. Once it reaches the uterus it is a ball of cells. The ball of cells implants itself in the walls of the uterus. It is here that the embryo begins to develop into a baby and the woman is now said to be **pregnant**. For the first two months the ball of cells is called an **embryo**.

After six weeks the embryo has a beating heart and a brain. It is about 1 cm long. The tiny embryo floats in a sac filled with watery liquid called **amniotic fluid** that protects it. The embryo cannot eat or breathe and so a link is formed between the embryo and the uterus to supply food and oxygen. The link is an organ called the **placenta**. The embryo is attached to the placenta by an **umbilical cord**.

? 2 Describe the journey an ovum takes from ovulation to implantation if it is fertilised by a sperm cell. *[Total 6]*

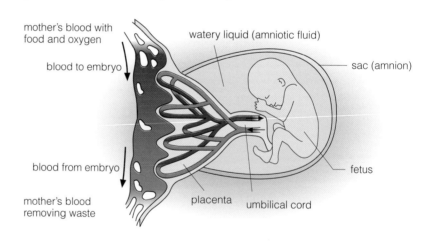

Figure 2.10 *Embryo and placenta.*

The placenta has a large network of capillaries. Food and oxygen diffuse from the mother's blood into the baby's. Waste products like carbon dioxide diffuse from the baby's blood into the mother's. The two blood supplies do not mix. The placenta acts as a barrier to some harmful substances. However some substances like the chemicals in cigarette smoke, alcohol and drugs can cross the placenta and harm the baby.

! Girls are given a rubella vaccine when they are about 11 to stop them from catching the disease rubella (German measles). If a woman catches rubella during the first 12 weeks of pregnancy, it can cause deafness, blindness and heart disease in the baby but does not greatly affect the mother.

After about two months the embryo has a head and torso and develops visible limbs. It is now called a **fetus**.

From embryo to fetus

The development of the fetus is shown in Figure 2.11. Some of the main stages are:

- 6 weeks: embryo 1 cm long, umbilical cord forming
- 7 weeks: embryo 2.5 cm long, limbs starting to form
- 3 months: fetus 7 cm long, body almost completely formed
- 6 months: 28 cm long, the fetus is moving around and kicking and will continue to grow until birth
- 9 months: fetus 50 cm long, fully developed and ready to be born.

Birth

Birth happens approximately nine months after fertilisation. A few days before birth the baby usually moves so that its head is near the cervix and can emerge first.

As the moment of birth approaches:

- the muscles in the uterus contract strongly (contractions)
- the muscles in the cervix relax
- the bag of fluid around the baby bursts
- the cervix widens
- strong contractions push the baby out through the vagina.

After birth, the baby's umbilical cord is cut to separate it from the placenta. The stub forms the navel or belly button. Shortly after that the muscles in the uterus contract again and push the placenta out. This is sometimes called the afterbirth.

6 weeks
approximate length 1 cm

7 weeks
approximate length 2.5 cm

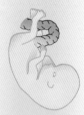

3 months
approximate length 7 cm

6 months
approximate length 28 cm

9 months
approximate length 50 cm

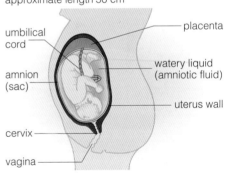

umbilical cord · placenta · amnion (sac) · watery liquid (amniotic fluid) · uterus wall · cervix · vagina

Figure 2.11 *Development in the uterus.*

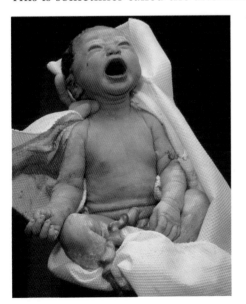

Figure 2.12 *New born baby with umbilical cord.*

> ! A newly born baby has strong automatic reflexes. It will respond by turning its head when its cheeks are touched and it will suck if a nipple is placed in its mouth. The more a baby sucks milk from its mother's breasts, the more milk is produced.

Twins

Twins may be formed in one of two ways.

○ Sometimes a woman's ovaries release two or more ova at the same time. If they all become fertilised they all develop into babies. Twins formed in this way are non-identical. They develop from different ova fertilised by different sperm.

○ Sometimes, after fertilisation, the fertilised ovum splits and divides into two balls of cells. Twins formed in this way are identical. They develop from the same ovum.

Identical twins have exactly the same physical characteristics such as the colour of their eyes, hair and skin, shape of their nose, attached ear lobes, blood group and gender. These characteristics are called **inherited characteristics** as they depend on information inherited from parents. Characteristics such as skill at sport and ability to speak a language result from environmental effects and may be different for the twins. Some characteristics, such as height, are the result of a combination of both inheritance and environment.

Summary

○ Cells can be made by mitosis or meiosis.

○ The female sex cell is called the ovum and is made in an ovary.

○ The male sex cell is called the sperm and is made in the testes.

○ Menstruation is the breaking down of the uterus lining.

○ Sexual intercourse allows ovum and sperm to meet in the woman's body.

○ Fertilisation is the point when the sperm enters the ovum and the two nuclei fuse, combining genetic material.

○ A fertilised ovum grows into a fetus inside the uterus

○ The fetus is protected by the amniotic fluid and the walls of the uterus.

○ The umbilical cord supplies the fetus with oxygen and nutrients and takes away wastes such as carbon dioxide and urea.

Questions

1 Copy and complete the following sentences.
The male reproductive cell is the _____,
the female reproductive cell is the _____.
An _____ is produced once a month in a
cycle called the _____ cycle. If the ovum is
not fertilised, then it and the _____ of the
uterus are passed out of the _____. This is
called a _____. _____ is where a
man and woman come together so that the
_____ can swim to the _____
and fertilise it. *[Total 5]*

2 a) List the different ways by which cells can
multiply. *[2]*
b) Briefly describe each of the ways listed in
part a). *[4]*
[Total 6]

3 a) What is asexual reproduction? *[1]*
b) Describe two different ways plants reproduce
asexually naturally. *[4]*
c) Describe two different ways plants reproduce
asexually artificially. *[4]*
[Total 9]

4 What are clones? *[Total 1]*

5 a) Where are sperm produced? *[1]*
b) What is semen? *[2]*
[Total 3]

6 Explain the meaning of the terms: erection
and ejaculation. *[Total 2]*

7 a) Where are ova made? *[1]*
b) What is ovulation? *[1]*
c) How often is an ovum released? *[1]*
[Total 3]

8 a) Describe what the uterus is. *[2]*
b) Explain what menstruation is. *[2]*
c) Briefly outline the menstrual cycle. *[5]*
[Total 9]

9 a) Explain what fertilisation is. *[2]*
b) At which point is a woman pregnant? *[1]*
[Total 3]

10 a) Explain the function of the placenta. *[2]*
b) Describe the difference between an embryo
and a fetus. *[2]*
[Total 4]

11 Using the information in Figure 2.11, draw a
graph to show the rate of growth of a fetus.
[Total 6]

12 a) When is a fetus ready to be born? *[1]*
b) List the things that happen as birth
approaches. *[5]*
[Total 6]

13 Explain how identical and non-identical
twins are formed. *[Total 4]*

5.3 Human development

What is puberty? Babies are born with reproductive organs but they do not fully develop until puberty. **Puberty** is the time when the reproductive organs become mature.

Puberty

This is the time between childhood and adulthood. A set of physical changes happen during puberty. For girls these changes start between the ages of 11 and 15, and for boys the changes start between the ages of 13 and 15.

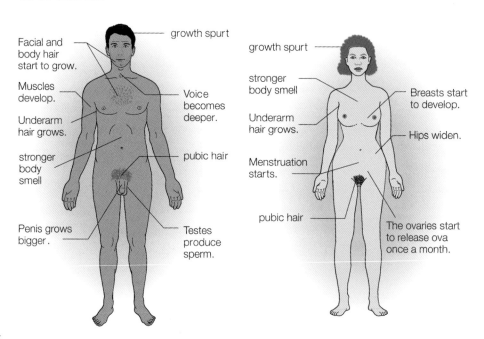

Figure 3.1 *Changes during puberty.*

The physical changes that are produced at puberty are called **secondary sexual characteristics**. They are necessary as individuals enter into the reproductive stage of their lives. Sex hormones control these changes. The main female hormone is called **oestrogen**. The main male hormone is called **testosterone**.

The physical changes are accompanied by emotional changes. Young people, at this stage of development are called **adolescents**. They become sexually mature and more independent from their parents. During puberty adolescents often become self-conscious about the changes in their bodies. They may suffer from mood swings and become irritable. Hormones also make these emotional changes happen.

? 1 Draw a table to compare how puberty affects girls and boys. Include similarities and differences. *[Total 8]*

Birth control

Sexual reproduction is an important part of a loving relationship. Couples who love each other often plan when they are to begin their family. In order to prevent conception or fertilisation they may use birth control measures. There are different methods of birth control which are commonly called **contraceptives**.

Contraceptives can be classified into one of three groups:

- barrier methods – these stop the sperm from reaching the ovum
- chemical methods – these stop the production of ova
- intrauterine devices (IUDs) – these stop the implantation of the fertilised ovum.

Contraceptive	Group	Description	Example
condom	barrier	A thin rubber cover that is placed over an erect penis. The condom is coated with a spermicide. A spermicide is gel which contains chemicals that kill sperm (95% reliable).	
diaphragm	barrier	A dome shaped rubber cover placed over the woman's cervix. Used with a spermicide (96% reliable).	
rhythm method	natural	Couple study the woman's menstrual cycle and avoid having sex near the time of ovulation (75% reliable).	
morning after pill (emergency contraception)	chemical	Two pills are taken by the female within 72 hours of sexual intercourse. The dose of two pills is repeated 12 hours later. The pills contain hormones which stop implantation taking place (99% reliable).	
pill	chemical	A pill is swallowed by the woman every day for 21 days of the 28-day cycle. The pill contains hormones which stop the ovaries releasing ova (98% reliable).	
coil	IUD	A plastic coil is fitted into the uterus. This stops the ball of cells implanting into the lining of the uterus (97% reliable).	

Table 3.1 *Examples of contraceptives.*

> **!** The chemicals in the contraceptive pill not only stop ova being released, but can also make the conditions inside the vagina hostile for sperm. This makes it difficult for the sperm to survive.

The decisions concerning which type of contraceptives to use can be very difficult for some couples. For some, there may be religious and moral issues which may prevent them using some types of contraceptives, or any contraceptives at all. Some contraceptives such as the pill are more reliable than others, like a diaphragm. For some couples, how reliable and reversible the contraceptive is may be an important aspect of their decision making. There are couples who are sure that they do not want to have children. One or both members of the couple may become sterilised and therefore not rely on contraceptives to prevent pregnancy. Sterilisation is nearly 100% effective but is difficult to reverse.

Sexually transmitted diseases

Some infections can be passed from one individual to another during sexual intercourse. Condoms help to prevent the spread of sexually transmitted diseases, because they prevent body fluids mixing. There are many different sexually transmitted infections. These infections include:

- Syphilis – caused by a type of bacterium. The sufferer may get sores on their **genitals** (external reproductive organs) and spots on their skin. It can be treated with antibiotics. If not treated it results in mental illness.
- Gonorrhoea – caused by bacteria. The sufferer may produce mucus from their reproductive opening and a burning sensation when urinating. It can be treated with antibiotics.
- AIDS – caused by a virus called HIV. HIV invades and damages white blood cells which help the body fight disease. If the number of white blood cells falls in the blood stream it is easier for bacteria and other viruses to invade. The sufferer may get pneumonia, skin cancer or a wide range of infections. Combinations of drugs can be taken to cure these diseases but there is no known cure for AIDS. HIV is passed on through mixing of body fluids, for example sexual intercourse or sharing needles. It can also pass across the placenta into a fetus.

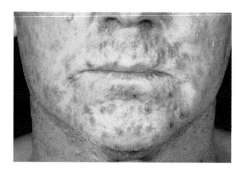

Figure 3.2 *A person with syphilis.*

Summary

- Puberty is the time when reproductive organs mature.
- During puberty physical and emotional changes take place.
- Contraceptives can be used to stop a sperm fusing with the ovum.
- Diseases such as syphilis, gonorrhoea and AIDS can be transmitted during sexual intercourse.

Questions

1 Copy and complete the following sentences.
Secondary sexual _____ develop during
_____. At this time physical changes such as
_____, _____, _____ and
_____ occur in boys and _____,
_____ and _____ happen in
females. After puberty individuals develop into
_____. Puberty is controlled by hormones
such as _____ in boys and oestrogen in girls.
[Total 5]

2 a) What is the difference between childhood,
puberty and adulthood? *[3]*
b) What role do the hormones oestrogen and
testosterone play in puberty? *[2]*
[Total 5]

3 Draw a table to show the physical changes that
happen to boys and girls during puberty. *[Total 10]*

4 a) Plot the data given in Table 3.2, drawing two
separate line graphs. *[5]*
b) Indicate on the graph the growth spurts
for each individual. *[2]*
c) Indicate which could be male and which
could be female. *[2]*
[Total 9]

Age (years)	Birth	2	4	6	8	10	12	14	16
	Height in cm								
A	36	88	100	116	138	142	156	176	184
B	34	90	104	119	140	150	161	178	192

Table 3.2

5 List and give the group of four different methods of
contraception. *[Total 4]*

6 a) What are sexually transmitted diseases? *[1]*
b) Draw up a table to show three sexually
transmitted diseases, their causes, symptoms
and how they can be treated. *[9]*
[Total 10]

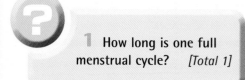
Reproduction and hormones

Hormones and menstruation

The menstrual cycle is controlled by several different hormones. Each one plays an important role in coordinating the events that occur in the uterus and the ovaries. **Oestrogen** and **progesterone** are the two main female hormones. Oestrogen controls the release of other hormones and also causes the lining of the uterus to thicken. Progesterone maintains the lining of the uterus – it is a drop in progesterone levels that causes menstruation to occur (a period). Both hormones are produced by the ovaries and their levels rise and fall in a particular pattern during one menstrual cycle (Figure 4.1). The release of an ovum from the ovaries (ovulation) happens at a specific point in the cycle.

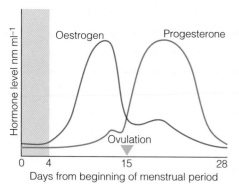

Figure 4.1 *Hormone levels during one menstrual cycle.*

The contraceptive pill

The **contraceptive pill** is a very widely used form of birth control. There are two main types of pill: the minipill which contains progesterone, and the combined pill which contains oestrogen and progesterone. The combined pill is

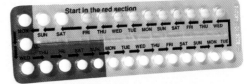

Figure 4.2 *The combined contraceptive pill.*

In ancient Egypt crocodile dung was used as a contraceptive.

the most commonly used type. The hormones present in the pill prevent ovulation and if no ovulation occurs, then there will be no ovum to fertilise and pregnancy cannot occur.

Implants

The contraceptive pill has been in use for over half a century. More recently, implants have been developed that are inserted under the skin and slowly release hormones over a long period of time. One type of implant, called Implanon, consists of a hormone-containing rod which prevents ovulation (and therefore pregnancy) for 3 years. At the end of the 3 years the rod is removed and a new one can be inserted.

Figure 4.3 *A contraceptive implant which is inserted underneath the skin.*

2 Women taking the pill are more likely to suffer from a heart attack than women not taking the pill. Despite this, the pill is still the most commonly used form of contraception in the UK. Why do so many women take the pill if it could cause them harm? [Total 2]

The menopause

As a woman gets older, the amount of oestrogen produced by the ovaries decreases and the levels in her blood start to drop. When these get very low, the monthly events of ovulation and menstruation stop. This is called the **menopause** and in the UK the average age at which it happens is 52. Low oestrogen levels can cause various side effects, the most common being hot flushes. A more serious consequence is the increased risk of osteoporosis. This is when bones become weaker and more likely to fracture.

Menopausal women can obtain extra oestrogen through hormone replacement therapy (HRT). This may involve either taking oestrogen tablets or wearing an oestrogen-containing patch on the skin. HRT reduces the chances of osteoporosis developing. There are some risks in using HRT though, such as an increased risk of developing some forms of cancer and an increased risk of having a stroke.

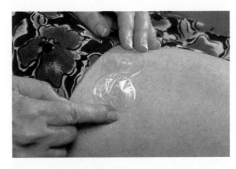

Figure 4.4 *A HRT Patch.*

Questions

1 A woman taking the combined pill takes a pill containing oestrogen and progesterone every day for 21 days and then she takes a pill that contains no hormones every day for 7 days.
   a) Sketch a graph to show how you might expect the levels of hormones to change during the 28 days. Use the same axes as the graph in Figure 4.1. *[2]*
   b) Why do you think pills containing no hormones are taken for 7 days? *[2]*
   c) What advantages are there to using a hormone implant such as Implanon instead of taking the combined pill? Are there any disadvantages? *[3]*
   [Total 7]

2 Suggest why many women use HRT, even though it has some risks associated with it. *[Total 3]*

3 Methods of contraception that involve hormones do not offer some of the benefits that condoms do. What additional benefits do condoms offer? *[Total 3]*

Hormones and fertility

Hormonal help

When a couple decide to have a baby it is not always straightforward. Sometimes either the man or the woman may have problems that make it very difficult or impossible to conceive naturally. The person who has the problem is said to be **infertile**.

Infertility in men may be a result of low sperm count or low sperm quality. In women, the most common cause of infertility is the failure to ovulate. Modern medicine is able to help women who do not ovulate.

IVF

IVF stands for **in vitro fertilisation**, which means that fertilisation of the ovum occurs outside of the woman's body. IVF is a common technique used to treat infertility. There are several steps involved:

a) The woman receives injections of an artificial hormone. This hormone stimulates her ovaries to develop many ova.
b) The ova are collected using a needle in a simple, quick operation.
c) The extracted ova are mixed with sperm in a dish, where fertilisation occurs.
d) The fertilised ova grow and divide to form embryos.
e) The healthiest embryos are selected and inserted into the uterus of the woman.
f) Hopefully at least one of the embryos will implant in the uterus and pregnancy will occur.

The success rate of IVF is typically around 20%, but this varies greatly depending on the age of the woman involved and the quality of the clinic in which it is carried out. Recent advances in a technique called **embryo screening** may lead to an improvement in these success rates.

> A normal sperm count is defined as a minimum of 20 000 000 sperm per millilitre of semen, and a minimum total number of 40 000 000 sperm in one ejaculation.

> 1 The typical cost of one cycle of IVF treatment is about £2500. Suggest why it is so expensive. [Total 2]

Figure 4.5 *The world's first IVF baby was Louise Brown, born in 1978.*

Embryo screening and genetic testing

When embryos are selected for IVF, they are chosen on the basis of appearance, how well they have grown and how regular the growth appears. Unfortunately, this does not always mean the best embryos are selected. This is because any problems with the DNA of the embryo cannot be detected under a microscope.

In embryo screening, a single cell is taken from the embryo, and it is then checked for any potential problems due to faulty DNA. This is called **genetic testing**. If the cell is normal, the embryo can then be inserted into the woman's uterus. Using only genetically healthy embryos increases the chances of a successful pregnancy occurring.

During embryo screening there is a small chance that the removal of a cell for testing might damage the embryo and prevent it from developing normally. A more recent technique gets around this problem and has given doctors hope for even higher success rates. This method involves screening the extracted ova for genetic defects before they are mixed with any sperm. Only healthy ova are used for the remaining stages and so the chance of success is high.

2 If genetic testing puts an embryo at risk, why do some people still want to have their embryos tested?
[Total 2]

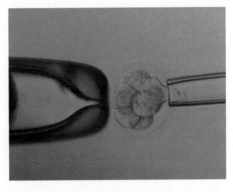

Figure 4.6 *Removing an embryo cell for genetic screening.*

Questions

1 There are a great number of children in the UK who are waiting to be adopted. Should infertile couples be forced to adopt instead of having IVF? Explain your answer. *[Total 3]*

2 Genetic screening can be used to ensure that babies do not have certain genetic diseases. It could also be used to select babies that have desirable characteristics.
  a) In 2008 a deaf couple petitioned to create a deaf embryo using IVF. What do you think the arguments for and against this might have been?
[3]

  b) Some people are worried that genetic screening might be used to create 'designer babies'. What sort of characteristics might parents want their children to possess? *[4]*
[Total 7]

3 IVF has been controversially used to help older women get pregnant. The oldest woman in the world to get pregnant and give birth through IVF was 70 years old. Write two lists of arguments for and against older women having IVF. *[Total 4]*

End of section questions

1 Which part of the flower:
 a) attracts insects [1]
 b) contains the female sex cell [1]
 c) contains the male sex cells? [1]
 [Total 3]

2 Draw and label a flowering plant. Include the functions of each part in the labels. [Total 10]

3 a) What is the difference between self-pollination and cross-pollination? [2]
 b) Describe two ways in which cross-pollination can take place. [2]
 [Total 4]

4 Describe how, after pollination, the nucleus of a pollen grain reaches the nucleus of the female sex cell. [Total 2]

5 Copy and complete Table 1 to compare insect- and wind-pollinated flowers. [Total 6]

Feature	Insect-pollinated flowers	Wind-pollinated flowers
petal size		
colour		
perfume		
nectary		
stamen shape		
stigma shape		

Table 1

6 a) What is fertilisation? [1]
 b) Where does fertilisation take place in a plant? [1]
 [Total 2]

7 Draw two labelled diagrams to show the stages of germination of a plant. Include the functions of each part in the table. [Total 6]

8 Name five different methods by which plants can reproduce vegetatively. [Total 5]

9 a) What are the four main methods of seed dispersal? [4]
 b) Explain how fruits and seeds are adapted to each method. [4]
 [Total 8]

10 What are the advantages and disadvantages of asexual reproduction? [Total 3]

11 a) Draw labelled diagrams to show:
  i) a female sex cell
  ii) a male sex cell. [6]
 b) Add to the labels on your diagram to show the adaptations each cell has to its function. [3]
 [Total 9]

12 Explain what happens to an ovum after it is released but not fertilised. [Total 3]

13 How does sexual reproduction make an individual unique? *[Total 3]*

14 Explain the functions of the placenta and the umbilical cord. *[Total 4]*

15 a) Explain why some methods of birth control are called barriers. *[1]*
   b) Give the names of the two other types of contraceptives and give an example of each type. *[4]*
   [Total 5]

16 Why is it important that couples discuss birth control before entering into a sexual relationship? *[Total 2]*

17 AIDS cannot be cured but syphilis and gonorrhoea can. Explain why. *[Total 4]*

18 Describe the changes that occur during puberty for girls and boys. *[Total 8]*

19 Explain how identical and non-identical twins are formed. *[Total 4]*

20 Find out about unusual methods of pollination.
   R

21 Find out how AIDS can affect an unborn child.
   P

22 Find out what the 'minimal legal age' means and which laws it applies to.
   P

23 Find out what the difference is between an annual, biennial and a perennial plant.
   P

24 Find out what a coleoptile is.
   P

25 Find out what drugs are available to treat hay fever.
   P

26 Investigate which factors affect the germination of a plant.
   P

27 Investigate the growth of pollen tubes under a microscope.
   P

28 Investigate whether the types and abundance of plants on the school field are affected by the level of moisture in the soil.
   P

29 Investigate how effective hormone rooting powders are on different plant cuttings.
   P

6.1 Classification and keys

Why are supermarkets set out in an organised way? Items that are similar are located near to each other. This makes it easier to find the items that we want and compare them. Scientists also arrange organisms into groups and this is called **classification**. The organisms in a group will have similar features and this makes it easier for scientists to study and compare them. The name of the group also gives us information about the organisms in the group.

Figure 1.1 *Super market classification*

Classification

There are millions of types of organisms on the planet. Scientists arrange them into groups based on how similar they are. The largest groups are called **kingdoms**. All organisms belong to one of the five kingdoms. The kingdoms are:

- **animal** – further subdivided into **vertebrates** (those with backbones) and many groups of **invertebrates** (animals without a backbone).
- **plant** – further divided into **flowering plants** (plants that have flowers) and many groups of non-flowering plants.
- **fungus** – these include moulds, mushrooms and yeast.
- **protist** – these are a wide variety of simple organisms, and many have only one cell.
- **monera** – these are single-celled organisms with no nucleus and include bacteria.

?

1 a) Where in a supermarket would you find fish fingers? [1]

b) How would you know to find them there? [1]

[Total 2]

2 a) How are you similar to the person sitting closest to you? [1]

b) How are you different? [1]

c) Suggest a way of classifying the members of your class in two groups. [1]

[Total 3]

?

3 Define the word 'classification'. [Total 1]

4 a) Which kingdom would you put 'humans' into? [1]

b) Why would you put humans into this kingdom? [1]

[Total 2]

5 a) What two groups can animals be most simply sorted into? [2]

b) What is the main difference between these two groups? [1]

[Total 3]

6 Suggest the name of:

a) a flowering plant [1]

b) a plant that does not have flowers. [1]

[Total 2]

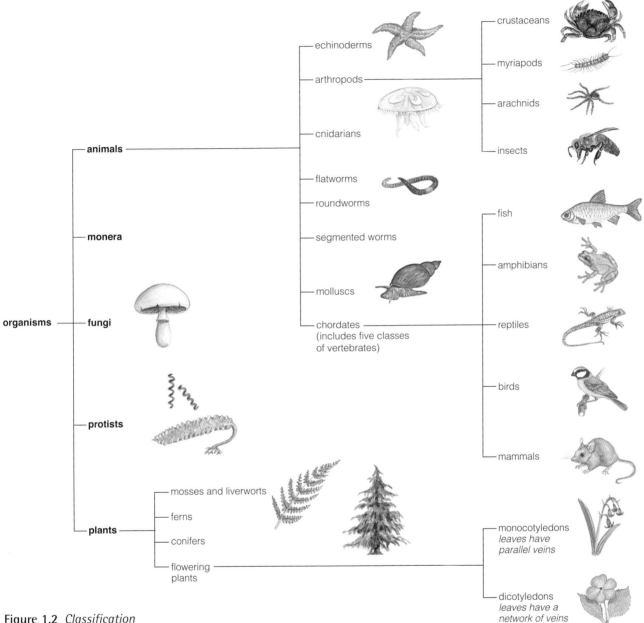

Figure 1.2 *Classification*

Kingdoms can be divided into smaller groups called **phyla**. These can then be subdivided into smaller groups called **classes**. Classes are divided into **orders**, orders into **families**, and families into **genera** (singular genus). Eventually you get to the smallest group called a **species**.

?

7 Make a list of all the phyla that only contain invertebrates. *[Total 2]*

8 Which of the groups shown in Figure 1.2 do humans belong to? *[Total 3]*

	Human	Honeybee	Corn	Field mushroom
kingdom	Animalia	Animalia	Plantae	Fungi
phylum	Chordata	Arthropoda	Angiospermophyta	Basidiomycota
class	Mammalia	Insecta	Monocotyledoneae	Agaricomycetes
order	Primates	Hymenoptera	Commelinales	Agaricales
family	Hominidae	Apidae	Poaceae	Agaricaceae
genus	*Homo*	*Apis*	*Zea*	*Agaricus*
species	*sapiens*	*mellifera*	*mays*	*campestris*

Table 1.1 *Hierarchy of groups. Note that the groups are given Latin names.*

! Horses and donkeys can mate and produce a mule but mules are not fertile. So horses and donkeys do not belong to the same species.

?

9 A liger is the offspring produced when a lion and a tiger mate. Would you expect ligers to be fertile? Explain your answer. *[Total 2]*

10 Humans are multicellular. What does this mean? *[Total 1]*

Species

The smallest group in the classification of organisms is species. A species is a group of organisms that are so alike that they can mate together and produce fertile young (offspring that can also reproduce).

Humans, horses and dandelions are examples of different species. Members of one species cannot naturally mate with members of another, for example cats cannot mate with dogs.

Animal kingdom

The animal kingdom contains organisms that are very complex. They are made of lots of cells (they are **multicellular**). The animal kingdom can be subdivided into smaller groups called phyla. We belong to a phylum called *chordata*. Nearly all the animals within this phylum are vertebrates. This means that they have backbones. The rest of the phyla in the animal kingdom are known as invertebrates because they do not have a backbone.

Vertebrates can be placed in one of five classes, as shown in Table 1.2.

Vertebrate class	Characteristics	Examples	Picture
fish	○ streamlined shape ○ breathe using gills ○ move using fins ○ skin has scales ○ live in water ○ eggs laid in water	shark, haddock, salmon, sea horse	
amphibians	○ can live under water breathing through skin ○ adults can live on land as they have lungs ○ moist soft skin ○ eggs laid in water	frog, toad, newt, salamander	
reptiles	○ dry scaly skin ○ breathe using lungs ○ eggs with a leathery shell laid on land	tortoise, crocodile, snake	
birds	○ breathe using lungs ○ warm-blooded ○ feathers ○ eggs with hard shells laid	eagle, sparrow, penguin, owl	
mammals	○ warm-blooded ○ young develop inside the mother ○ young feed on milk from the mother ○ breathe using lungs ○ fur or hair	bat, human, horse	

Table 1.2 *Vertebrate classification.*

The invertebrates can be subdivided into many phyla, as shown in Table 1.3.

Table 1.3 *Invertebrate classification.*

Invertebrate phyla	Characteristic	Examples	Picture
echinoderms	○ armour-plated skin covered in spines ○ body has five-part radial symmetry	starfish, sea cucumber, sea urchin	
arthropods	○ hard outer skeleton ○ segmented body ○ jointed walking limbs	crab, tick, beetle ladybird	
cnidarians	○ two-layered organism with a body like a bag	jellyfish, hydra, sea anemone	
flatworms	○ flat body	planarian, tapeworm, liver fluke	
roundworms	○ smooth worm-like body	nematode	
segmented worms	○ segmented worm-like body	earthworm, leech	
molluscs	○ soft body protected by hard parts (e.g. a shell) ○ use a large muscle to move or feed with	snail, limpet, mussel, cuttlefish	

There are more species of arthropod than any other type of animal. Arthropods can be subdivided into four classes, as shown in Table 1.4.

11 a) Draw a table to show three differences between insects and arachnids. [3]
b) An animal has 14 legs. Which class would you put it into? [1]
[Total 4]

Arthropod class	Characteristic	Examples	Picture
insects	○ three pairs of legs ○ body divided into three parts	grasshopper, dragonfly, stag beetle	
arachnids	○ four pairs of legs ○ no antennae ○ body divided into two parts	spider, scorpion, harvestman	
crustaceans	○ two pairs of antennae ○ five to seven pairs of legs ○ hard chalky shell	crab, lobster, water flea	
myriapods	○ long, thin segmented body ○ many pairs of legs	centipede, millipede	

Table 1.4 *Arthropod classification.*

Plant kingdom

Plants are multicellular organisms that contain **chlorophyll**. Chlorophyll is a green chemical, which absorbs light energy. The light energy can be used to make food for the plants. Some groups of plants produce seeds and some do not.

The seedless plants include:

◯ Mosses and liverworts. These have no true roots or **xylem** tissue (in which water is carried). They are very small and reproduce by **spores**. A spore is a reproductive cell that has a thick wall around it.

◯ Ferns have roots and xylem tissue. They also reproduce by spores.

The seed-producing plants include:

◯ Conifers, which reproduce using seeds found inside cones. They have no true flowers and have needle-like leaves.

◯ Flowering plants, which bear flowers. The flowers then turn into fruits that contain seeds.

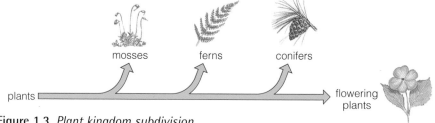

Figure 1.3 *Plant kingdom subdivision.*

Fungi

Fungi do not contain chlorophyll and cannot photosynthesise. Most fungi are multicellular. Yeast is the exception as it is **unicellular**. Uniellular organisms are made of one cell.

Fungi are usually made up of fine branched threads called **hyphae**. The hyphae spread out in a network called a **mycelium**, like bread mould. When the mycelium reaches a certain size it forms reproductive structures that contain spores. Some fungi such as mushrooms produce large structures called fruiting bodies. These are bundles of hyphae joined together. The fruiting body is in two parts: the stalk and the cap. The cap contains gills, which produce spores.

Figure 1.4 *Bread mould and mushrooms.*

Most fungi are decomposers called **saprobionts**. They feed on dead matter, decomposing it. A few may feed as **parasites** in living tissues and can cause diseases such as ringworm in humans.

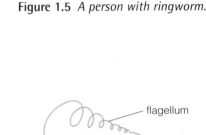

Figure 1.5 *A person with ringworm.*

Protists

Protists live in water and damp places. Some are unicellular and all have a nucleus in each cell. The unicellular protists have developed rather special ways to move their bodies. Some move by making the contents of their cell flow. Many, like the *Amoeba*, push out parts of their cells to form temporary arm-like projections called **pseudopodia**. The pseudopodia are then used to catch food, which is usually other protists or bacteria.

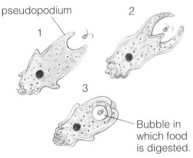

pseudopodium

1

2

3

Bubble in which food is digested.

Figure 1.6 *An amoeba.*

Some, like the *Euglena*, have chlorophyll and so gain energy from photosynthesis. However they move in a different way to amoeba. *Euglena* have a long hair-like projection called a **flagellum**. They move by lashing the flagellum like a whip to propel themselves forward through water.

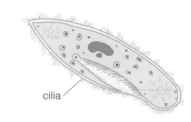

flagellum

Figure 1.7 *Euglena.*

Other protists such as *Paramecium*, have tiny hairs called cilia over the surface of their bodies. They flick the cilia backwards and forwards in a wave-like motion, to push their bodies through the water. The currents of water they generate also suck food into their mouths.

The protist kingdom also contains some algae such as seaweeds.

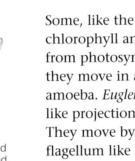

cilia

Figure 1.8 *Paramecium.*

Monera

These organisms are single celled (unicellular). Their cells do not have a nucleus. All of their genetic material is free in the cytoplasm of the cell. This group can be subdivided into two smaller groups: bacteria and Archaea.

- **Bacteria** – most are decomposers. They can be classified according to their shape: rounded, coiled or rod shaped. They may be able to live on ther own but may cause serious diseases, e.g. cholera. The ones that cause serious diseases are usually parasitic.
- **Archaea** are even simpler than bacteria.

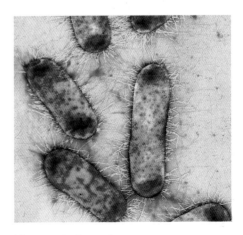

Figure 1.9 *Bacteria.*

There are about three times as many species of insects as all other kinds of animals put together.
40% of insects are beetles – about 350 000 different species. Scientists think that there are millions of species of beetles that are as yet undiscovered.

Identifying organisms

More than 1 500 000 different types of organism have been found and identified. Every day more are discovered. Individual scientists cannot remember the names of every organism. When they want to find out which species an organism belongs to or its name, they use a device called a **key**. A key is a special chart, which consists of descriptions and information that make identifying organisms easier.

There are different types of keys. A 'statement key' has numbered questions with two possible alternative answers. The answer for each question leads on to another question or the name of the organism. Eventually the name of the unknown organism is found.

To use the key you must look at the drawings carefully. Read the first pair of questions. Decide which description fits, and if the arrow does not point to a name it will point to another question. That is the next question to read and then work your way through the key until the organism has a name.

15 Use the statement key to work out the names of the beetles, A – F. [Total 6]

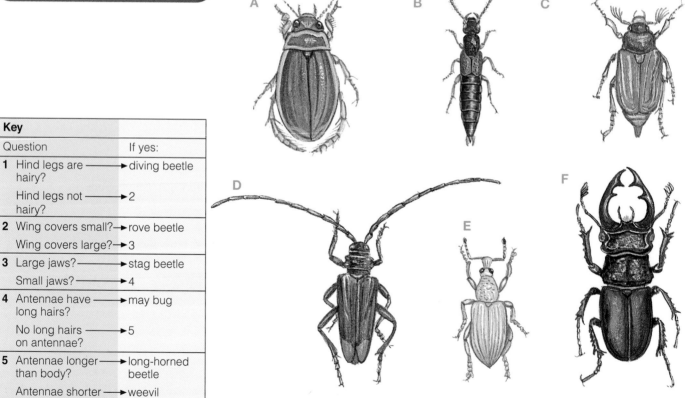

Key	
Question	If yes:
1 Hind legs are hairy?	→ diving beetle
Hind legs not hairy?	→ 2
2 Wing covers small?	→ rove beetle
Wing covers large?	→ 3
3 Large jaws?	→ stag beetle
Small jaws?	→ 4
4 Antennae have long hairs?	→ may bug
No long hairs on antennae?	→ 5
5 Antennae longer than body?	→ long-horned beetle
Antennae shorter than body?	→ weevil

Figure 1.10 *Identifying beetles using a key (not to scale).*

Another type of key is the 'branching' or 'spider key'. As you read each question you are given a choice of two branches to follow. You need to follow the route that is the best match until the organism has a name. You still need to look at the drawings carefully.

?

16 Use the branching key to work out the names of the plants, A – F. *[Total 6]*

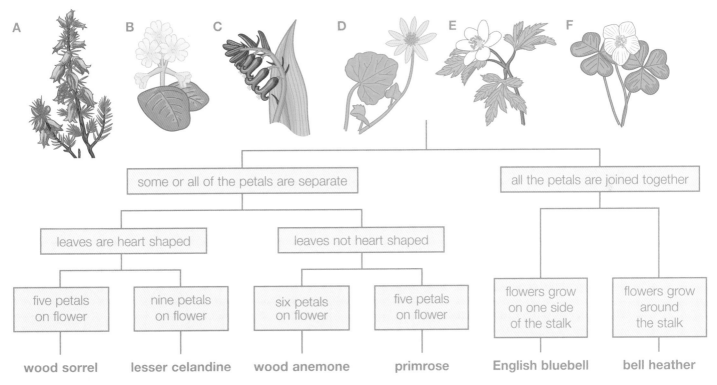

Figure 1.11 *Branching key to identify some wild flowers.*

Summary

- Organisms can be classified into groups according to their main characteristics.
- The groups are kingdom, phylum, class, order, family, genus and species.
- There are five different kingdoms: plants, animals, fungi, protists and monera.
- A key can be used in the identification of an organism.

Questions

1 Copy and complete the following sentences. All living things can be _____ into groups. The _____ major divisions are called _____. A _____ can help you identify and name an organism. *[Total 3]*

2 a) What does classification mean? *[1]*
b) What do scientists look for when classifying organisms? *[1]*
c) In classification, what is a kingdom? *[1]*
[Total 3]

3 What determines if an animal is called a vertebrate or an invertebrate? *[Total 1]*

4 Explain what a species is. *[Total 3]*

5 Which group of animals have wings and six legs? *[Total 1]*

6 What class of animal is a snake? *[Total 1]*

7 a) Which animals can breathe on land and in water? *[1]*
b) Explain how they are able to do this. *[2]*
[Total 3]

8 A reptile and an amphibian both lay eggs. Describe how they are different. *[Total 2]*

9 Which types of sea animals have armour-plated bodies? *[Total 1]*

10 What is chlorophyll and which kingdom contains it? *[Total 2]*

11 What are spores and where are they found? *[Total 3]*

12 Explain the differences between mosses and conifers. *[Total 3]*

13 Why are fungi in a different group to plants? *[Total 1]*

14 List a difference and a similarity between monera and protists. *[Total 2]*

15 What are pseudopodia, flagellum and cilia used for? *[Total 1]*

16 Explain why a botanist (plant biologist) might use a key. *[Total 1]*

17 Make a branched key for the six shapes in Figure 1.11. *[Total 3]*

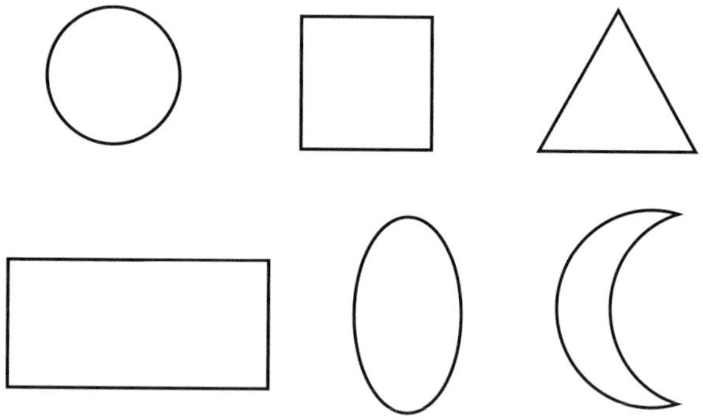

Figure 1.12

18 Make a statement key for the four pond animals in the diagram. *[Total 3]*

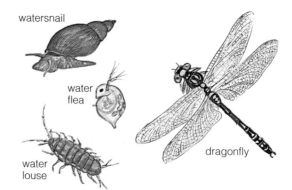

watersnail

water flea

water louse

dragonfly

Figure 1.13

6.2 Why do organisms vary?

Why do we all look different? Humans have different features, such as eye colour, hair colour or blood groups. These are called **characteristics**. The characteristics of all humans are similar because we belong to the same species, *Homo sapiens*. Members of one species live in similar ways, move in similar ways, need similar food and can breed together to produce fertile offspring.

The differences we find between organisms are called **variation**. There is much greater variation between members of different species than between members of the same species.

Figure 2.1

Types of variation

There are two types of variation: **continuous** and **discontinuous**.

If you measured the heights of all the pupils in your class, some would be shorter, some tall and some in-between. This type of variation is called **continuous variation**, as the characteristic (height) can vary in tiny amounts between individuals.

The bar chart shows the variation in heights in a large group of 12 year olds. The 'bell shape' pattern is called the **normal distribution**.

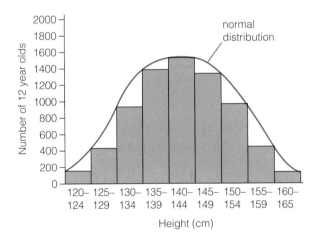

Figure 2.2 *Heights of pupils.*

1 Describe one of your characteristics that shows discontinuous variation between people. [Total 1]

2 What sort of variation do these characteristics show:
a) shoe size
b) blood group
c) height
d) foot length
e) being able to roll your tongue. [Total 5]

3 Describe what is meant by 'normal distribution'. [Total 2]

4 People's arm lengths vary. Sketch a graph to show what you would expect the 'left arm length' distribution to look like, for all adults in the UK. [Total 2]

If you asked all the people in your class to roll their tongues some would be able to do it and the others would not. There would be no one in-between. This type of variation is called **discontinuous variation**. Other examples of discontinuous variation include the attachment of ear lobes (are they attached or not?), blood type and inherited genetic diseases such as cystic fibrosis.

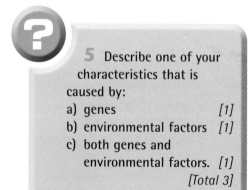

Figure 2.3

Causes of variation

Most of the characteristics that you have are passed on to you from your parents, through **genes**. Genes are small sections of DNA that control a particular characteristic. For example genes control the colour of your eyes.

Some characteristics are due to factors around us, for example how much food we eat. Diet can affect height, weight and other features. This type of variation is caused by **environmental factors**.

Many characteristics depend partly on genetic factors and partly on environmental factors. This is so for most organisms, e.g. two trees may have the same genes. However, one may grow better than the other because it receives a better supply of water or more light.

Figure 2.4 *Identical twins with variation caused by environmental factors.*

Variation between species

In addition to variation between individuals within a species, variation also occurs between species. Some organisms look the same at first. If you look at them closely there are differences between them.

Two horses have more in common with each other than a horse with a monkey. However, some species do have similarities with others, as they are closely related to them.

Figure 2.5 *Different species of woodlice.*

Figure 2.6 *Monkeys, lemurs and tree shrews are all related.*

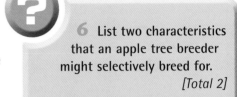

Selective breeding

Animals and plants of the past were very different from those we see today. Over the years people have tried to breed organisms with certain characteristics – a process called **selective breeding**. For example, a greyhound owner wants fast greyhounds. Very fast dogs are mated with each other. The offspring should also be fast runners. The fastest of the offspring are then mated with other fast greyhounds, which will hopefully produce even faster dogs. The process is called selective breeding because only animals with certain characteristics are selected for breeding.

6 List two characteristics that an apple tree breeder might selectively breed for.

[Total 2]

Figure 2.7 *Greyhounds have been selectively bred for speed.*

Figure 2.8 *Bulldogs were selectively bred in the thirteenth century for 'bull baiting' where people would watch a dog attack a bull, for fun! The nose is upturned so that the dog can breathe when its jaws are clamped down around a bull's nose.*

Figure 2.9 *Ornamental cabbages selectively bred for their colours.*

7 A greyhound and a bulldog are crossed. Describe what characteristics the offspring might have.

[Total 2]

Cross-breeding is when two breeds, both with desirable characteristics, are bred together. For example, a farmer may have a cow that produces a lot of milk. He may know of a bull that has fathered cows that produce very creamy milk but not much of it. He can breed the cow and the bull together and hope that the calves will eventually produce lots of creamy milk.

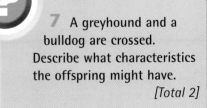

Summary

- A species is a group of organisms with very similar features that can breed together and produce fertile offspring.
- Variation can be continuous e.g. height, or discontinuous, e.g. blood type.
- Variation between species is greater than the variation within a species.
- Variation can be caused by environmental factors and/or genes.
- Closely related species have similar characteristics.

Questions

1 Copy and complete the following sentences. Humans are all different, and our differences are called _____. It may be one of two types, _____ or _____. Variation can be caused by genes or _____ factors.
[Total 2]

2 a) What is variation? *[1]*
b) Explain the difference between the two different types of variation. *[2]*
[Total 3]

3 What does the term 'normal distribution' mean?
[Total 2]

4 What are the causes of variation? *[Total 2]*

5 Explain why there is more variation between species than within a species. *[Total 1]*

6 a) What is selective breeding? *[1]*
b) Why is selective breeding important to farmers? *[2]*
c) Explain how a farmer would selectivly breed tomatoes to produce plants with the largest yield (i.e. greatest number of tomatoes in a year). *[3]*
[Total 6]

7 Suggest two characteristics a farmer might want to select when breeding:
a) chickens *[2]*
b) sheep *[2]*
c) pigs. *[2]*
[Total 6]

8 Some people can roll their tongues but others cannot.
a) Sketch a bar chart to show what you think the proportion of tongue rollers versus non-tongue rollers will look like. *[1]*
b) What information did you base your chart on? *[1]*
c) How would you find out if your proportion is correct? *[1]*
d) What sort of variation is shown by tongue rolling? *[1]*
e) What do you think causes some people to be able to roll their tongues and others not to be able roll their tongues? *[1]*
[Total 5]

6.3 Patterns of inheritance

What are genes? Why are they so important? We know that some characteristics of an organism are inherited from its parents. When genes are mixed during sexual reproduction variation occurs.

DNA

The human body contains billions of cells. Each cell has a specific function. Most cells have a **nucleus** that controls them. The nucleus of a cell contains long, threadlike strands called **chromosomes**. There are 46 chromosomes in each human nucleus. Chromosomes carry pieces of information called **genes**. Chromosomes and genes are made of a large molecule called deoxyribonucleic acid (**DNA**). The DNA molecule is arranged like a twisted spiral ladder called a **double helix**. (A helix is any spiral-shaped object.) Each 'rung' on the ladder consists of a pair of **bases**.

The genetic instructions are carried in the sequence of DNA bases that make up each gene. This sequence is a code that controls the order in which amino acids are joined together to produce **proteins**. The proteins are used for the growth of cells and as enzymes that control all the chemical reactions in the body. It is the proteins that genes produce that control our characteristics.

Each human cell contains about 2 m of DNA strands forming a double helix.

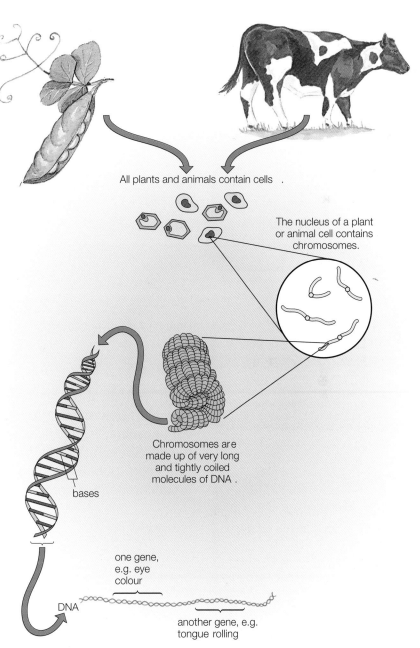

All plants and animals contain cells.

The nucleus of a plant or animal cell contains chromosomes.

Chromosomes are made up of very long and tightly coiled molecules of DNA.

bases

one gene, e.g. eye colour

DNA

another gene, e.g. tongue rolling

Figure 3.1 *Cells, chromosomes and DNA. Genes are sections of chromosomes.*

Chromosomes

All human cells except for the sperm and the egg cell (ovum) contain 23 *pairs* of chromosomes. A sperm contains a single copy of each of the 23 types of chromosomes of the father. The ovum contains a single set of chromosomes from the mother. At fertilisation these two sets of chromosomes are brought together. The fertilised egg then contains 23 pairs of chromosomes, one of each pair from each parent. These pairs of chromosomes are called **homologous pairs**.

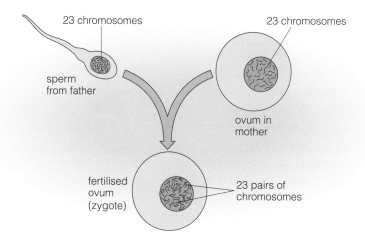

Figure 3.2 *Most of our cells have two copies of each chromosome.*

Genes

Short sections of the DNA in a chromosome make up each gene. The many genes are arranged in a particular sequence along each chromosome. Each gene consists of thousands of bases. Genes control the development of inherited characteristics in individuals. Different genes control hair colour, eye colour, and nose shape as well as the production of hormones such as insulin.

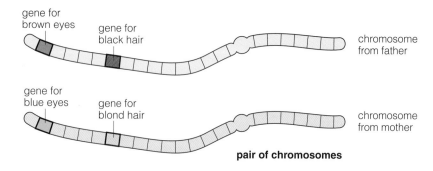

Figure 3.3 *Chromosomes in a homologous pair carry the same genes but the genes can come in different forms.*

?

1 In what part of a cell are chromosomes found?
[Total 1]

2 If a buffalo sperm cell contains 30 chromosomes, how many chromosomes will be found in a buffalo body cell? [Total 1]

3 Kangaroos have six different types of chromosomes. Draw a diagram, like Figure 3.2, to show how many chromosomes kangaroo gametes and zygotes have.
[Total 3]

!

Scientists estimate that humans have a total of about 25 000 different sorts of genes.

?

4 Where are genes found? [Total 1]

5 A gene that controls eye colour may come in two types? Suggest what these two types are. [Total 2]

6 Genes contain information in the form of a code. What substances are used to make this code? [Total 1]

Genetics

Genetics is the branch of science that studies genes. We all inherit some characteristics from each parent. When ova and sperm are produced by meiosis each gamete receives a different selection of the parental genes.

Each chromosome in a homologous pair carries the same genes. We therefore have a copy of each gene from our father and one copy from our mother. A gene always 'codes' for one characteristic but it can have different forms (e.g. one gene may cause blood type A, and another may cause blood type B). For example, some people can 'roll their tongue' and some people cannot (Figure 3.4). The alternative forms that the gene can take are called **alleles**.

Some alleles are always seen in an individual. These are called **dominant** alleles and tongue rolling is a dominant allele. If your mother gives you an allele for tongue rolling and your father gives you an allele for 'not tongue rolling', you will be able to roll your tongue. The allele whose effect is not seen is called a **recessive** allele and 'not tongue rolling' is a recessive allele.

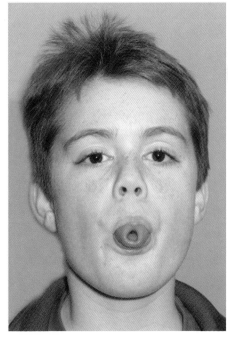

Figure 3.4 *Tongue rolling.*

Occasionally mistakes happen when cells divide. Information in chromosomes may be lost, changed or added to. This change in the DNA is called a **mutation**. Some chemicals and radiation can damage DNA causing mutations. Exposure to radiation may result in the cells dividing very quickly over and over again causing a lump called a tumour or cancer. Mutations are not always harmful and are important as a source of variation if passed on to offspring.

Sometimes DNA changes happen in a sperm or ovum. These changes can be mutations or the addition or loss of whole chromosomes. For example, individuals with Down's Syndrome have an extra chromosome (47 rather than 46).

?

7 What process produces sperm and ova? *[Total 1]*

8 What is an allele? *[Total 1]*

?

9 a) Michael has inherited two 'not tongue rolling' alleles. Do you think he is able to roll his tongue? *[1]*

b) Do you think his parents will be able to roll their tongues? Explain your answer. *[1]* *[Total 2]*

10 Sonia has a disease called cystic fibrosis. It is caused by inheriting two copies of a mutated gene – a recessive allele, called CFTR F508. Explain how Sonia can come to have the disease but neither of her parents have it. *[Total 1]*

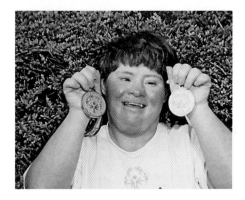

Figure 3.5 *A child with Down's Syndrome.*

11 What combination of sex chromosomes do you have? [Total 1]

Sex determination in birds works the other way around from mammals. In birds, the females have two different sex chromosomes (Z and W) and the males have two Z sex chromosomes.

12 How many sex chromosomes are found in a sperm? [Total 1]

13 a) Draw out a Punnett square for a male and female chicken. [2]
   b) What percentage of their chicks will be male? [1]
   [Total 3]

Sex determination

Sexual reproduction involves the joining together of a sperm and ovum. This is **fertilisation**. The sex of an individual is determined by the chromosomes inherited from the parents. One pair of chromosomes is known as the **sex chromosomes**. Body cells in a male have one 'X' sex chromosome and one 'Y' chromosome. Females have two 'X's. So, in males, half the sperm carry an X chromosome, the other half carry a Y chromosome. All ova have one X chromosome. When fertilisation takes place, the X and Y chromosomes of the sperm determine the sex of the offspring. There is a 50:50 chance the child will be a boy or a girl.

Table 3.1 is called a Punnett square. It tells you which chromosomes come from the father and which from the mother. In this case we can see that when the chromosomes combine there is an equal chance of the baby being a boy or a girl.

		Father's sex chromosomes	
		X	Y
Mother's sex chromosomes	X	XX Female	XY Male
	X	XX Female	XY Male

Table 3.1 *A Punnett square.*

Figure 3.6 *An American crocodile.*

Not all offspring have their sex determined in this way. Environmental factors can play an important role. Temperature can be involved in deciding whether a fetilised ovum will develop as a male or female. This is known as **temperature-dependent sex determination (TSD)**. It occurs mainly in reptiles like alligators and crocodiles and some species of turtles. The sex of the offspring depends upon the temperature of the fetilised ovum as it develops. In alligators, cool temperatures result in females and high temperatures cause male offspring. The opposite is true for turtles.

Summary

- A cell nucleus contains chromosomes.
- A normal human cell contains 23 pairs of chromosomes.
- Chromosomes are made up of genes.
- Genes are made of DNA.
- A dominant allele will always express its characteristic.
- Mutations are changes that appear in gene structure.
- Males carry a pair of sex chromosomes called XY.
- Females carry a pair of sex chromosomes called XX.

Questions

1 Copy and complete the following sentences. The nucleus of a cell contains _____ which carry _____. Chromosomes are made of _____. Each pair of genes controls a particular _____. *[Total 2]*

2 What is the function of the nucleus? *[Total 1]*

3 a) What are chromosomes? *[1]*
b) How many chromosomes are there in each of the following human cells: *[4]*
cheek, sperm, fertilised ovum? *[Total 5]*

4 a) What are genes? *[1]*
b) What do genes do? *[1]*
c) Explain what genetics is. *[1]*
[Total 3]

5 What is an allele? *[Total 1]*

6 Outline what the term 'mutation' means. *[Total 2]*

7 Explain how the sex of a baby is determined. *[Total 2]*

8 What do you think causes two alleles to be different to one another? *[Total 1]*

9 Huntington's disease is caused by a dominant allele called 'H'. The normal allele is called 'h'. Janette has alleles H and h. Her partner, George, has alleles h and h.
a) Will either Janette or George have Huntington's disease? Explain your answer. *[3]*
b) What percentage of their children would have the disease? Draw a Punnett square to work out your answer. *[5]*
[Total 8]

10 Tay-Sachs disease is caused by a recessive allele called 't'. The normal allele is called 'T'. Jackson has alleles T and t. His wife, Asha, has alleles T and t.
a) Will either Jackson or Asha have Tay-Sachs disease? Explain your answer. *[3]*
b) What percentage of their children would have the disease? Draw a Punnett square to work out your answer. *[5]*
[Total 8]

6.4 Evolution

Fossils

How can fossils tell us about the past? Fossils are the remains of plants or animals that lived millions of years ago and are mainly found in rock. They reveal to us small fragments of what happened a long time ago.

Figure 4.1

When an organism dies, micro-organisms very quickly begin to decompose it. Fossilisation only takes place under certain conditions that either prevent decay or the destruction of the organism's structure occurring. Fossils have been found in the ice of the Arctic, tar pits in the Caribbean, peat bogs in Europe and tree resin. Many microorganisms do not grow well in these environments. many microorganisms grow best where there is oxygen, moisture, warmth and a suitable pH.

A fossil can be dated by looking at the layer of rock in which it is found. Older rocks are usually deeper in the ground, and so contain the oldest fossils. For the exact dating of rock, a process which measures traces of radioactive elements that are in the rock needs to be used. This involves the elements uranium, lead, rubidium and strontium. We can track how organisms have changed over millions of years by looking at fossils.

Figure 4.2 *Fossils in amber (fossil tree resin) and stone.*

! The study of fossils (palaeontology), is attributed to a close friend of Queen Victoria, Sir Richard Owen. He invented the name 'dinosaurs' based on two Greek words *deinos* (fearfully great) and *sauros* (lizard).

?
1 Why don't dead animals decay very quickly in Antarctica? [Total 1]
2 a) What is amber? [1]
   b) Why don't dead animals decay very quickly when they are trapped in this substance? [1]
   c) What sort of animal fossils would you expect to find in amber? [1]
   [Total 3]

! In 1986, two archaeologists, Tim White and Donald Johanson, found 302 pieces of a female of the species *Homo habilis* (an ancestor of modern humans). It was 1.8 million years old. It was the first time that bones from the limbs of *Homo habilis* had been found. The specimen was about 1 m tall and far more ape-like than expected!

Conditions on Earth

Conditions on the Earth are always changing. About 3000 million years ago simple unicellular (single-celled) life forms developed. 2000 million years ago worm like animals emerged. 2500–1500 million years ago oxygen was building up on the planet rapidly because of photosynthesising bacteria. The oxygen was poisonous to most early forms of life. As time passed more organisms developed, the landmasses moved and temperatures changed. Only organisms that adapted to the new conditions survived. If they could not adapt to the conditions, they became **extinct**.

Figure 4.3

Natural selection

All living things have characteristics that help them to survive. Individuals in a species show many differences. This variation is a result of the alleles inherited. There is competition between individuals for food, space and other resources. This leads to a struggle for survival. The individuals that can compete successfully for resources are most likely to survive. This is known as the '**survival of the fittest**' or more properly as **natural selection**. If variation gives individuals a greater ability to compete for resources, then those individuals will have a better chance of survival, and so live to breed and produce offspring. This ensures that their genetic material is passed on to the next generation.

3 Explain briefly why species become extinct.
[Total 2]

4 What do individual members of an animal species compete for? List two things. [Total 2]

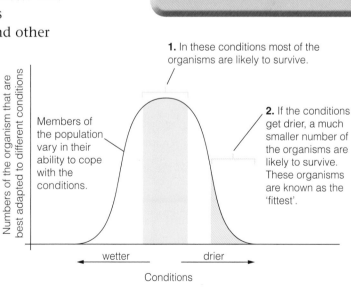

1. In these conditions most of the organisms are likely to survive.

Members of the population vary in their ability to cope with the conditions.

2. If the conditions get drier, a much smaller number of the organisms are likely to survive. These organisms are known as the 'fittest'.

Numbers of the organism that are best adapted to different conditions

wetter   drier

Conditions

Figure 4.4 *Natural selection often takes place as a result of environmental change.*

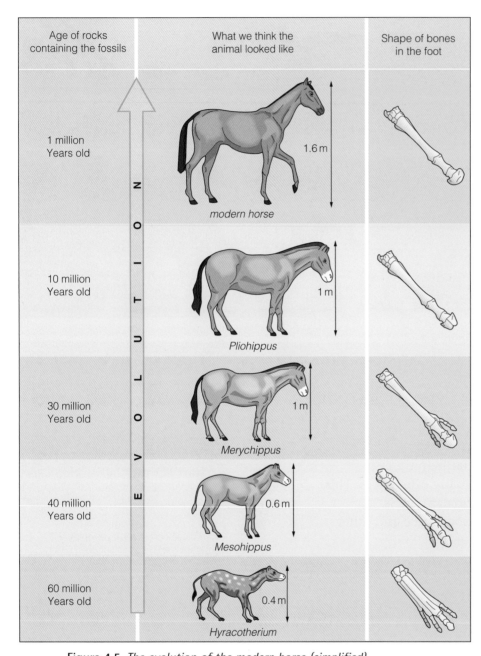

Figure 4.5 *The evolution of the modern horse (simplified).*

Evolution

Natural selection happens continuously and can lead to the formation of new species. The gradual change of the characteristics of an organism over time is called **evolution**.

An example of evolution

Organisms evolve because the environments in which they live change over time and so the organisms need different characteristics to survive. A good example of this is the evolution of the horse.

Hyracotherium was an animal the size of small dog. It lived about 60 million years ago in what is now North America. It was adapted to living in a marshy habitat by having toes that were spread out, to stop it sinking into the ground. It avoided predators by hiding behind bushes in the marshes.

Over millions of years, the marshy ground was replaced by drier and drier grassland and there were fewer bushes to hide behind. Natural selection favoured animals that could run faster to get away from predators. Running on fewer toes is faster. So, over millions of years natural selection favoured animals that had fewer toes touching the ground. Today's horses run on hooves.

?

1 State two differences between *Mesohippus* and modern-day horses.
2 How many toes did *Hyracotherium* walk on?

Horses evolved in what is now North America and spread to other parts of the world by crossing a piece of land that used to connect Alaska with Russia. However, horses became extinct in America about 6 million years ago. One theory to explain this suggests that a new type of grass started to cover the grasslands. This grass was very tough and wore down the horse's teeth quickly, meaning that they did not live very long.

Summary

- Fossils are the preserved remains of animals or plants which existed millions of years ago.
- Life on earth has been changing ever since it formed.
- Evolution is the slow change of organisms over time.
- Evolution may result in the formation of new species.
- The survival of well-adapted organisms is called natural selection.

Questions

1 Copy and complete the following sentences.
_____ are formed when animal or plant remains are preserved in rock for millions of years. Natural _____ is the process in which organisms that are best suited to the _____ in their environment are most likely to survive. If the _____ changes, failure to _____ results in extinction. _____ is the change in the characteristics of a population over time.
[Total 3]

2 a) What are fossils? [1]
   b) List four environments where fossils have been found. [4]
   [Total 5]

3 List the conditions in which microorganisms grow well. [Total 4]

4 What is the theory of evolution? [Total 3]

5 Explain the term 'survival of the fittest'. [Total 1]

6 Modern horses are much taller than the animals that they evolved from. Suggest one reason why. [Total 1]

7 Look at Figure 4.5. Some aspects of the drawings are based on evidence and some are based on educated guesses.
   a) Suggest one aspect of the drawings that is based on evidence. [1]
   b) Suggest one aspect of the drawings that is based on educated guesses. [1]
   [Total 2]

8 Look at the fact box above.
   a) When horses became extinct in America, why didn't they spread back into America from Russia? [1]
   b) What evidence would you expect to find if the theory about tough grasses and teeth is correct? [1]
   [Total 2]

Ideas about variation and inheritance

Carl Linnaeus

Until the eighteenth century scientists in different countries all referred to plants and animals using different names. A Swedish botanist and naturalist, Carl Linnaeus (1707–1778), decided to try to create a system that would make it easier for scientists from different parts of the world to communicate with each other about plants. Linnaeus travelled widely throughout Europe studying and collecting plants. He attempted to classify every known plant and animal. Linnaeus sorted all living things according to similarities in their structure.

In the eighteenth century the most widely understood language among scientists was Latin. So he gave each plant and animal a two-part Latin name. This system is called a **binomial** system. Binomial means two names. The binomial system created by Linnaeus is still used today. Each organism has a genus name that is written with a capital letter and a species name that starts with a small letter. As the name is Latin it is written in italics. Using the binomial system, horses are known as *Equus caballus*. We are known as *Homo sapiens*.

Mendel

Gregor Mendel (1822–1884) was an Austrian monk. He studied mathematics and natural history. Mendel was interested in botany (the study of plants) and wanted to teach biology, but he failed his biology exam twice. He was, however, an excellent mathematician and so taught mathematics and Greek in the local secondary school.

After teaching for a few years, Mendel had to return to the monastery. There he was in charge of the garden. He began to experiment with the plants that he grew. He became interested in how features of pea plants were passed from one generation to another. He monitored the height of the pea plants, blossom colour, position of the flowers on the stem, leaf type, differences in seed colour and shape, and variations in the appearance of the pods. His observations enabled him to suggest how characteristics were inherited. This gave an explanation of how parents pass on their characteristics to their offspring.

Figure 5.1 *Gregor Mendel.*

Ideas about variation and inheritance

Mendel deduced from his experiments that the characteristics of the plants were controlled by an inherited factor. He worked out and concluded that there were two parts to the inherited factor. One part (or 'particle' as he called them) comes from each parent. It was not until the twentieth century that scientists described these 'particles' as genes.

He worked for eight years carrying out thousands of experiments. He conducted his research in a mathematical way, which many people found hard to understand. Some scientists later believed that as Mendel was such a good mathematician he actually fixed some of his results!

Mendel wrote a scientific paper about his work and this was published in a scientific journal. However, it was not widely read at the time. It was only in the 1900s that Mendel's discoveries became well known when three independent botanists, Carl Corren in Germany, Hugo de Vries in Holland and Erich von Tschermak-Seysenegg in Austria, drew attention to them.

Figure 5.2 *Pea plants.*

Questions

1 What area of science did Linnaeus study? *[Total 1]*

2 In which century did Linnaeus live? *[Total 1]*

3 What work has Linnaeus been remembered for? *[Total 1]*

4 What sort of naming system did he create? *[Total 1]*

5 What does binomial mean? *[Total 1]*

6 How are living things labelled using this system? *[Total 1]*

7 a) Who was Gregor Mendel? *[1]*
   b) What subjects did he study? *[1]*
   c) What type of experiments did he carry out? *[1]*
   d) Which type of organism did he use as a focus for his experiments? *[1]*
   [Total 4]

8 List some of the different characteristics that Mendel monitored. *[Total 4]*

9 Why did some people at the time of Mendel find it difficult to understand the nature of his work? *[Total 1]*

10 What conclusions did Mendel make about inherited characteristics? *[Total 2]*

11 In his findings Mendel referred to particles in the plants. What do we now call these? *[Total 1]*

12 When did Mendel's discoveries become well known? *[Total 1]*

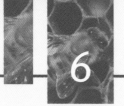

6 Evolution

An evolving theory

Until the seventeenth century, most scientists in the UK thought that humans were not part of the natural world. They also believed that God created the Earth and its organisms (which did not change over time).

In 1644, a church minister called John Lightfoot (1602–1675) claimed to have worked out that God created the Earth on Sunday September 12th 3929 BCE. According to him, humans were created at 9 am the following Friday.

Swedish scientist, Carl Linnaeus (1707–1778), designed our way of classifying organisms. In his book, *Systema Naturae*, he grouped humans with apes and monkeys. This suggested that humans were part of nature and closely related to apes and monkeys. Linnaeus said that he was just classifying God's creations.

Georges Louis Leclerc, Comte de Buffon (1707–1788) published a science encyclopedia called *Histoire naturelle*. In it he stated his belief that environments could cause species to change. However, in his lectures he said that he did not believe that species could change into new species.

James Burnett, Lord Monboddo (1714–1799) was a Scottish judge who had a great interest in how languages changed. He said that, just as languages have evolved, humans evolved from apes. Most people thought Monboddo was mad, not helped by the fact that he thought that some people must be born with tails and had an obsession for finding people with tails.

Jean-Baptiste Lamarck (1744–1829) was one of the first to develop a theory of how evolution happened. Lamarck believed that organisms developed new characteristics, which they passed on to their offspring. He reasoned that wading birds got long legs by stretching them out, so that their bodies could remain dry. Once a bird had stretched its legs, it would pass on the long legs to its offspring. He had, however, little evidence to support this theory.

In 1831 Charles Darwin (1809–1882) set off on an expedition to South America. In the Galapagos Islands he noticed differences between the mockingbirds on different islands. This led him to develop his 'theory of evolution by natural selection'.

Figure 5.3 *John Lightfoot.*

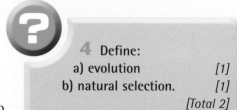

1   What would Linnaeus and Buffon's books be called in English?   [2]

2   Linnaeus upset many people with his grouping of humans. Why do you think people were upset?   [1]

3   State the main difference between Buffon's and Monboddo's thoughts.   [1]

[Total 4]

4   Define:
   a) evolution   [1]
   b) natural selection.   [1]

[Total 2]

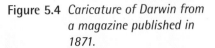
He thought that mockingbirds produced more offspring than could survive, and those with the best adaptations for the conditions would be more likely to survive. So, over time, the species would change. If groups of the same species were separated they would evolve differently, depending on the conditions. The mockingbirds evolved differently because the conditions on each island were different.

Over the years he collected more and more evidence, until he finally published a book, *The Origin of Species*. In the book, he says that he knew of Buffon's ideas. He also says that he was influenced by an economist called Thomas Malthus (1766–1834). Malthus had written a famous essay about how children would die of starvation if people had too many children.

Figure 5.4 *Caricature of Darwin from a magazine published in 1871.*

? 5 Why do you think caricatures showed Darwin as an ape? [2]

Questions

1 a) How would Lamarck have explained why giraffes have long necks? [1]
  b) If Lamarck were correct, what would happen to the offspring of a bird with a missing leg? [1]
  [Total 2]

2 a) List the ways in which the scientists on these pages told each other about their work. [2]
  b) List the ways in which scientists tell each other about their work today. [2]
  [Total 4]

3 a) How did Monboddo apply knowledge of one subject to another? [1]
  b) Draw a caricature of Monboddo. [1]
  [Total 2]

4 Mockingbirds are still found on the Galapagos Islands. State one difference between the mockingbirds in the photographs. [Total 1]

Figure 5.5 *Española Island mockingbird (left) and Santiago Island mockingbird (right).*

6 Variation and inheritance

End of section questions

1 Name three kingdoms in the biological classification system. *[Total 3]*

2 Explain what biological keys are. *[Total 1]*

3 State which group the following organisms belong to (be as specific as you can):
a) jellyfish *[1]*
b) crab *[1]*
c) lobster *[1]*
d) earthworm *[1]*
e) tapeworm *[1]*
f) whale *[1]*
g) dolphin *[1]*
h) bacteria *[1]*
i) newt *[1]*
j) salamander. *[1]*
[Total 10]

4 Find out the heights and arm spans of all the pupils in your class.
a) Record them in a table. *[4]*
b) Draw a chart or graph of your findings. *[4]*
c) From what you have found out, do taller pupils have wider arm spans? *[1]*
[Total 9]

5 Suggest whether the variation in each of the following might be caused by genes, environmental factors or both:
a) eye colour *[1]*
b) life span *[1]*
c) hair colour *[1]*
d) the language a person speaks *[1]*
e) height *[1]*
f) blood group *[1]*
g) intelligence *[1]*
h) skin colour *[1]*
i) how fast a person runs. *[1]*
[Total 9]

6 Explain the difference between a gene and a chromosome. *[Total 3]*

7 a) Draw a graph or chart of the data shown in Table 1. *[4]*
b) What does it show you? *[1]*
[Total 5]

Shoe size	3	4	5	6	7	8	9	10	11	12
Number of people	1	2	4	7	8	2	2	1	1	0

Table 1

8 a) Where are genes found in the body? *[1]*
b) Genes are in pairs. Where do the genes in each pair come from? *[1]*
[Total 2]

9 Describe the shape of the DNA molecule. *[Total 1]*

10 A town has a population of 600 000 people.
a) How many are likely to be female? *[1]*
b) Explain your answer. *[1]*
[Total 2]

11 List the similarities and differences between natural selection and selective breeding. *[Total 4]*

12 Read the following passage and then answer the questions.

A species of moth called the peppered moth is normally light coloured but from time to time a black variety is produced. These moths rest on lichen-covered tree trunks and they blend into their backgrounds. Their main predators are birds. In large industrial towns the black moth often forms 90% of the population. The pollution not only kills many species of lichen but the tree bark and the lichen darken with sooty deposits.
a) Why has the black coloured moth become so successful? *[2]*
b) Explain why this is an example of natural selection. *[1]*
c) Suggest a source of the sooty deposits. *[1]*
d) What might happen to the number of black moths if the large towns become less polluted? *[1]*
[Total 5]

13 Whales are descended from animals that lived on land. Look at where the nostrils are on the skulls, circled in Figure 1.

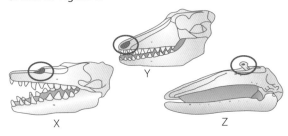

Figure 1

a) Which of the skulls belongs to a modern whale? Explain your choice. *[2]*

b) Which of the skulls belonged to the animal that lived on land? Explain your choice. *[2]*

c) List the skulls in order, from oldest to youngest. Explain your choice. *[2]*

d) The three skulls were found as fossils in bands of rock. Which skull would most likely be found in the deepest band of rock? Explain your choice. *[2]*

[Total 8]

14 The Punnett square shows the alleles of Tamsin and Tres. Tres suffers from a genetic disease called phenylketonuria (PKU). Tamsin does not.

		Possible alleles in Tres' sperm	
		p	p
Possible alleles in Tamsin's ova	P		
	p		

a) Where are alleles found? *[1]*

b) Is PKU caused by a recessive allele or a dominant allele? Explain your answer. *[2]*

c) Copy and complete the Punnett square. *[2]*

d) Use your Punnett square to predict what percentage of their children will have PKU. *[1]*

[Total 6]

15 Only very few organisms ever become fossilised. Suggest a reason for this. *[Total 3]*

16 Rats are killed with a poison called warfarin. Some rats are immune to the poison and their numbers are increasing. Explain why this is happening. *[Total 3]*

17 The graph in Figure 2 shows the percentages of male turtles that hatch, after turtle eggs have been incubated at different temperatures.

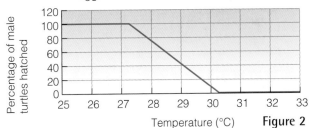

Percentage of male turtles produced from turtle eggs incubated at different temperatures

Figure 2

a) What percentage of hatchlings are male when the incubation temperature is 27 °C? *[1]*

b) What percentage of the hatchlings are female when the incubation temperature is 29 °C? *[1]*

c) At what temperature will an equal number of male and female turtles hatch? *[1]*

[Total 3]

18 R Find out about sickle cell anaemia, a disease caused by a gene mutation.

19 R Find out about some of the other evidence Darwin used to develop his theory of evolution.

20 R Investigate the relationship between head circumference and ear length or hand span and length of middle finger.

21 P Investigate how you could classify all the plants that grow in and around water.

7.1 Health

How do you keep healthy? Humans are complex organisms. To maintain a healthy body you need to eat the right foods, take some exercise, not take in harmful substances, sleep and be free from disease. Plants need to stay healthy too. They make their own food using photosynthesis but they are sensitive to chemicals and pollutants. Plants need the right amounts of water, light and heat to grow healthily.

Maintaining a healthy body can be difficult and requires a **balanced diet**. Some adults are extremely overweight or **obese** because they consume more food than they need. Others may be extremely thin and not consume enough food, because they think they are overweight. There are also individuals who abuse their bodies by using drugs and those who take very little exercise. An unhealthy lifestyle can cause illness and damage vital organs in the body.

Diet and exercise

Taking regular exercise and eating a balanced diet of different foods helps people become fitter and more healthy. During exercise our muscles work hard. As the muscles work harder more energy is needed. The energy the body needs is stored in food. Energy is released from foods such as sugar (particularly a sugar called glucose), during a chemical process called **aerobic respiration**. The word equation is:

$$\text{glucose} + \text{oxygen} \rightarrow \text{carbon dioxide} + \text{water } (+ \text{ energy})$$

During aerobic respiration, the glucose is broken down to release the energy locked in it.

Figure 1.1 *A balanced body!*

As well as glucose, we also need oxygen for aerobic respiration. When we exercise hard we cannot always breathe fast enough to get the oxygen to the muscles in the bloodstream because it is being used up so fast. In fact muscle cells can respire without oxygen for a short time, in a process called **anaerobic respiration**. When this happens, a substance called **lactic acid** is produced in the body and builds up in your muscles. Lactic acid is a toxin and makes the muscles ache. Therefore, after exercising the lactic acid must be broken down. Oxygen is needed to do this. So after exercise you continue to breathe fast and pant to get extra oxygen into the blood to break down the lactic acid.

As people do more exercise they get fitter:

- the heart gets stronger and pumps blood more efficiently.
- the lungs get bigger, which helps with breathing.
- the body gets stronger and more supple because muscle is built up.

During the last 20 years the US Government has found out that the average amount of energy consumed has gone down (i.e. people are eating less). However, they have also found that the number of obese children has risen. It has been suggested that a reason could be a lack of exercise. To help change this situation, health camps for children have been established.

Figure 1.2

Drugs

Drugs are chemicals that change the way the body works. **Medicines** are drugs that cure illness or ease **symptoms**. Medicines include painkillers such as aspirin. Drugs that are taken for pleasure (e.g. alcohol, caffeine, cocaine) are called **recreational drugs**. These drugs all affect the workings of the brain and the nervous system. Prolonged use of some of these drugs can cause unnecessary diseases. Recreational drugs that are dangerous are often illegal.

When some drugs are taken regularly the body becomes used to the presence of the chemical. The body starts to become **dependent**, that is, it always needs the drug. The person is then **addicted**. If an addict tries to stop taking the drug they can suffer from effects such as sweating, shaking, and feeling sick. These are called withdrawal symptoms.

Drugs that slow down reactions are called **depressants**, and those that make people more alert are called **stimulants**. Caffeine is a stimulant and alcohol is a depressant. Drugs that cause people to see things that are not there are called **hallucinogens**.

4 a) Sort these drugs into two groups: aspirin, alcohol, caffeine, cocaine, ibuprofen. [1]
   b) How have you sorted the drugs? [1]
   [Total 2]

5 Copy and complete this sentence. If someone is dependant on the nicotine from tobacco, we say that they are _____ to it. [Total 1]

6 Cocaine speeds up reactions. Is it a stimulant or a depressant? [Total 1]

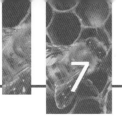

Drug	Form	Category	Effect
amphetamine (speed)	pills	stimulant	depression, heart damage
cannabis (marijuana)	smoked with tobacco	depressant and hallucinogen	cancer, liver damage
cocaine	sniffed, injected, smoked	stimulant	brain damage, destroys soft tissue in nose if sniffed
ecstasy	pills	stimulant	confusion, excessive thirst, epilepsy/heart attack
heroin	injected	depressant	highly addictive, liver damage (HIV infection as a result of the use of infected syringes)
LSD	liquid, pills	stimulant and hallucinogen	mental disturbance, liver and brain damage

Table 1.1 *Some common illegal drugs.*

Anything you drink may be taken and used in evidence.

DRINKING AND DRIVING WRECKS LIVES.

Figure 1.3

Alcohol

The proper chemical name for the 'alcohol' found in some drinks is **ethanol**. Alcohol gets into the blood through the stomach. When it reaches the brain it affects the nervous system. Alcohol can cause slow reactions and is a **depressant**. People often feel relaxed after drinking alcohol. A large amount of alcohol in the blood can result in people losing self-control and their reactions and judgement are affected. Too much alcohol can also kill you because it depresses the rate of breathing and heart rate.

In most countries it is legal to buy alcohol. However, because of the effect that alcohol has on reaction times, governments set limits on the permitted amount of alcohol in the bloodstream when a person is driving.

The liver breaks down alcohol. One of the major functions of the liver is to remove harmful substances from the body. Excessive drinking can lead to damage and scarring of the liver tissue called **cirrhosis**. People who become dependent on alcohol increase the risk of heart disease, stomach ulcers and brain damage.

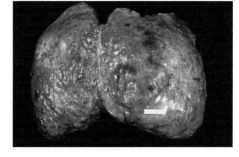

Figure 1.4 *A healthy (top) and a damaged liver (bottom).*

Smoking

Smoking cigarettes is considered to be one of the most preventable causes of death in the United Kingdom. Every year approximately 80 000 people die of smoking-related illnesses.

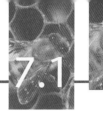

Cigarettes contain many chemicals such as tar, carbon monoxide, hydrogen cyanide and the drug **nicotine**. Nicotine is very addictive and that makes it hard to give up smoking. Nicotine also causes **heart disease** because it narrows blood vessels in the body. This increases blood pressure, making the heart work harder. Increased blood pressure can also put more strain on the blood vessels, which supply the heart's muscles with blood.

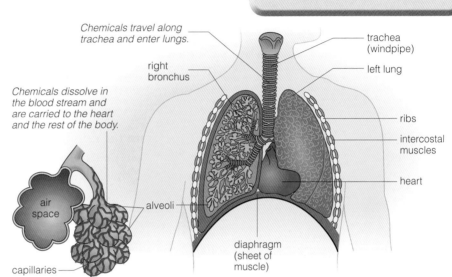

Chemicals travel along trachea and enter lungs.

Chemicals dissolve in the blood stream and are carried to the heart and the rest of the body.

right bronchus

air space

alveoli

capillaries

trachea (windpipe)

left lung

ribs

intercostal muscles

heart

diaphragm (sheet of muscle)

Figure 1.5 *How smoke enters the bloodstream.*

The chemicals in tobacco affect many organs. The **tar** damages the bronchi and alveoli, and builds up in the lungs. This makes it harder to get oxygen into the blood. The tar can cause the uncontrolled growth of cells in the lung, resulting in cancer. If not treated, the cancer can spread to other parts of the body. Lung cancer or other types of cancer can be fatal so the Government requires cigarette manufacturers to put a health warning on the packets.

Carbon monoxide from cigarettes stops the blood carrying oxygen efficiently. This puts more strain on the heart, which increases the risk of a **heart attack**. It combines with the oxygen–carrying substance (**haemoglobin**) in the blood so that less oxygen can be carried. A pregnant woman who smokes does not give as much oxygen to the baby as normal and the baby, on average, does not grow as much. The 'low birth weight' baby is more likely to get infections in the first few months of life.

Smokers are also at risk of developing a smoker's cough, bronchitis or emphysema. A smoker's cough happens when the **cilia** (fine hair like structures in the **trachea**) are damaged by cigarette smoke and cannot work to remove mucus and dirt from the lungs. The build-up of mucus in the lungs causes smokers to cough.

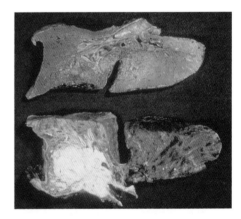

Figure 1.6 *Sections through a healthy lung and a cancerous lung.*

7 Look at the lower photograph in Figure 1.6.
a) What do you think the black stuff is? [1]
b) What do you think the white lump is? [1]
[Total 2]

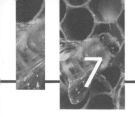

8 Describe a symptom of:
a) bronchitis [1]
b) emphysema. [1]
  [Total 2]

9 Look at Figure 1.8.
a) The government ran an advertising campaign warning of the dangers of solvent abuse in February 1992. Do you think the campaign worked? Explain your answer. [2]
b) In 1999, the government passed a law banning the sale of lighter refill gas to people under the age of 18. Was the law successful? Explain your answer. [2]
c) If you looked only at deaths from lighter refill gas from this time, what do you think you will find? [1]
  [Total 5]

Bronchitis is a disease caused by bacteria infecting the bronchi. It results when the lining of the bronchi becomes sore due to the chemicals in the smoke. Because the smoke also stops the cilia working, bacteria and dirt particles will be trapped in the mucus but not be removed. The bacteria cause the infection. The air passage gets smaller and this causes difficulty in breathing ('wheezy breathing').

In **emphysema** the cells in the alveoli are irratated by cigarette smoke and become inflamed. Then the cells are attacked by the body's immune system. The cells are destroyed so bigger holes appear in the lungs. There is a smaller surface area because some of the alveoli have been destroyed.

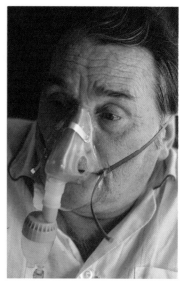

Figure 1.7 *Emphysema sufferers need extra oxygen.*

This means that gas exchange is difficult and the smoker gets very short of breath. An emphysema sufferer has to take a cylinder of oxygen with him or her. This will help oxygen get into the blood. The oxygen will help the breathing but the damage to the lungs can not be repaired.

Solvents

The **solvents** found in glue and aerosols are designed to evaporate easily and can be inhaled. The fumes are absorbed into the blood through the lungs and reach the brain. The use of solvents slows reaction times. Solvents are **depressants**. Solvent abusers who inhale deeply may become unconscious and even die due to heart failure. They can also die of suffocation from inhaling solvents through plastic bags or choking on their own vomit. Solvent abuse can lead to permanent damage to the brain, lungs and liver.

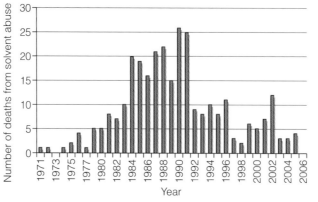

Figure 1.8 *Deaths from solvent abuse in UK for 11–14 year olds.*

Summary

- A balanced diet is needed to sustain good health.
- Exercise needs energy.
- Energy is stored in food and released during respiration.
- Cannabis, heroin, cocaine and amphetamines are all drugs that can change the way the body works and can damage body organs.
- Drinking alcohol can damage the liver, heart and stomach.
- Smoking can cause cancer, heart disease and lung diseases such as emphysema.
- Inhaling solvents can cause lung and brain damage.

Questions

1 Good health is not just the absence of disease it also involves eating a _____ _____. _____ is used by the body to provide energy. Respiration involves the release of _____ from glucose. Chemicals that may alter the way the body works are called _____. The body may be damaged when substances such as _____ are taken excessively. *[Total 3]*

2 How does exercise affect the heart? *[Total 2]*

3 What is the word equation for aerobic respiration? *[Total 1]*

4 Name two illegal drugs and in each case state how it could damage your health. *[Total 2]*

5 Suggest ideas why some drugs are illegal. *[Total 2]*

6 Why are cigarettes not sold to people under 18? *[Total 1]*

7 Suggest reasons why people should not drink and drive. *[Total 2]*

8 Look at the apparatus shown in Figure 1.9.
   a) Which piece of apparatus represents the lungs? *[1]*
   b) What do you think you might see in the U-tube after the cigarette has been finished? *[1]*
   [Total 2]

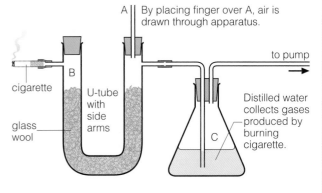

Figure 1.9

9 Name and describe the symptoms of two diseases caused by smoking. *[Total 4]*

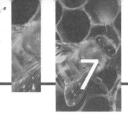

7.2 Microorganisms and disease

How can something that we cannot see cause so much pain and harm? In the seventeenth century the Dutch scientist van Leeuwenhoeck discovered 'little creatures'. Two hundred years later the French scientist Pasteur proved that these 'little creatures' are present in the air, in water and in our bodies. Today we call them **microorganisms** or **microbes**.

Pasteur attempted to show that microorganisms cause decay and that they can invade the body and cause **disease**. We now know that not all microorganisms cause disease, and not all diseases are caused by microorganisms. The microorganisms that do cause disease are called **pathogens**. Some pathogens produce poisonous waste substances called **toxins**.

Microorganisms

There are four main types of microorganism:

- viruses (although not strictly living, we consider them to be microorganisms)
- bacteria
- protozoa (types of protist)
- fungi (some types only).

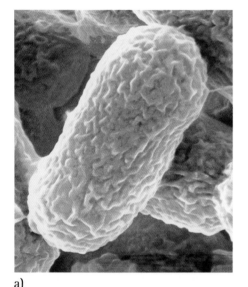

a)

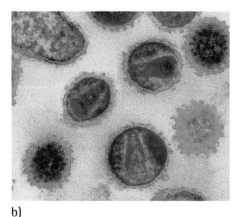

b)

c)

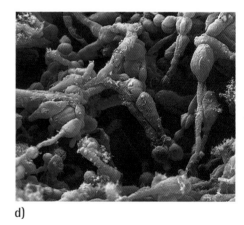

d)

Figure 2.1 a) *A bacterium (×30 000).*
b) *Virus particles (×150 000).*
c) *Protozoa (×15 000).*
d) *A fungus (×500).*

Viruses are the smallest of the microorganisms. They can only be seen using the most powerful microscopes. Viruses invade and then destroy living cells. They can only live inside the cells of other living organisms. Viruses are responsible for many diseases, such as: influenza, measles, chickenpox, smallpox and AIDS.

Bacteria are single-celled organisms. They are able to live in body tissues between the cells. They need food, warmth and moisture to grow. They can multiply very quickly by cell division if conditions are right. Bacteria cause diseases such as whooping cough, tuberculosis (TB), pneumonia and cholera. Salmonella is a bacterium that can cause food poisoning.

Protozoa are single-celled organisms like amoeba. They are larger than viruses and bacteria. Protozoa feed by absorbing nutrients from their surroundings. Malaria and amoebic dysentery are caused by protozoa.

Fungi are the largest of the four types of microorganism. Some fungi (e.g. moulds) make fine threads, which invade cells and absorb nutrients from them. Other fungi are single-celled (e.g. yeast). Fungi can live on decaying substances or in living tissue. The diseases caused by fungi include athlete's foot, ringworm and thrush.

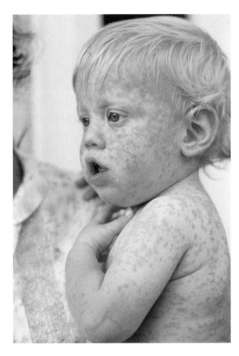

Figure 2.2 *Measles.*

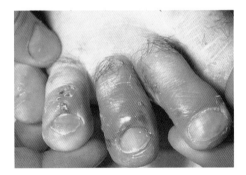

Figure 2.3 *Athlete's foot.*

Figure 2.4 Penicillium *mould.*

All individual microorganisms are very small, but we can see microorganisms when they are grouped together. A group of microorganisms is called a **colony**. The blue-green mould that we see on an orange that has gone bad is a colony of Penicillium.

! Acquired Immune Deficiency Syndrome (AIDS) is caused by a virus called HIV. White blood cells form part of the body's immune system, which defends the body. HIV attacks some white blood cells and the immune system stops working. The HIV virus cannot live outside the body. It is passed from one person to another in liquids: semen or vaginal fluids during sexual contact or blood during exchange of syringes when injecting drugs. Using condoms during sexual intercourse and drug users not sharing syringes reduces the risks of contracting AIDS. Currently, there is no known cure for AIDS.

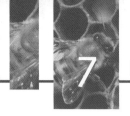
> **!** There is some dispute about where the sexually transmitted disease syphilis came from. The general view is that it was brought back to Europe from the Americas by Christopher Columbus. However, there is some evidence (which is disputed), that traces of the effects of syphilis have been found on human remains from the Roman town of Pompeii in Italy.

> **!** In the nineteenth century London had three very large outbreaks (epidemics) of cholera. Dr John Snow thought that the disease had been caused by contaminated water. By plotting where deaths had ocurred on a map, he was able to locate the source as a water pump in Broad Street. Snow convinced the authorities to remove the handle of the pump. The epidemic decreased dramatically after that. It was later discovered that the Broad Street pump took water from a shallow well. The water supplying the well had been contaminated with sewage and rubbish.

> **?** **3** State one disease caused by:
> a) a fungus [1]
> b) a virus [1]
> c) a bacterium. [1]
> [Total 3]

Spreading of disease

Diseases that are easily passed on are called **infections**. Microorganisms are passed on from people in a number of different ways. The microorganisms can get into the body through openings such as the nose or mouth, or breaks in the skin like cuts and scratches.

Method of transmission	Examples
actual contact with an infected person	impetigo, smallpox, blood poisoning (septicaemia), sexually transmitted diseases
contact with an infected person's belongings	athlete's foot, ringworm
droplets in the air, coughs and sneezes	influenza, tuberculosis, measles, chickenpox
contaminated food, prepared unhygienically	typhoid, food poisoning
contaminated water, which has been in contact with sewage	typhoid, cholera
carried by animals	malaria, bubonic plague, rabies

Table 2.1 *How some diseases are spread.*

Controlling disease

The spread of many diseases has been reduced by the control of microorganisms. Many diseases in the world are spread through contaminated water. On a small scale, washing your hands after using the lavatory and before handing food can cut down the spread of infections. However, clean water is essential. When water becomes contaminated with sewage, diseases such as cholera may be caught. Drinking water can be made safe by filtering and chlorinating it. This is a large-scale and expensive process.

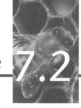

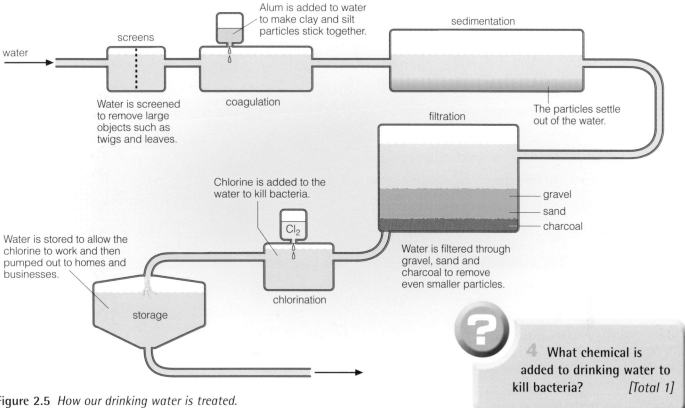

Figure 2.5 *How our drinking water is treated.*

Alum is added to water to make clay and silt particles stick together.

sedimentation

screens

water

Water is screened to remove large objects such as twigs and leaves.

coagulation

The particles settle out of the water.

filtration

Chlorine is added to the water to kill bacteria.

gravel
sand
charcoal

Water is stored to allow the chlorine to work and then pumped out to homes and businesses.

Cl₂

Water is filtered through gravel, sand and charcoal to remove even smaller particles.

storage

chlorination

The spread of microorganisms can also be controlled with the use of chemicals. **Disinfectants** are chemicals that kill microorganisms. Some are corrosive and many contain chlorine. They are powerful and often cannot be used on skin. **Antiseptics** are usually weaker and can be used safely on the skin. They stop microorganisms from growing and multiplying.

Antibiotics

The prevention of disease is not always possible. Sometimes medicines are needed to treat a disease. A group of medicines that have been very successful in treating diseases are **antibiotics**. The mould Penicillium produces an antibiotic called penicillin. Antibiotics kill bacteria. They do not damage body cells and work very quickly. Antibiotics have no effect on viruses.

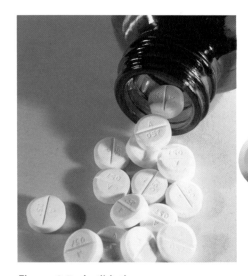

Figure 2.7 *Antibiotics.*

4 What chemical is added to drinking water to kill bacteria? [Total 1]

Figure 2.6 *A range of disinfectants and antiseptics.*

5 What is the difference between a disinfectant and an antiseptic? [Total 1]
6 Give the name of an antibiotic. [Total 1]

Summary

- Microorganisms are microscopic organisms.
- There are four main types of microorganism: viruses, bacteria, protozoa and fungi.
- Microorganisms that cause disease are called pathogens.
- Infections are easily transmitted through the air, by contact and by eating contaminated food.
- The treatment of water can control the spread of many diseases.
- Disinfectants and antiseptics are used to kill microorganisms.
- Antibiotics are used to kill bacteria.

Questions

1   Copy and complete the following paragraph. Microorganisms are everywhere: there are four types, _____, viruses, _____ and _____. Many of them are useful, but some cause serious _____. Viruses are the smallest type. They can only be seen with an electron microscope as they are so small. _____ kill bacteria.   *[Total 3]*

2   a) 'Colds' are caused by viruses. Write down two symptoms of having a cold.   *[2]*

     b) Why would a doctor not prescribe antibiotics to treat a cold?   *[1]*
                            [Total 3]

3   Design a poster warning people going on holiday of the ways in which diseases are transmitted.   *[Total 6]*

4   Measles is an infectious disease.
     a) What is an infectious disease?   *[1]*
     b) How is measles spread?   *[1]*
     c) What sort of microorganism causes measles?   *[1]*
                            [Total 3]

5   What is an antibiotic?   *[Total 2]*

6   Diphtheria is a bacterial disease. The number of cases reported in England and Wales is shown in Table 2.2.
     a) Plot the results on a chart or a graph.   *[3]*
     b) Suggest when you think vaccination against diphtheria was introduced.   *[1]*
                            [Total 4]

Year	Number of reported cases in England and Wales
1935	70 000
1940	60 500
1941	61 834
1950	6 672
1955	780
1970	4

Table 2.2

7   List all the ways in which bacteria have been stopped from getting into your body today.
                            [Total 1]

7.3 Microorganisms and food

Can microorganisms be helpful as well as harmful? Microorganisms are everywhere. Some microorganisms are harmful and cause diseases, and others make food go bad. However, not all microorganisms are harmful. Many are used effectively in the brewing, baking and dairy industries.

Food preservation

Bacteria and fungi often spoil our food, making it decay. The microorganisms produce substances called **enzymes** that enter the food. The enzymes work by breaking the food down quickly. The microorganisms also produce poisonous substances (**toxins**). These poisons cause us to be sick if we eat the food. The most dangerous bacteria that cause food poisoning include E. coli, Salmonella, and Clostridium botulinum. To stop microorganisms from damaging food they need to be killed or the conditions they need for growth must be removed. They need food, water and warm conditions to grow and multiply.

One in Three Chickens Contain Salmonella Bug!

E. coli kills yet more

Food Poisoning Strikes Young and Elderly

Soft Cheeses Blamed for Listeria Scare

Figure 3.1 *Food poisoning can affect many people.*

There are a number of different ways to preserve food. The methods chosen will depend on the type of food. Some methods change the taste and appearance of the food. Preservation does not always change a food's nutritional content. Types of food preservation are shown in Table 3.1.

Figure 3.2 *Food can be heat treated, vacuum-packed, dried, canned or frozen.*

?

1 Name one industry that uses microorganisms.
[Total 1]

2 a) What do microorganisms produce to break down food? *[1]*

b) In what conditions would you expect the amount of these substances to increase most rapidly? Explain your answer. *[2]*
[Total 3]

3 What is a toxin? *[Total 1]*

!

Botulinum toxin, produced by *Clostridium botulinum*, is one of the most powerful poisons that we know of. Just a millionth of a gram can kill someone. Very, very tiny amounts can be injected into people's faces to reduce wrinkle lines.

?

4 Suggest the names of two foods that are preserved by:
a) freezing *[1]*
b) heating *[1]*
c) canning. *[1]*
[Total 3]

5 Make a list of the preserved foods that you have eaten so far today.
[Total 1]

Aim	Method	Example
kill microorganisms – high temperatures and take away oxygen	canning	baked beans
kill microorganisms – high temperatures or gamma radiation	bottling/sterilisation	baby food
kill microorganisms – high temperatures 70 °C	pasteurisation	yoghurt, milk
kill microorganisms – ultra high temperatures 135 °C	ultra-heat treatment	long-life milk
slow growth of microorganisms – low temperatures 4 °C	refrigeration	meat
stop growth of microorganisms – very low temperatures –20 °C	freezing	vegetables
slow down growth – remove water	freeze drying	herbs
slow down growth – remove water	smoking	bacon
slow down growth – conditions are changed	preserving adding salt, sugar or acid (vinegar)	fish, jam, pickled onions
stop growth – no water or oxygen	vacuum packing	ground coffee

Table 3.1 *Types of food preservation.*

In 1800, the French leader Napoleon Bonaparte offered a huge reward for anyone who could invent a way of preserving food for the French army. The prize was won by Nicholas Apert in 1810. He'd invented canning.

Although food can be preserved and stored safely, food poisoning still happens. If people handle food with contaminated hands, do not cook food for long enough or leave food out uncovered, then microorganisms reproduce rapidly. Food poisoning can be avoided by following good hygiene habits.

Figure 3.3

6 a) Why do canned baked beans last longer in a can than in air? [2]
b) Instant coffee is often freeze dried. How does this stop the coffee going off? [1]
[Total 3]
7 Why do you think long-life milk lasts longer than ordinary milk? [Total 1]
8 Things can still go off in a fridge. Why do you think this is? [Total 2]

Uses of microorganisms

Sewage treatment

Microorganisms play an important role in recycling chemicals around us, because they can break down waste materials effectively. Raw sewage is treated with millions of microorganisms in sewage works. The treatment makes the sewage safe enough to be placed back into rivers.

Dairy products

The dairy industry uses microorganisms to make cheese by mixing bacteria with milk. When left, lumps form, which are called curds; the liquid part of the milk is called whey. During cheese making, an enzyme called rennin is added to make more curds form quickly. An enzyme is a substance that speeds up a chemical process. The curds are then skimmed off and made into cheese. Yoghurt is also made from milk using bacteria.

Antibiotics

The commonly prescribed antibiotic, penicillin, is obtained from a fungus, blue Penicillium mould.

Production of alcohol

Yeast is a single-celled fungus. Yeast is able to respire with or without oxygen (anaerobically). When yeast uses anaerobic respiration it feeds on sugar and produces a toxin called ethanol or alcohol. This process is called **fermentation**. During fermentation the gas carbon dioxide is also produced. If the alcohol content of the drink is too high it kills yeast. Distillation is used to make strong drinks such as whisky and vodka. Wine and beer can be made into vinegar using bacteria.

Making bread

Yeast is also used in the baking industry. Bread making uses yeast mixed with a little sugar, flour and water to form dough. The dough is 'kneaded' to get lots of air into it. The yeast respires and the carbon dioxide gas forms bubbles inside the dough that cannot escape. This makes the dough swell and expand. The yeast mainly respires aerobically but will also respire anaerobically. Any ethanol produced evaporates when the dough is baked in a hot oven.

Each day, about 11 million tonnes of sewage is flushed down the toilets of the UK.

Figure 3.4 *Cheese being made.*

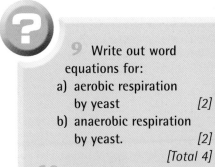

Figure 3.5 *Made by microorganisms.*

9 Write out word equations for:
a) aerobic respiration by yeast [2]
b) anaerobic respiration by yeast. [2]
[Total 4]

10 Look at Figure 3.5. For each product say which microorganisms have been used to make it.
[Total 6]

?

11 a) What sort of microorganism is Quorn® made out of? [1]

b) What substance does the microorganism use for food? [1]

c) The vats that the microorganism is grown in must be kept sterile. Why? [2]

d) What sort of respiration does the microorganism use? [1]

[Total 5]

12 Give as many reasons as you can why someone might buy Quorn® nuggets as opposed to chicken nuggets. [Total 2]

!

A new baby has no bacteria in its intestines and so cannot make vitamin K. So, new babies are often given an injection of vitamin K shortly after they are born.

?

13 Give two uses for bacteria in your intestines. [Total 2]

14 How do you think bacteria get into your intestines? [Total 1]

15 Why might a newborn baby bleed more from a cut than a baby who is 1 month old? [Total 2]

Single cell protein (SCP)

This is made from the cells of microorganisms that have been grown to make food for humans or animals.

An example is **mycoprotein**, which is produced when the fungus Fusarium venanatum is grown on glucose. The fungus is grown in huge vats that contain glucose, vitamins and minerals. Sterile air is pumped into the vats to provide a source of oxygen. It is made into Quorn®, which is used as vegetarian replacement for meat.

Figure 3.6

Microorganisms are important in the digestive process in many animals. The stomachs of mammals such as cows and sheep contain bacteria that produce very powerful enzymes. The most important enzyme is cellulase. It breaks down cellulose in plant material so that the animal can absorb the nutrients locked in the material. We have microorganisms in our gut too, which help our digestion. Some of them also produce vitamin K, which is needed to help your blood to clot and form scabs.

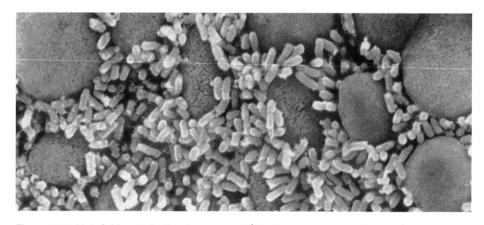

Figure 3.7 *Helpful bacteria live in your gut. (Bacteria are coloured yellow).*

Summary

- Microorganisms need food, water and warm conditions to grow.
- The destructive effect of microorganisms on food can be prevented using preservation methods.
- Microorganisms are used in many industries including brewing, baking and cheese and yoghurt making.
- Wine, beer, bread, vinegar, yoghurt and cheese are all made with microorganisms.

Questions

1 Copy and complete the following sentences.
_____ such as yeast and bacteria can be useful to humans. We make medicines such as _____, drinks such as _____, as well as foods such as cheese and _____.
When yeast is added to sugar solution a chemical process called _____ happens.
_____ can also spoil food.   *[Total 3]*

2 The milk sold in supermarkets is pasteurised.
  a) What is the effect of pasteurisation on microorganisms?   *[1]*
  b) Why do you think milk is pasteurised?   *[1]*
  c) Unpasteurised milk cannot be sold in supermarkets. What do you think of this law?   *[1]*
          [Total 3]

3 a) When Quorn® was first marketed it was described as being 'mushroom in origin' What does this mean?   *[1]*
  b) Why do you think that the marketing people chose to use this phrase?   *[1]*
  c) Why do you think the Advertising Standards Authority objected to this way of describing Quorn®?   *[1]*
          [Total 3]

4 Some cheeses have holes in them, others blue veins. What could have caused these characteristics? *[Total 1]*

5 How does cooking help in the prevention of food poisoning?   *[Total 1]*

6 Look at the graph in Figure 3.8.
  a) In which year were the lowest number of *E. coli* food poisoning cases recorded?   *[1]*
  b) Frances has concluded from the graph that 'there is no overall trend up or down in the levels of *E. coli* food poisoning in the UK.' What do you think of this conclusion?   *[1]*
  c) There are usually more cases of food poisoning in the summer. Why do you think this is?   *[1]*
          [Total 3]

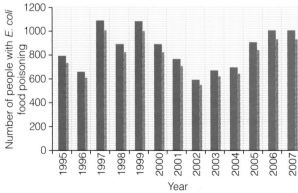

Figure 3.8 *Data from the Chartered Institute of Environmental Health.*

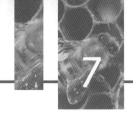

7.4 Immunisation

How does the body protect itself from microorganisms? Microorganisms are all around us. The body needs to protect itself in many ways.

Natural defences

The human defence system is often compared to that of a castle. With a castle the first form of defence is the outer wall. If a hole occurs in the wall soldiers work quickly to plug the holes. They are second in the line of defence. If some invaders get through they are then faced with the third form of defence, the inner barricade, which contains highly skilled defenders. The skin is our first line of defence. It acts as a barrier to prevent invading microorganisms from entering the body. If we cut the skin, the blood produces clots to seal the cuts.

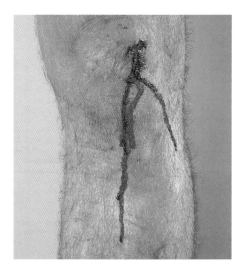

Figure 4.1 *Cuts allow bacteria into the body.*

The third line of defence in the body is white blood cells. These deal with the microorganisms once they are inside. This defence mechanism is called the **immune system**. Sometimes the body's natural immune system cannot deal with all the microorganisms it encounters and so medicines called **antibiotics** are used to assist the body to fight against the microorganisms that cause diseases.

As well as the skin and the blood, there are other ways the body can defend itself against disease. For example, our eyes make an enzyme called lysozyme which kills bacteria and prevents eye infections. The acid in our stomach helps to kill bacteria in food.

The immune system

As there are many microorganisms around us, it is not difficult for them to invade the body. Once they invade, they can multiply quickly. The body must react quickly and destroy them. This is the job of the white blood cells. There are many types of white blood cell. The job of some is to search for and recognise the invading bacteria or viruses. This is fairly easy as the invaders (or foreign bodies) have a protein coating that is different from the proteins on the surfaces of human cells. These proteins are called **antigens**.

Some invaders also produce harmful toxins. **Lymphocytes** are a type of white blood cell that produce antitoxins to neutralise the toxins. They then produce **antibodies**. Antibodies are proteins that stick to the invading microorganisms. The antibodies lock onto the antigens and cause the bacteria or viruses to clump together.

> **!** Our immune systems can sometimes go wrong and start attacking foreign bodies that are not harmful. That's what happens if you have an allergy to something. The immune system can also start attacking the body's own cells and this is what happens in auto-immune diseases (e.g. rheumatoid arthritis).

> **?**
> 1 Why is it important for a scab to form quickly over a cut? [Total 1]
> 2 Antibodies are said to be 'specific' for a certain microbe. Explain what this means. [Total 1]

This action then makes it easier for **phagocytes** (another type of white blood cell) to surround and digest the microorganisms.

The lymphocytes make a unique antibody for each type of invading antigen they encounter. Once a lymphocyte has made an antibody against a microorganism, it will be able to quickly produce this antibody again. This means that if the person is ever infected again by the same microorganisms the body is already prepared to fight, and extra antibodies are produced very quickly. The body is then said to have **immunity** to that microorganism.

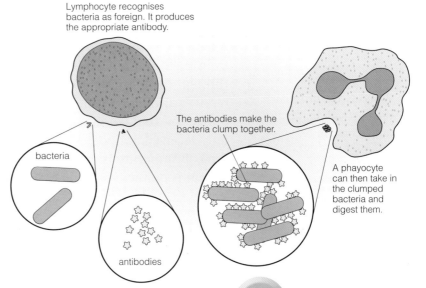

Lymphocyte recognises bacteria as foreign. It produces the appropriate antibody.

bacteria

The antibodies make the bacteria clump together.

A phayocyte can then take in the clumped bacteria and digest them.

antibodies

Figure 4.2 *White blood cells destroy bacteria.*

Vaccinations

Doctors can now stimulate a person's immune system before they contract a serious disease. This is known as **immunisation**. When a person is immunised a **vaccine** is passed into the blood. Getting the vaccine into the blood is called **vaccination** and usually involves an injection. Vaccines can be made up of different things:

- antigens, e.g. polio
- weak strains of a microorganism, e.g. TB
- toxins of the microorganism that have been made harmless, e.g. diphtheria.

These vaccines cause the body to make new antibodies. This results in the body's natural immunity being increased. The lymphocytes will then react quickly to produce huge amounts of the correct antibodies if the antigen appears again. This 'active immunity' can protect a person for a long time.

Figure 4.3 *Vaccinations help to protect us.*

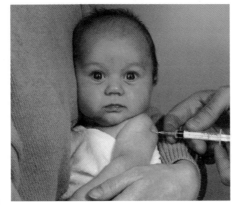

Thanks to immunisation, a terrible disease called smallpox no longer exists. The last natural case was in 1977 in Somalia. The last ever case was in Birmingham in 1978, when researchers allowed some of the virus (which they were studying) to escape. It killed Janet Parker, a photographer who was working near the researchers.

3 Polio vaccine is made from antigens. What does this mean? [Total 1]

4 a) Explain why you should not get measles again if you have had it already. [2]

b) Explain why you should not get measles if you are vaccinated against it. [2]

[Total 4]

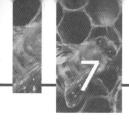

?

5 What is the difference between activity immunity and passive immunity?

[Total 2]

Passive immunity

A baby in its mother's uterus receives protection against some diseases from their mothers. This is due to antibodies passing from the mother, through the placenta, to the baby. Once the baby is born it still receives antibodies from its mother through breast milk. The protection that young babies have is short lived because they have only received antibodies and have not made any for themselves. This type of immunity is called **passive immunity** as the baby's immune system is not active in the making of antibodies.

Immunisation programme

Babies and young children are very susceptible to diseases. In many countries, individuals are protected against some diseases by being given a course of vaccines at a very early age. The immunity of a young person is then gradually built up. Occasionally the vaccine makes the person feel unwell for a few days.

!

We know that antibiotics kill bacteria and have no effect on viruses. However there are some bacteria that are resistant to antibiotics. Some strains of *Staphylococcus aureus* are called superbugs. A superbug is a bacterium that is resistant to most antibiotics, even methicillin, which is one of the strongest. MRSA (methicillin-resistant *Staphylococcus aureus*) attacks wounds and can cause fatal blood poisoning (septicaemia). MRSA is now present in many hospitals.

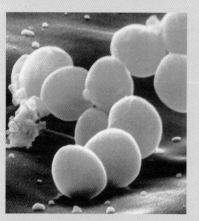

Figure 4.4 Staphylococcus aureus.

Age	Immunisation
2 months	diphtheria, tetanus, whooping cough, polio, Hib, pneumococcal infection
3 months	diphtheria, tetanus, whooping cough, polio, Hib, meningitis C
4 months	diphtheria, tetanus, whooping cough, polio, Hib, meningitis C, pneumococcal infection
12 months	Hib, meningitis C
13 months	MMR (mumps, measles and rubella), pneumococcal infection
3-5 years	diphtheria, tetanus, whooping cough, polio
12-14 years	tuberculosis (BCG)
12-13 years	rubella (girls only), cervical cancer (girls only)
13-18 years	diphtheria, tetanus, polio
adult	tetanus every 5-10 years

Table 4.1 *Typical vaccination course. Some vaccines are given more than once so that the body can produce high levels of antibodies.*

Summary

- Microorganisms are everywhere. They are not all harmful. However, if the skin is broken, microorganisms can quickly invade the body.

- The body has many natural protective barriers.

- Many changes take place in the body to kill microorganisms, e.g. blood clotting, the destruction of microorganisms by white blood cells, the production of antibodies and the production of antitoxins to neutralise the antigens of the invading microorganisms.

- Once antibodies have been produced, the body develops a natural immunity to a disease.

- We can be immunised against diseases. Vaccines contain dead or harmless microorganisms that are similar to harmful ones.

- Antibiotics are used to help the body fight disease. Antibiotics kill bacteria and have no effect on viruses.

Questions

1 Copy and complete the following sentences.
_____ can enter the body through one of many natural openings or a cut. The body has natural defences such as the skin, and _____. Some of these cells can surround _____ and kill them. Other white blood cells produce antitoxins and _____. Immunisation is a way to increase the body's natural _____. This usually takes the form of an injection called a _____.
[Total 3]

2 List the natural defences the body uses to keep out bacteria and viruses. *[Total 3]*

3 a) What are antigens? *[1]*
   b) What are toxins? *[1]*
   c) What is the job of antibodies? *[1]*
   [Total 3]

4 a) Why are white blood cells important? *[1]*
   b) Name two different types of white blood cells. Explain what each one does. *[4]*
   [Total 5]

5 How does the clumping of invading microorganisms help the body defend itself? *[Total 2]*

6 Why is it unlikely that a person will suffer with measles twice? *[Total 2]*

7 a) Explain the difference between natural and artificial immunity. *[1]*
   b) How are babies naturally protected from disease? *[1]*
   [Total 2]

8 Find out why only girls are vaccinated against rubella at 13. *[Total 1]*

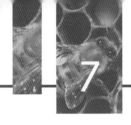
7.5 Genetic modification and biotechnology

Can the genes from a human work in a bacterium? Genes are sections of DNA. The DNA code is very similar in many organisms. This means that one organism can understand the genes of an other. This makes **genetic engineering** or **genetic modification** possible.

Genetic engineering

This involves scientists adding genetic material to, taking genetic material away from, or transferring genetic material between organisms. Genes can be cut out of the DNA of one organism using enzymes and then added into the DNA of a bacterium. The added gene is then copied by the bacterium many times.

Insulin is a hormone that lowers the concentration of sugar in the blood. It is made in an organ called the **pancreas**. People with **diabetes** do not produce enough insulin. In the past insulin was taken from the pancreases of pigs (and cows) after they died. This was a difficult procedure. In 1978, an American company called Genentech succeeded in producing human insulin using bacteria. They inserted the gene for healthy human insulin into bacteria. The bacteria then produced lots of human insulin. This is now widely available as Humulin® (human insulin).

! In 2009, scientists at the Massachusetts Institute of Technology in America, announced that they had genetically modified a virus so that it could help to build electrical batteries!

?

1 Suggest some advantages of making insulin from bacteria rather than extracting it from pigs and cows. [Total 2]

2 Explain why a scientist only needs to put a single gene for human insulin into a single bacterium in order to make a lot of insulin. [Total 2]

3 What are used to cut and rejoin pieces of DNA? [Total 1]

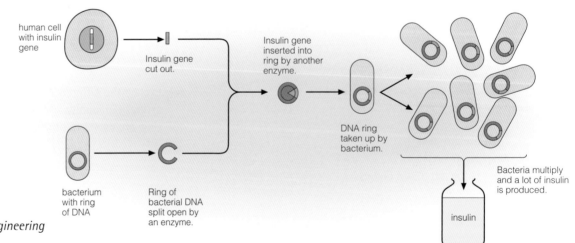

Figure 5.1 *Genetic engineering of insulin.*

human cell with insulin gene

Insulin gene cut out.

Insulin gene inserted into ring by another enzyme.

DNA ring taken up by bacterium.

Bacteria multiply and a lot of insulin is produced.

insulin

bacterium with ring of DNA

Ring of bacterial DNA split open by an enzyme.

Cystic fibrosis is a genetic disease, which causes thick mucus to be produced in the lungs and gut. This makes breathing difficult and, as the mucus is a good breeding ground for microorganisms, cystic fibrosis sufferers tend to get lung infections easily. The disease is caused by a faulty gene. Scientists have genetically modified viruses to contain copies of the normal gene, which they hope will be able to be used in a nasal spray to introduce the normal gene into lung cells.

Human eggs (ova) can be taken out of a woman's body, fertilised and then put back. While the ovum is outside the body, theoretically, genes could be transferred to cells so that they produce certain characteristics. This could be used to stop babies being born with cystic fibrosis. However, this has not yet been done in the UK as it is illegal to alter the set of genes in ova or zygotes.

> **!** About one in every 25 white people in the UK are carriers for cystic fibrosis. Carriers only have one copy of the faulty gene and so do not get the disease. The faulty gene is much less common in black and Asian people.

Cloning

Cloning is a method of reproduction that results in genetically identical offspring being produced. Plants have been cloned for a long time. When plant growers develop a variety of a plant that has features that they want to preserve, they often clone the plant, so that all the offspring have those special features. A simple way of doing this is to 'take a cutting'.

British scientists have now developed a method of cloning animals. They first began work cloning frogs, and then in 1996 the first adult mammal was cloned, Dolly the sheep.

Dolly the sheep was the first successful clone out of 277 attempts. An udder cell was removed from a fully grown sheep. An ovum from another sheep was taken and its nucleus was removed. The nucleus of the udder cell was put into the empty ovum and the whole cell was implanted in a third sheep. It grew into Dolly. Dolly was a **clone** of the sheep that donated the udder cell – this means that Dolly was genetically identical to her parent.

Figure 5.2 *Dolly the sheep (1996-2003).*

> **?** 4 What is a clone? *[Total 1]*
>
> 5 When DNA is copied many times by bacteria, it is known as 'molecular cloning'. What does this term mean? *[Total 1]*

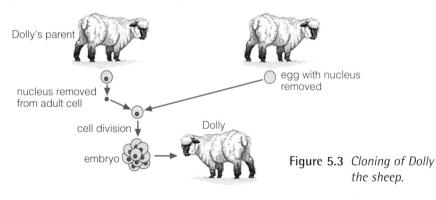

Dolly's parent

nucleus removed from adult cell

egg with nucleus removed

cell division

Dolly

embryo

Figure 5.3 *Cloning of Dolly the sheep.*

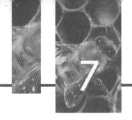
Organ transplants

Today, some people with damaged organs, such as a heart, kidney or liver can have them replaced. Unfortunately there are not enough human organs to supply all the people who need them. Although the idea of transplants has been around for a long time, it was not until the twentieth century that transplantation became successful. Medicines were developed to prevent the immune system rejecting the new organ. Techniques for matching tissue were also developed so that the implanted organ matched the rest of the body tissue as closely as possible.

Xenotransplantation is the transplanting of cells, tissues or organs from one species to another. Since there are not enough human organs available for transplants, scientists are working on breeding animals that could provide these organs. Research is concentrated on using pigs because their organs are similar to ours. Parts of pig hearts are already used to repair human hearts but transplanting a whole pig heart into a human has never been done successfully. This is because the human immune system attacks the pig heart. So, genetically modified pigs are being developed, which will contain human genes that will prevent this from happening.

Genetically modified food

More than 60 plant species have now been genetically modified. Commercial crops such as oilseed rape, maize, potatoes, tomatoes and soya have been modified.

Plants are genetically engineered so that they can be resistant to diseases, to improve their nutritional value, or improve their ability to survive in different conditions such as drought, flood or frost. For example, maize has been genetically modified so that it can make a toxin from the bacterium Bacillus thuringiensis. This toxin kills an insect that is a major threat to the maize. Soya has been modified to make it tolerant to certain weedkillers (herbicides). This means that the crop only needs to be sprayed once with the herbicide. Everything except the soya is killed. This means that less herbicide is used by the farmer.

Genetic engineering has many positive uses. It can be used to help produce cures for diseases and can help in food production. If plants are genetically immune to pests then fewer chemicals will need to be used in the countryside. However, there may be many unknown side-effects. The action of removing genes from one organism and putting them into another organism could have unexpected effects. The issue of genetic engineering in embryos raises many questions about **ethics** and **morals**. It is a subject which will continue to be debated.

Figure 5.4 *An organ transplant taking place.*

> **!**
>
> According to legend, in about 500 BC a Chinese doctor, called Pien Chi'ao, swapped hearts between a man with 'a strong spirit and a weak will' and a man with 'a strong will but a weak spirit'. He was attempting to achieve a balance of characteristics in the two men.

> **?**
>
> 6 In 1984, surgeons put a baboon heart into a baby who had been born with a faulty heart. 'Baby Fae' only survived for 20 days.
> a) Suggest why Baby Fae only survived for 20 days. *[1]*
> b) What do you think about this surgery? Was it right or wrong? Try to explain why you think this. *[1]*
> *[Total 2]*
> 7 a) What is the advantage for a farmer in planting maize that produces a toxin from *Bacillus thuringiensis*? *[1]*
> b) Suggest a disadvantage. *[1]*
> *[Total 2]*

Summary

- Genes are sections of DNA.
- Genetic engineering involves the altering of genes and so altering the instructions of a cell.
- Genetic engineering can be used to produce human proteins e.g. insulin.
- Cloning is the process of making copies of living things.
- Animal organs could be genetically modified to be used in xenotransplants.
- Plants can be genetically modified to make them more resistant to pests, diseases and droughts.

Questions

1 Copy and complete the following sentences.
All organisms have genes that use the same DNA code. So the _____ from one organism can be used by another. Genetic engineering can involve _____ the genes from the cells of one living thing and _____ them into the cells of another. Genetically identical offspring of a parent are called _____. *[Total 2]*

2 What is genetic engineering? *[Total 2]*

3 a) How can insulin be genetically engineered? *[2]*
 b) What are the advantages of using this method? *[2]*
 [Total 4]

4 a) What is cystic fibrosis? *[1]*
 b) How might it be treated with genetic engineering? *[1]*
 [Total 2]

5 a) What is cloning? *[1]*
 b) Why are plants cloned? *[1]*
 [Total 2]

6 a) After a transplant a patient is given drugs to prevent their immune system working properly. Why do you think that this is done? *[1]*
 b) Why is it a potential problem? *[1]*
 [Total 2]

7 Waiting lists for organ transplant operations in the UK are growing by 15% a year. How could these lists could be shortened? *[Total 2]*

8 Why is it thought that pig organs can be used in humans? *[Total 1]*

9 In the film *Gattaca*, parents can choose the characteristics of their children by going to a geneticist and asking for certain characteristics to be added to or removed from a zygote.
 a) How would characteristics be added to or removed? *[1]*
 b) What do you think of this idea? Should it be allowed? Try to explain why you think this. *[2]*
 [Total 3]

10 Some people do not make enough Human Growth Hormone (hGH). The hormone used to be collected from dead bodies and then injected into people who needed it. Since 1985 it has been made using genetically modified bacteria.
 a) Draw a diagram to show how bacteria are engineered to produce hGH. *[3]*
 b) Suggest some advantages of using genetically modified bacteria to produce hGH. *[2]*
 [Total 5]

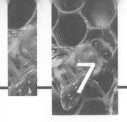
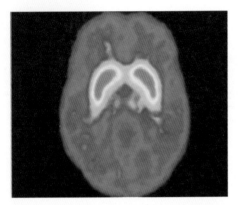

Figure 6.1 *A PET scan of a normal brain. Red parts show greater brain activity than yellow parts.*

> **!** When invented in 1886 Coca-Cola® contained cocaine (from coca leaves) and caffeine (from kola nuts).

> **?** 1 Why is money spent doing brain scans on drug abusers? [Total 1]

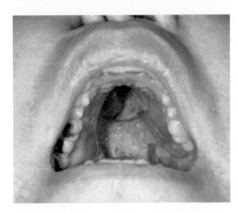

Figure 6.4 *The hole in the roof of this man's mouth has been caused by cocaine use.*

Drugs and addiction

Addiction

When people are addicted to things, they feel that they cannot cope without them. They also have **withdrawal symptoms** if they cannot get hold of the thing to which they are addicted. These signs of addiction are fairly easy to spot but recently developed brain scanning methods have been used to try to find out what addiction really is.

The brain scan in Figure 6.1 shows up the parts of the brain that learn about pleasure. Using cocaine affects this area and causes pleasure. However, some scientists think that cocaine also damages this area, meaning that addicts use more and more cocaine to get the same effects.

Many other drugs, including nicotine, affect the same part of the brain and may also damage it. Scientists also think that drugs damage other parts of the brain. Some effects may be permanent.

Since many drugs affect the 'pleasure' part of the brain, some scientists think that experimenting with less dangerous (or 'soft') drugs, like cannabis, will lead to using 'hard' drugs to get the same pleasurable effects. Other scientists disagree and research in this area is still continuing.

Signs of drug abuse are not just found inside the body. Drugs can also cause bad skin, shakes, vomiting, reduced reaction times and obvious damage to parts of the body (e.g. Figure 6.4).

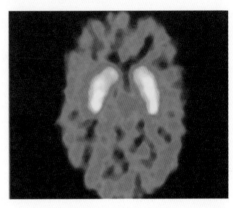

Figure 6.2 *A PET scan of a brain from a cocaine user.*

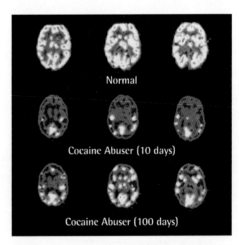

Figure 6.3 *PET scans of a) a normal brain, b) a cocaine addict after 10 days without cocaine, c) the addict after 100 days without cocaine.*

Breaking the addiction

Scientists think that if they can find out how drugs cause their effects, they could design chemicals to help people give up drugs.

Methadone can be given to heroin addicts. It acts on the same part of the brain as heroin and so reduces cravings, but it does not give a 'high'. It can also prevent heroin causing a 'high' if any heroin is injected after taking methadone.

In 2007, scientists in California found that smokers who suffered damage to a part of the brain, called the insula, could stop smoking without any cravings. So, some scientists think that damaging the insula on purpose could help smokers to quit. This is not possible yet because the insula controls other processes. However, doctors have successfully damaged a part of a brain to treat Parkinson's disease (which causes loss of control over body muscles).

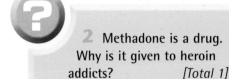

2 Methadone is a drug. Why is it given to heroin addicts? *[Total 1]*

Solving the problems

Drug abuse can cause misery for addicts and also leads to people committing crime. In the UK, people found in possession of 'hard' drugs can be sent to prison. In prison, many addicts are put on drug **rehabilitation** courses. The authorities in parts of Switzerland have tried a different approach. They give heroin addicts free heroin, although not enough to make the addicts 'high'.

Questions

1 Look at Figures 6.1 and 6.2.
  a) What do the scans suggest happens when people use cocaine? *[1]*
  b) Why is the use of just two pictures poor evidence? *[1]*
  c) How would you collect better evidence? *[1]*
  d) If your answer to part a) is correct, what would you expect to find? *[1]*
  e) How else could the two photos be interpreted? (Hint: Think about whether some people are more likely than others to become drug abusers.) *[1]*
      [Total 5]

2 a) Why might methods to help people quit cocaine also help smokers to quit? *[1]*
  b) What surgical procedure might be tried in the future to help smokers quit? *[1]*
  c) What are the dangers of this? *[1]*
      [Total 3]

3 Suggest:
  a) two advantages *[2]*
  b) two disadvantages of the Swiss system. *[2]*
      [Total 4]

Controlling diseases

Throughout history people have tried to stop diseases spreading. However, they often didn't know the causes of the diseases or how they were spread.

At the end of the fifteenth century, the church in Italy banned public bathing because it was thought that syphilis was transmitted in water. During an **epidemic** of the plague in 1576 in Venice, it was thought that 'vampires' spread the disease. A 'vampire' was thought to be an undead person (someone who had died but behaved as if alive). Bricks were pushed into the mouths of bodies that were suspected of being vampires, to make sure they starved. Around the same time in London, people thought that the plague was caused by foul-smelling air. They thought that if they breathed in heavily scented herb oils they would not get the disease.

Some methods worked. In 1665, plague arrived in the village of Eyam in Derbyshire. The villagers stopped contact with any outsiders; they put themselves in **quarantine**. Although 260 of the 350 villagers died, the disease was prevented from spreading to neighbouring villages.

Modern epidemics

In the mid-nineteenth century, French scientist Louis Pasteur made the link between microbes and disease. Since that discovery, scientists have worked out the causes of most infectious diseases and how they are spread. We now know that droplets from sneezes or coughs transmit plague, carrying the bacterium from one person to another.

There are still outbreaks of plague today. People who are found to have the disease are quickly put into quarantine. However, doctors now have another tool at their disposal to defeat the bacteria – **antibiotics**.

Figure 6.7 *This plate has bacteria growing all over it. Each disc contains an antibiotic. There is no 'ring' around the antibiotic discs to which the bacteria are resistant.*

Figure 6.5 *The remains of a suspected 'vampire'.*

? 1 Explain why the plague did not spread out of Eyam. [Total 2]

! One of Pasteur's pupils, Alexandre Yersin, discovered the bacterium that causes plague in 1894. It is named in his honour – *Yersinia pestis*.

Figure 6.6 *The plague bacterium* Yersinia pestis.

Unfortunately antibiotics are starting to lose their effectiveness because they have been misused. In any population of bacteria there is **variation** and some bacteria may be naturally **resistant** to an antibiotic. This is useful for the bacteria. The antibiotic will not kill the resistant bacteria, which can then spread to other people and cause infections that cannot then be treated with the antibiotic. The genetic material that causes resistance can also be passed from bacterium to bacterium. There are now many bacterial infections that are difficult to treat with antibiotics because they are resistant (e.g. MRSA). Scientists are actively looking for other ways of treating diseases.

2 a) Which antibiotic (A–N) in Figure 6.7 is the most effective? [1]
   b) Explain your answer. [2]
   [Total 3]

Flu

Flu (or influenza) is caused by a virus and certain strains can spread around the world, causing a **pandemic**. Governments are very worried by these pandemics and take precautions to try to stop them spreading. Figure 6.8 shows part of a leaflet distributed to all households in the UK in the spring of 2009 to try to prevent 'swine flu' from Mexico spreading. However, the 'swine flu' was declared a pandemic in June 2009.

Name of pandemic	Date	Deaths
Spanish flu	1918–20	40 million
Asian flu	1957–58	1.5 million
Hong Kong flu	1968–69	0.1 million

Table 6.1 *Flu pandemics in the twentieth century. Note that the word 'pandemic' only refers to the spread of the virus and not how dangerous it is.*

Figure 6.8 *Part of the government 'swine flu' leaflet.*

Questions

1 Why aren't antibiotics used to treat people with flu? [Total 1]

2 a) Explain why the plague did not spread out of Eyam. [2]
   b) There was an outbreak of plague in western India in 1994. Flights to the area were stopped. What was the point of stopping the flights? [1]
   [Total 2]

3 a) Why can't a flu epidemic be treated in the same way as a plague epidemic? [1]
   b) What is the reasoning behind the advice from the government leaflet? [2]
   c) What other advice do you think it contained? [1]
   [Total 4]

4 Why didn't a ban on public bathing stop the spread of syphilis? [Total 1]

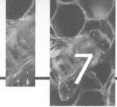

Drug development

New drugs

In 1928 Alexander Fleming (1881–1955) noticed mould growing in a dish he was using to grow bacteria. He observed that the bacteria did not grow near the mould.

Fleming thought that the mould produced a chemical that harmed the bacteria. He was right. Howard Florey (1898–1968) and Ernst Chain (1906–1979) purified the substance and made the first antibiotic – penicillin.

Different antibiotics harm different bacteria. Some antibiotics are made by chemically altering penicillin to make it effective against different bacteria. One of these antibiotics is methicillin. Bacteria that are not harmed by an antibiotic are resistant. MRSA stands for methicillin-resistant Staphylococcus aureus. Scientists are trying to develop new antibiotics to attack this bacterium (which causes problems in hospitals).

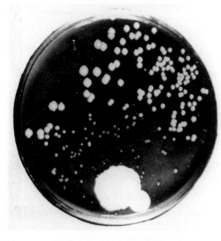

Figure 6.9 *One of Fleming's dishes.*

Figure 6.10 *Prof. Brian Austin is developing a new antibiotic from bacteria that grow on seaweed. His results suggest that it can kill MRSA.*

Before a drug can be sold, it needs to be tested to make sure that it is safe and that it works. The first stage is often to test the drug on human cells, grown in a laboratory. If the cells appear to be unharmed, the drug is then tested on animals, usually rats or mice.

If the drug doesn't harm the animals it is tried out on healthy humans. After this, it is tested on people with the problem that it is meant to treat. If it seems to be working it is tested on a large group of people with that problem – half the test group take the drug and the other half take a dummy treatment (called a **placebo**). The people do not know which they are taking. If the drug has the right effects, and is safe, it can be made available to people with the problem. Doctors continue to monitor newly available drugs to make sure that they are completely safe.

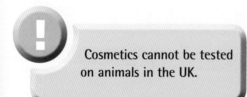

Cosmetics cannot be tested on animals in the UK.

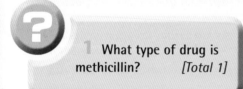

1 What type of drug is methicillin? *[Total 1]*

When testing goes wrong

In the 1950s, many pregnant women took a drug called thalidomide. It caused many babies to have deformed limbs, although the drug had appeared to be safe when tested on animals. Thalidomide was banned in the UK in 1961. The company that made the drug has to pay compensation – about £18,000 per victim per year. However, many victims feel that this is not enough.

In 1982, Opren (an anti-arthritis drug) was banned in the UK because it seemed to cause liver and kidney problems. In 1991, Halcion (a sleeping drug) was banned in the UK because it seemed to cause memory problems.

Sometimes the testing goes wrong. In 2006, a drug called TGN1412 was tested on healthy volunteers at a London hospital. Six of the volunteers, who had been paid £2000 each, became very seriously ill and nearly died.

Figure 6.11 *Thalidomide victims*

Figure 6.12 *many of the volunteers in the TGN1412 trial suffered tissue damage similar to frostbite.*

? 2 Suggest two reasons why people might volunteer to take part in a drug trial. [Total 2]

Questions

1 a) What theory did Fleming come up with?   [1]
   b) What evidence supported this theory?   [1]
   [Total 2]

2 Draw a flowchart to show how Prof. Austin's new drug would be tested before it could be sold.
   [Total 3]

3 Suggest a reason why someone might:
   a) object to animal-testing   [1]
   b) be in favour of animal-testing.   [1]
   [Total 2]

4 Why are placebos used in drug trials?   [Total 1]

5 Why do you think some companies are unwilling to publish results of their drug trials?   [Total 1]

6 Sometimes, scientists are paid by drug companies to carry out work on new drugs. If the scientists publish their work, do you think they should say that they were paid by the drugs company? Explain your reasoning.   [Total 2]

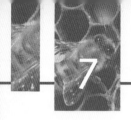

Smallpox and Edward Jenner

Smallpox was a disease caused by a virus. The sufferers developed rashes, spots and scabs filled with pus. Pus is a thick yellowish liquid produced by infected tissue. The Chinese developed an immunisation procedure in the tenth century that involved dried pus being taken from the sores and put up the noses of healthy people. This method, called **variolation**, was quite successful. It gave people a milder form of the disease and only killed around 2% of those who had the procedure. This compared with the 20–30% of people who died from getting smallpox naturally.

In 1716, Edward Wortley Montagu was made ambassador to Turkey. His wife, Lady Mary, went with him to Istanbul. There she learnt about variolation, which she became very interested in because smallpox had scarred her and also killed her brother. She had both her children variolated. Back in Britain, in 1721, the method was tried on some prisoners. Several months later, the prisoners were exposed to smallpox. None of them got the disease and so the procedure started to become popular in Britain. However, the procedure still killed some people, including George III's son, Octavius.

In the eighteenth century, an English doctor, Edward Jenner (1749–1823), noticed that milkmaids who had caught a disease called cowpox did not get smallpox. He began to study farm workers who came into regular contact with cows. He found that they were **immune** to smallpox. Jenner thought that the liquid from a cowpox sore could protect people from smallpox. In 1796 he experimented with a small boy who had never had cowpox. Jenner gave the boy cowpox by putting pus from a cowpox sufferer into cuts on the boy's arm. The child developed cowpox. A few months later Jenner took pus from a smallpox sufferer and placed this into the boy's cuts. The boy did not contract smallpox. He then began to inject people with the cowpox virus. Jenner had made a **vaccine** for smallpox.

Shortly afterwards, efforts were made to immunise people on a large scale. In 1803, the Spanish sent an expedition to South America led by Francisco Javier de Balmis. To keep cowpox alive as he crossed the Atlantic, he sailed with 22 orphaned boys who were infected with cowpox in turn. Balmis travelled extensively, vaccinating local people. In 1853 the British government made it compulsory for people to be immunised against smallpox. Other countries also made similar efforts

> **!** Spanish explorers were said to have introduced smallpox into America in the sixteenth century. The native American population was reduced by approximately 6 million people by smallpox after it was introduced to the continent.

> **!** The word 'vaccine' comes from the Latin for 'cow' – vacca. It was called this because the first vaccine was developed from a disease that infects cows.

Figure 6.13 *A cartoon of Edward Jenner at work.*

to immunise people and by the start of the twentieth century smallpox was rare in Europe. However, in other parts of the world it was still killing millions each year.

In 1959 the World Health Organisation (WHO) launched a huge effort to **eradicate** smallpox using vaccinations. They employed 200 000 health workers in 40 different countries. The last case of naturally caught smallpox occurred in Somalia in 1977 but the infected man survived. There was one further case (see page 179).

In 1980 WHO officially announced that smallpox had been eradicated. Samples of the virus are still kept for research purposes. The hope is that the virus will not be allowed to escape from any work done on these samples, and that the samples will not be used to create biological warfare weapons.

In 1853, some people objected to compulsary smallpox vaccinations. They thought that the vaccine could harm their children and demanded the freedom to choose whether to have their children vaccinated. Public marches were held but the law was not changed and people were fined for not having their children vaccinated.

Today, people still worry about vaccinations. In 1998, Dr Andrew Wakefield claimed that MMR vaccinations could cause autism (a brain development disorder). Many people stopped having their children vaccinated but other studies found no link. Later, Wakefield was accused of manipulating his data to make the link between MMR and autism look more significant. One journalist even claimed that Wakefield was being paid by a lawyer who was trying to sue the makers of the vaccine.

Figure 6.14 *A child with smallpox.*

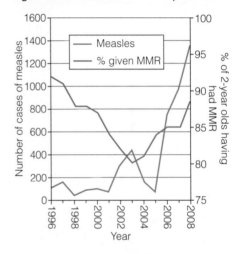

Figure 6.15 *The percentages of children given MMR and the number of cases of measles. 10% of measles cases need hospital treatment and one in 5000 are fatal.*

Questions

1 Explain why Balmis took 22 orphans on his voyage to vaccinate South Americans. *[Total 2]*

2 In what way might smallpox be used as a biological weapon? *[Total 1]*

3 In 1853 was it a good or a bad idea to fine people for not getting their children vaccinated? Explain your reasoning. *[Total 1]*

4 Suggest some reasons why a scientist might manipulate or invent data. *[Total 2]*

5 a) What was the effect of Andrew Wakefield's claim, which was widely reported in newspapers? *[1]*
 b) What effect did this have on the numbers of cases of measles? *[1]*
 c) In some parts of America, children without vaccinations are banned from school. Why do you think this is? *[1]*
 d) Do you think that banning unvaccinated children from schools is a good or a bad idea? Give your reasons. *[1]*
 [Total 4]

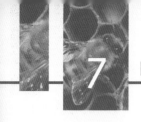
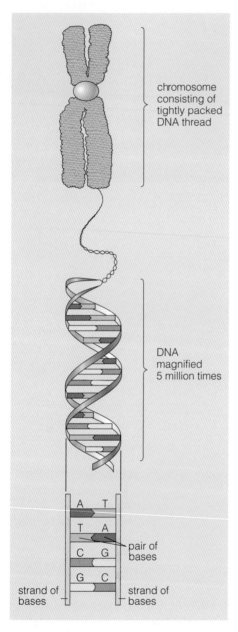

chromosome consisting of tightly packed DNA thread

DNA magnified 5 million times

pair of bases

strand of bases — strand of bases

A   T
T   A
C   G
G   C

Figure 6.16 *DNA.*

Diseases and genes

Decoding the book of life

In all organisms, the combination of genes that are inherited from parents determines their characteristics. Genes combine to make the **genome** or genetic blueprint of an organism. Each gene is made up of part of a DNA molecule. In 1953, two scientists, James Watson and Francis Crick, worked out the structure of DNA. It is made from **bases** that are arranged in a pattern that forms a code. The code contains the instructions that make up all living things. Each DNA molecule consists of two strands of bases that are coiled up into a spiral shape, called a double helix.

Each strand of human DNA can be written down in a code. The code is an arrangement of four letters (bases): A, C, T and G. It has taken scientists almost 50 years, after Watson and Crick first described DNA, to identify the complete code for a human.

The achievement of mapping the human genome was made by scientists from around the world working on the human Genome Project. This work could lead to endless possibilities in the field of gene-based medicine. For example:

- personalised medicines – people respond differently to medicines they are prescribed. In the future, individuals could go to the doctor with their own gene map and the doctor would know exactly which medicines to prescribe.
- correcting mutant genes – doctors may be able to correct faulty genes linked to diseases before a baby is born.

The list could go on as gene technology appears to have limitless potential. The use of gene technology raises many important social and ethical questions.

Selective breeding

All living things have characteristics that they inherit from both parents. It is possible to breed new varieties of an organism by taking advantage of variation. Three thousand years ago the Egyptians created wheat from wild grasses.

People often try to breed animals with special characteristics, e.g. horses that can run fast. This is called **selective breeding**. Selective breeding involves selecting a useful characteristic of an organism and

breeding it with another showing a similar feature. The offspring should develop the same feature but hopefully even better. These offspring are then bred again with similar individuals until the ideal plant or animal has been produced. Most domestic animals and many fruits and vegetables that we use today are the result of selective breeding. Fruits can be bred that ripen slowly, and that keep well. Animals can be bred to gain weight quickly and have lean meat.

Selective breeding has been very useful in helping farmers produce plants with a bigger yield, which are resistant to disease or drought and which grow quickly. The results have led to great advances in agriculture in many countries of the world.

Figure 6.17 *A Basset hound.*

Selective breeding can also have disadvantages. This is because if you keep breeding animals within the same family you increase the risk of a genetic disease. For example, in the 1980s guide dogs for visually impaired people were bred from only a small number of dogs. Many of the dogs had the disease PRA (progressive retinal atrophy). This is an inherited disease, which causes blindness in dogs. It was caused by a **reccessive** gene that all the dogs had. A reccessive gene is one that only has an effect if there are two copies of it.

Selective breeding can also cause problems because it enhances a certain characteristic. For example Basset hounds have problems with their backs because of their long bodies and short legs. Cows can have problems with swollen udders due to excess milk.

Figure 6.18

Questions

1 Explain what you think gene technology is. *[Total 1]*

2 a) What is selective breeding? *[1]*
   b) How long have humans been using selective breeding? *[1]*
   c) Why does selective breeding take such a long time? *[1]*
   [Total 3]

3 Describe two ways in which selective breeding has improved food production? *[Total 2]*

4 Doctors could soon be able to take a fertilised ovum and alter a gene in it, so that a disease will not affect the baby.

   a) Suggest a benefit of doing this. *[1]*
   b) Suggest a danger of doing this. *[1]*
   [Total 2]

5 In 2009 the BBC refused to broadcast a famous dog show called Crufts. The RSPCA also pulled out of the event. Chief vetinary advisor to the RSPCA, Mark Evans, explained that: 'There is compelling scientific evidence that the health and welfare of hundreds of thousands of pedigree dogs is seriously compromised as a result [of their breeding].'

   a) Why do you think the BBC and the RSPCA pulled out of Crufts 2009? *[1]*
   b) Do you think they were right or wrong to do so? Explain your reasoning. *[2]*
   [Total 3]

Figure 6.19 *Strawberry plants produce runners from which clones can grow.*

?

1 What is a clone?

[Total 2]

Figure 6.20 *Bernann McKinney and one of her cloned dogs.*

Figure 6.21 *Dr Brigitte Boisselier.*

Ethics and cloning

Cloned mammals

A **clone** is an identical copy of an organism, and will have the same genetic information as its parent. Plants often clone themselves and this is called **asexual reproduction**. When you 'take a cutting' from a plant, you are cloning the plant. Most fields of crops contain thousands of clones because then the farmer can be sure of the characteristics of all the plants.

Some animals can also clone themselves. Many of these animals are very small and simple but some are large, like some types of gecko (a type of lizard).

Mammals do not clone themselves. However, **biotechnology** has allowed us to clone them. The first cloned mammal was Dolly the sheep (born in 1996). A cloned cat, called 'cc' (copy cat) was born in 2001. The births of these animals were kept secret until scientists were sure that they had succeeded in producing a clone. The scientists then wrote up their experiments in 'papers' that were published in 'journals'. Before a paper can be published it is read by other scientists to make sure that the results are real and that the science is correct.

Today there are many examples of cloned mammals. In 2008, Bernann McKinney paid £25 000 to have her pet pit bull terrier cloned. The dog had died and Miss McKinney had one of the dog's ears frozen. DNA was taken from the ear and used to produce five puppy clones.

Cloned humans

On 27 December 2002, Dr Brigitte Boisselier (director of a company called Clonaid) gave a press conference and announced that a human had been cloned for the first time. She claimed that the baby, Eve, had been born the day before. Scientists wanted to test the DNA of the baby and the person she was cloned from, but Clonaid has never allowed this. Clonaid wants to clone people so that we can all live forever.

Dr Panayiotis Zavos works in a secret lab in the Middle East and is also trying to clone humans. He claims that he is trying to develop the technique so that he can help people who cannot have children to have them.

Other scientists are interested in 'therapeutic cloning'. In this form of cloning, cells from someone with a problem would be taken and used to make an embryo clone. 'Embryonic stem cells' would then be taken

from the embryo and used to make replacement tissues for the person, hopefully curing them. This method has the advantage that the cells are from the patient, and not from someone else, so there is no danger of the tissue being rejected by the immune system.

? 2 Why do you think Dr Zavos works in secret?

[Total 2]

! Some scientists are trying to recreate extinct animals (e.g. the woolly mammoth) using cloning.

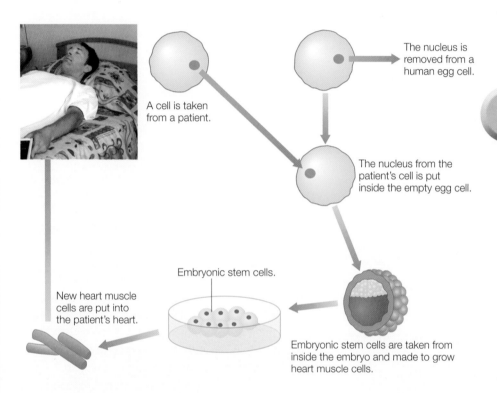

A cell is taken from a patient.

The nucleus is removed from a human egg cell.

The nucleus from the patient's cell is put inside the empty egg cell.

Embryonic stem cells.

New heart muscle cells are put into the patient's heart.

Embryonic stem cells are taken from inside the embryo and made to grow heart muscle cells.

Figure 6.22 *How therapeutic cloning could help someone with a damaged heart.*

Questions

1 What sex do you think all the gecko clones will be? Explain your answer. *[Total 2]*

2 a) Give one difference between the way that scientists told people about 'cc' the cat and how Clonaid told people about 'Eve'. *[1]*
  b) How do you think scientists should announce their discoveries? *[1]*
  c) Why do you think this? *[1]*
  [Total 3]

3 a) Why did scientists want to test the DNA of 'Eve' and the person she was cloned from? *[1]*
  b) Suggest why Clonaid never allowed this. *[1]*
  [Total 2]

4 a) Do you think that human cloning to produce fully-grown clones should be allowed? Explain your reasons. *[2]*
  b) Do you think that human cloning to produce new tissues for treatments should be allowed? Explain your reasons. *[2]*
  [Total 4]

End of section questions

1 Why are most public buildings 'non-smoking' buildings? [Total 2]

2 What is the 'health warning' found on cigarette packets? [Total 1]

3 a) What is a balanced diet? [1]
   b) Suggest three things that you can do to make sure that you have a balanced diet. [3]
   [Total 4]

4 What are some of the effects of an unhealthy diet? [Total 2]

5 How does alcohol affect a person's behaviour? [Total 2]

6 Suggest reasons why the minimum age for the purchasing of alcohol is 18. [Total 2]

7 What is high blood pressure and how is it caused? [Total 2]

8 What does the term addicted mean? [Total 1]

9 Why must we cover our mouths and noses when we cough or sneeze? [Total 1]

10 Vectors are animals that carry disease. Name three vectors. [Total 3]

11 Give two reasons why you put a plaster on a cut. [Total 2]

12 Why is chlorine added to drinking water? [Total 1]

13 Why is it better to keep butter in a refrigerator and not on the kitchen table? [Total 1]

14 Why is important that all cooks wash their hand regularly especially after handling raw meat? [Total 1]

15 What are toxins? [Total 1]

16 List five different methods of preserving food. Explain how each works. [Total 10]

17 Explain why we wrap food in cling film before placing it in the refrigerator. [Total 1]

18 a) Why do pets brought in from other countries need a passport to enter the UK? [1]
   b) What kind of diseases could they bring in? [1]
   [Total 2]

19 List two inherited diseases which could be prevented using genetic engineering. [Total 2]

20 John Snow thought that cholera was a disease spread in water. In those days people got their water from pumps in the street. In 1854 he drew a map of an area of London, marking each death from cholera on it.
   a) Snow told the authorities to remove the handle from one of the pumps shown on the map. Which one? Explain how you worked out your answer. [2]
   b) If Snow was right, what do you think the effect of removing the pump handle was? [1]
   [Total 3]

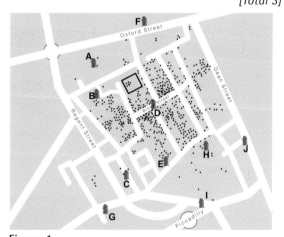

Figure 1

21 Table 1 shows the pulses of two girls while they were exercising for 5 minutes.

a) Plot a chart or graph to show the pulse rate of Sarah and Jane. *[3]*

b) Which girl is fittest? *[1]*

c) Explain your answer. *[1]*

[Total 5]

Time (min)	Pulse rate (beats per minute)	
	Sarah	Jane
0	65	75
5	150	160
7	100	130
10	75	100
15	65	90

Table 1

22 The graph shows the number of deaths from infectious diseases in the UK for the last hundred years.

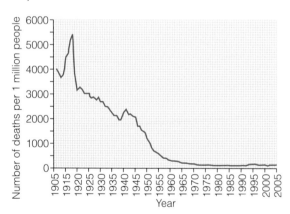

Figure 2

a) If there were 44 million people living in the UK in 1923, work out roughly how many people died of an infectious disease in 1923. *[1]*

b) Describe the main trend that the graph shows. *[1]*

c) Write down as many ways you can think of why this trend has occurred. You should write down at least four reasons. *[4]*

d) In which period of 10 years does the death rate decline the most rapidly? *[1]*

e) Give one reason why the death rate drops most dramatically during this time. *[1]*

f) There were two periods when the death rates went up again. Suggest one reason why these increases happened. *[1]*

[Total 9]

23 R Present a balanced argument about genetically modified food. Include at least three advantages and three disadvantages.

24 R Outline the social and moral implications of cloning humans.

25 R Find out about the different methods used by people wishing to give up smoking.

26 R In Holland people can buy and smoke cannabis in some coffee shops.

a) Find out about this and how these coffee shops are controlled.

b) Would you want these coffee shops in the UK? Explain your reasons.

27 R Find out about the most recent flu pandemic.

a) Why aren't people who already have had flu immune to it?

b) What precautions did the government take and did they work?

28 R Investigate what factors affect the growth of microorganisms.

29 R Investigate which antiseptic handwash is best at killing bacteria.

30 R Investigate the factors that affect the rising of bread dough.

8.1 Food chains and webs

Figure 1.1 *An abandoned field habitat.*

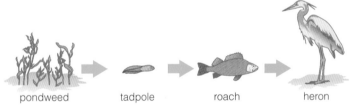

how it gets energy	traps energy	**herbivore** (eats plants), **prey** of roach	**carnivore** (eats animals), **predator** of tadpoles, prey of herons	carnivore, predator of roach (eats animals)
trophic level	producer	primary consumer	secondary consumer	tertiary consumer
how it gets energy	traps energy	herbivore, prey of fox	carnivore, predator of rabbits	

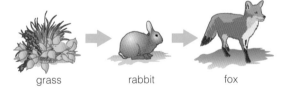

Figure 1.2 *Food chains.*

How does energy flow through an **ecosystem**?

A **community** is a group of organisms of different species that live in the same place (**habitat**). Sometimes one animal will eat another. The transfer of energy from one organism to another in the community is modelled using **food chains** and **food webs**.

Food chains

Plants and animals need energy. Plants trap light energy using a green substance called **chlorophyll**. Plants use the energy to make large molecules like glucose, starch, fat and proteins. Plants are called **producers** because they are the first organism in a food chain and make energy-rich, large molecules.

Animals get their energy from other organisms. The sequence of organisms that eat each other is called a **food chain**. The arrows linking the organisms always point in the direction that the food (energy) goes. Animals that eat producers are called **primary consumers**. Animals that eat primary consumers are called **secondary consumers**. The position that an organism has in a food chain is said to be its **trophic level**.

Food chains are usually short. This is because each animal in the food chain uses up most of the energy it receives. Only a small amount of the energy in the food (about 2%) goes into the growth of the animal. The rest of the energy is released by respiration and used for movement, digestion or heat. Some energy is also lost in waste materials. Some animals use more than 70% of their energy to keep themselves warm (Figure 1.3).

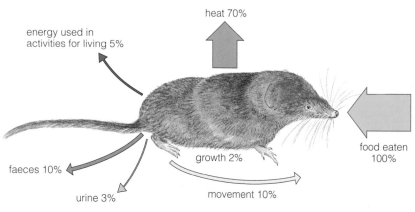

heat 70%

energy used in activities for living 5%

faeces 10%

urine 3%

growth 2%

movement 10%

food eaten 100%

Figure 1.3 *Use of energy entering a mammal. Values are approximate and vary between species.*

Think about the food chain grass → rabbit → fox. It will take more than one grass plant to feed a rabbit and more than one rabbit to feed a fox. This is the same for all food chains. The number of individuals at each trophic level goes down as you go along the food chain. The decrease in number is shown as a pyramid (Figure 1.4). It is called a **pyramid of numbers**. The reason the numbers decrease is because only the energy used by an organism for growth is passed onto the next trophic level. Most of the energy is lost as heat or is excreted. After four or five trophic levels there is not enough energy to support another predator.

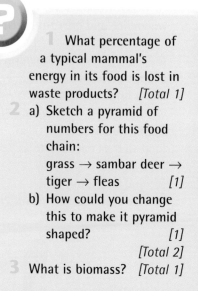

1 What percentage of a typical mammal's energy in its food is lost in waste products? [Total 1]

2 a) Sketch a pyramid of numbers for this food chain:
grass → sambar deer → tiger → fleas [1]

b) How could you change this to make it pyramid shaped? [1]
[Total 2]

3 What is biomass? [Total 1]

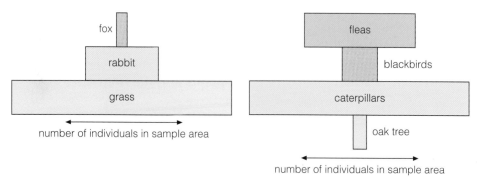

fox

rabbit

grass

number of individuals in sample area

fleas

blackbirds

caterpillars

oak tree

number of individuals in sample area

Figure 1.4 *Pyramids of numbers for simple food chains.*

Figure 1.5 *Inverted pyramid of number.*

In some food chains, the organisms are very different sizes (e.g. an oak tree is much larger than the caterpillars feeding on it). If the numbers of organisms are counted then there is not a regular pyramid (Figure 1.5). An inverted pyramid is formed.

It is better to use the **biomass** of the organisms instead of the number. Biomass is the mass of the organisms at each trophic level. A **pyramid of biomass** is usually a regular pyramid (Figure 1.6).

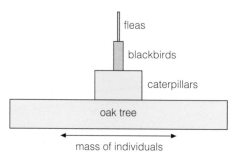

fleas

blackbirds

caterpillars

oak tree

mass of individuals

Figure 1.6 *A pyramid of biomass is usually a pyramid shape.*

Food webs

In a community, an organism usually feeds on several different types of food. Instead of one simple food chain there are many food chains that share the same organisms. If all the food chains are put together a **food web** is made (Figure 1.7). The arrows show the direction in which the energy flows.

A food web is usually arranged with the producers at the bottom. As far as possible, organisms at the same trophic level are shown level with one another. This is not always possible since an organism might be at different trophic levels in two different food chains.

A food web can show **omnivores**. These are animals that rely on both plants and animals for food. The animals at the ends of food chains are called **top predators** and these will be found at the tops of food webs.

If you carefully study one area, for example a pond, you can draw a food web and plot a pyramid of biomass for the whole area (Figure 1.8). There are usually very few predators in the pond. If you look at the pyramid of biomass you can see why. The biomass gets smaller at each trophic level. There is not enough biomass (or energy) to support lots of predators.

Decomposers

Simple food chains and food webs contain herbivores and carnivores. In real life not all plants are eaten by a herbivore and not all animals are eaten by a carnivore. Animals and plants also die from disease or old age.

There are many types of organism that eat dead material. These are grouped together as **decomposers**. Decomposers are organisms that gain their energy from organisms that have died. The main decomposers are bacteria and fungi. They respire like all other organisms and therefore some energy is lost to the environment as waste heat. Although energy is lost, decomposers allow material to be recycled through an ecosystem. Decomposers break down large molecules in the dead material and return nutrients to the soil. Bacteria and fungi

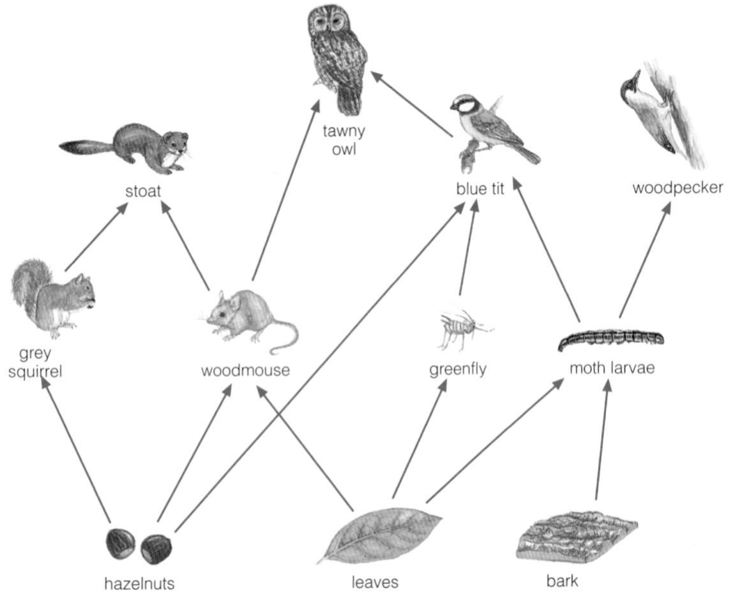

?

4 Look at the food web in Figure 1.7.
a) Write out the longest food chain starting with leaves. [2]
b) From your food chain, write down the name of a:
   i) top predator
   ii) herbivore
   iii) consumer
   iv) producer
   v) omnivore. [5]
   [Total 7]

5 At which trophic level are woodmice and grey squirrels? [Total 1]

6 In Figure 1.7 which organism is both a secondary consumer and a primary consumer? [Total 1]

7 State two advantages of a food web as opposed to a food chain for showing feeding relationships between organisms. [Total 2]

Figure 1.7 *A typical food web for a woodland.*

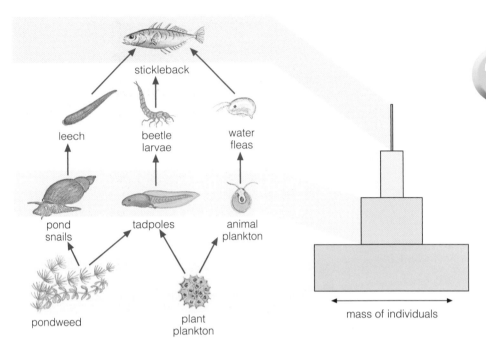

mass of individuals

Figure 1.8 *A pond food web with the pyramid of biomass.*

8 From where do decomposers gain their energy? [Total 1]

9 Why are there far fewer top predators in a habitat than there are primary consumers? [Total 2]

are important in recycling carbon and nitrogen compounds. A food web should include decomposers as they are part of the community but because they are small or microscopic they are often missed out.

Figure 1.9 *Fungi feeding on a rotting log.*

Summary

- A food chain shows the passage of energy between organisms.
- A producer traps energy from its surroundings.
- Energy passes from producer to primary consumer, to secondary consumer and on to tertiary consumer.
- Energy is lost from food chains, mainly as heat.
- Pyramids of number show the decrease in number of individuals along a food chain.
- Pyramids of number can be inverted if the organisms are of different sizes.
- A pyramid of biomass shows the decreasing amount of matter available along a food chain.
- A food web shows all the feeding relationships in a community.
- Dead matter from organisms is decomposed, mainly by bacteria and fungi.

Questions

1 Copy and complete the following sentences.
Plants are usually the _____ organisms in a food chain. They get their energy from _____. Arrows represent the _____ passing along a food chain. At each link in the food chain some of the energy is lost through _____. This limits the number of links in the chain. A pyramid of _____ shows the number of organisms at each trophic level. Sometimes the different _____ of organisms causes the pyramid to be inverted. *[Total 3]*

2 a) Put the following in the correct order: *[1]*
   tertiary consumer   producer
   secondary consumer   primary consumer.
 b) Pair the terms in part a) with the following feeding types: *[4]*
   traps energy   herbivore   carnivore *[Total 5]*

3 List six ways that energy can be used by an animal that has eaten food. *[Total 6]*

4 a) What is biomass? *[1]*
 b) Why is a pyramid of biomass sometimes more useful than a pyramid of numbers? *[2]*
   [Total 3]

5 a) Use your knowledge of the sizes of the organisms to sketch rough pyramids of numbers for the following food chains:
   i) grass → snail → thrush → sparrowhawk
   ii) pondweed → water fleas → minnow
      → perch → pike
   iii) sycamore tree → greenfly → ladybird
      → blue tit *[6]*
 b) Name the trophic level which the pike occupies. *[1]*
 c) Explain why one of the pyramids is not regular. *[1]*
 d) Draw the pyramid of biomass for the inverted pyramid of numbers. *[2]*
   [Total 10]

6 Why are most food chains limited to about 4 links? *[Total 1]*

7 From the food web shown in Figure 1.7:
 a) write a food chain of four organisms *[1]*
 b) list the producers *[2]*
 c) list the omnivores. *[1]*
   [Total 4]

8 State two types of decomposer organism. *[Total 2]*

9 What roles do the decomposers play in the community? *[Total 2]*

10 Look at the food web in Figure 1.10.

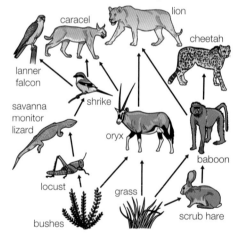

Figure 1.10

 a) What eats grass? *[1]*
 b) What do caracals eat? *[1]*
 c) From the food web, write down one of the two longest food chains in the food web. *[2]*
 d) Write a list of the organisms in your food chain from part c). Describe what each one is by writing one or more of these words next to it:
   carnivore consumer herbivore omnivore
   producer top predator *[5]*
   [Total 9]

11 Why are plants called producers? *[Total 1]*

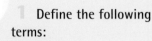

8.2 Population changes

What is a population? A group of organisms, which have the same features and can breed together successfully, is called a **species**. The total number of individuals of one species, which live in one area, is called the **population**. In a population individuals die but they also reproduce. Sexual reproduction means that there is variation within the population and this can lead to evolution (see Section 6.4).

Population size is limited by:

- the amount of space available for breeding
- the amount of food available
- build up of wastes produced
- disease
- predators
- the physical environment.

Space and food

In a habitat there is only a certain amount of space for organisms to live. For example, there can only be a certain number of oak trees in a wood. Each tree competes for space, light and nutrients with the other trees.

In the branches of an oak tree, there is only a limited space for nest sites for birds. The birds must also compete for food. The **competition** for resources depends on the population size. If there are only a few birds to catch caterpillars, there is more food to go round and the bird population will grow. If there are too many birds then there will be more competition between the birds for food. Some will starve and the population will decrease.

Figure 2.1 *Plants in dense woodland compete for light.*

Figure 2.2 *Birds compete for food in order to feed themselves and their young.*

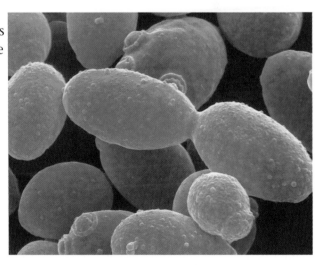

Figure 2.3 *Yeast cells reproduce by producing a growth called a 'bud'. The bud grows and separates from the original cell. Increase in number of cells can be very rapid.*

?

1 Define the following terms:
  a) species [1]
  b) population. [1]
    [Total 2]

2 Explain how predators can limit the size of an animal population. [Total 2]

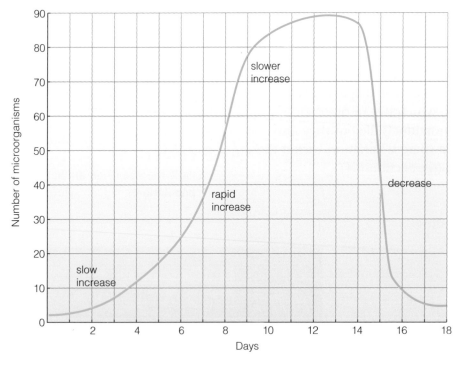

Figure 2.4 *Growth curve of microorganisms.*

Microorganisms also compete. Yeast cells reproduce by **budding** (Figure 2.3) but most other microorganisms reproduce by dividing into two (**binary fission**). Bacteria are grown in fermenters to make food, e.g. yoghurt. Using a few bacterial cells to start the fermentation the number of cells will increase slowly at first as they get used to the conditions. Soon the numbers double for each generation. The growth cannot continue for long because the bacteria run out of food. Waste products also build up, which poison the bacteria. The growth rate (population increase) slows down because of the competition and poisoning. When more cells die than are being produced, the population decreases.

Disease

A major cause of death in plants and animals is disease. Microorganisms can invade plants or animals to use them as food (Figure 2.5). The rapid growth of the invading microorganisms causes illness or death of the larger organism. Microorganisms can spread between individuals very easily when they are tightly packed in one area, for example crops in a field. Death by disease is usually density-dependent because disease spreads more rapidly when organisms live closer together.

Predators

The close relationship between a predator and its prey can be seen in Figure 2.6. If there are not many predators, the numbers of prey will increase. However, the increase in prey provides more food for the predators. The number of predators then increases. Predators start to eat more prey than are being produced. The prey numbers start to go down. There is less food for the predators and more predators starve to death or move away from the area. The predator numbers go down until there are so few that the prey population increases again. This pattern is shown by the lynx and snowshoe hare in Canada.

Figure 2.5 *A potato plant suffering from potato blight. This fungus caused a great famine in Ireland in the 1840s.*

Number of prey (hares) increases rapidly when predators (lynxes) are few.

— snowshoe hare
— lynx

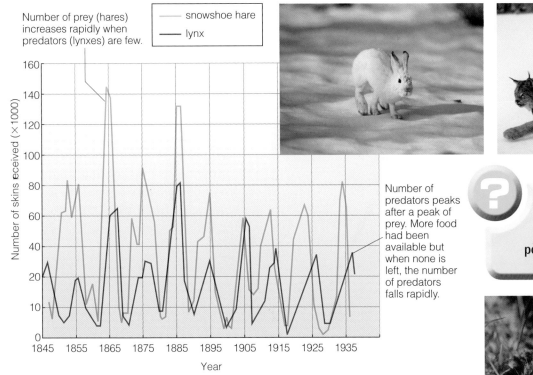

Number of predators peaks after a peak of prey. More food had been available but when none is left, the number of predators falls rapidly.

Figure 2.6 *Graph showing populations of snowshoe hare and lynx based on the number of skins supplied by trappers.*

Some animal populations show variation with increases and sudden crashes. Studies on lemmings in Scandinavia show that after three or four years of ample food supply there is an increase in population number. After a while space becomes short or the food supply decreases. There is such competition that many of the lemmings migrate. Whilst migrating many die due to starvation, being eaten or by having accidents. Due to migration, the original populations fall to a lower level.

Physical environment

The weather in a particular habitat will vary from year to year. If one year is colder than another, more animals or plants may die. If there is a drought or fire then organisms will die. The temperature of the environment, water shortages and fires are **physical factors**; they are non-living factors that can affect things.

A food web of a hedgerow (Figure 2.8) shows some of the feeding relationships. If the numbers of snails were to increase because of a wet year then there may be fewer brambles. There might be fewer caterpillars because there are less brambles to eat. However, the hedgehogs and thrushes may eat more snails than caterpillars and so

3 Suggest three factors that might decrease the population of lynx. *[Total 3]*

Figure 2.7 *A lemming.*

There is a myth that lemmings commit suicide when their populations get too great. This myth was also in a Walt Disney film from 1958 called *White Wilderness*. In the film, the footage of the lemmings was faked ... the lemmings did not jump but were pushed. Nor was the sequence filmed anywhere near the Arctic Ocean. Have a look at it on YouTube!

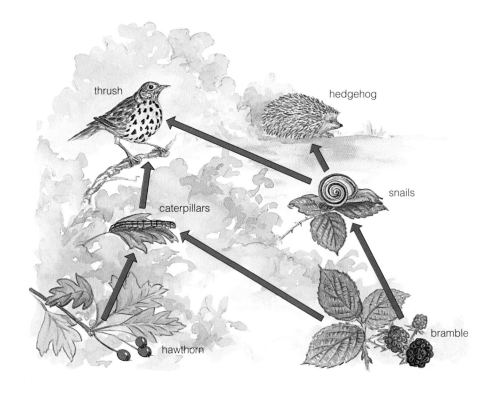

Figure 2.8 *Foodweb from a hedgerow.*

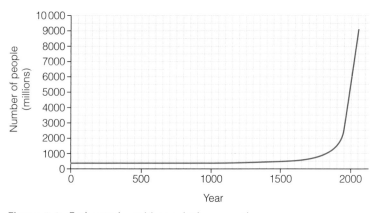

Figure 2.9 *Estimated world population growth.*

the caterpillars might survive better. In the end the number of caterpillars might stay the same as for other years. Both suggestions are equally likely to be right.

Human populations

The world human population is growing so quickly that many people are worried that there will not be enough food. In the year 1000 there was a population of about 310 million. By 1850 it had risen to 1300 million and by 2000 it was over 6000 million.

The population is rising because more people are surviving for longer, i.e. the death rate is decreasing. This is due to:

- better medicines and health care
- better hygiene so diseases do not spread as quickly
- better farming methods in some parts of the world which increase the amount of food available.

Changes in the world's climate or natural disasters could cause an increase in the death rate. The human population remains under the control of natural forces however much we protect ourselves in the developed world.

?

4 What is the estimated population of the world:
a) now [1]
b) in 2050? [1]
[Total 2]

Summary

○ A population is the total number of individuals of one species in a defined area.

○ Competition for resources limits the population size.

○ Major population limitations are food, predators, disease and physical factors.

○ In a predator-prey situation the population numbers change in a regular way. The prey population reaches a peak before the predator population does.

○ Human populations are no longer limited by disease or food in many parts of the world.

Questions

1 Copy and complete the following sentences.
A _____ is a group of the same species living in an area. The number of organisms varies because of the living factors (food, _____ and predators) and _____ factors (_____, toxins, temperature and water). In a simple food chain the number of a prey species varies with the number of _____. As the predator numbers _____ the prey number will decrease. *[Total 3]*

2 List the factors that limit the population size. *[Total 6]*

3 Explain what is meant by 'competition for resources'. *[Total 2]*

4 Suggest two reasons why populations of some animals might suddenly crash. *[Total 2]*

5 Explain how three physical factors could affect the populations of organisms. *[Total 3]*

6 Give three reasons why the human population is increasing. *[Total 3]*

7 Look back at Figure 2.8. If the hedgehogs all die of a disease, what might be the effect of this on the thrush population? Explain your answer. *[Total 2]*

8 Table 2.1 shows the population size of bacteria feeding on a rotting leaf.
a) Draw a graph of the population size against time. Choose suitable scales for the axes and label them carefully. *[5]*
b) What is the population size after:
   i) 4 days
   ii) 10 days
   iii) 20 days? *[3]*
c) Suggest why the number of bacteria remains about the same from day 24 to day 27. *[1]*
d) What may happen to the bacteria after day 30? *[1]*
[Total 10]

Day	Number of bacteria (million)
1	0.3
5	0.5
9	1.2
13	4.8
17	19.2
21	76.8
25	78.0
29	78.2

Table 2.1 *Population size of bacteria feeding on a leaf.*

8.3 Human influences

How have we changed our environment? Humans have been on the Earth for about 200 000 years. They have interacted with the environment in the same way as all other species. However, in recent years, the effects of humans on the environment have been increasing. This has meant that some organisms are in danger of disappearing and this will affect food webs. Also some endangered plants and animals have been found to contain chemicals that could be useful to humans. For example, an anti-cancer drug has been extracted from the leaves of the Madagascan periwinkle.

Figure 3.1 *A red panda*

Competition for space

In many regions of the world the human population has increased so much that the original habitat has been destroyed. Humans are winning the competition for space.

To grow more food people cut down forests and use the land for crops or grazing. Unfortunately, the area of destroyed forest provided homes for a great many different types of plants and animals. If the whole of one species is lost permanently we say that the species has become **extinct**.

Today, about a third of the world's land is used for agriculture.

Competition for space can be seen if too many animals are grazed in one area. **Overgrazing** occurs and plants cannot re-grow. When there are too few plants the soil is eroded more easily. Normally, plant roots hold the soil together. Heavy rainfall may wash the soil away or it could dry out and be blown away by the wind.

Figure 3.2 *Forest habitat destroyed during felling.*

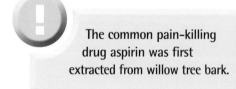

The common pain-killing drug aspirin was first extracted from willow tree bark.

Land is used to build towns and cities and this means that less space is available for plants and animals. The area around housing is compacted or covered in concrete so that the original inhabitants cannot live there. Having many buildings also causes problems with drainage of rainwater. Soil will absorb rainwater but concrete will not. The water runs into rivers faster and rivers flood more often (Figure 3.3). The planners try to understand the systems and build in measures to protect areas that humans value.

Figure 3.3 *Flooding in October 2000.*

Sometimes human influence can help a species. The presence of buildings has created new habitats for animals. Bats may live in roofs instead of caves or trees. The use of salt on the roads in winter to keep them free of ice has let seaside plants grow along the roadside (Figure 3.4).

Competition for resources

The work involved in obtaining the raw materials for our lifestyle causes damage to the environment. An open-cast mine is a visual eyesore and the dust, noise and road or rail network to transport people or products all reduce the ability of other organisms to live around the mine. Dust falls on the plants and stops some of the light getting to leaves. The plants are weakened and are more likely to get diseased just as we are when we breathe in dust.

Climate change

Non-renewable energy resources like coal, oil and uranium are being used to power our lifestyle (Figure 3.5).

hydroelectric 1.3%
oil 1.2%
wind 1.3%
other renewables 2.7%
nuclear 16.1%
coal 34.8%
natural gas 41.9%

Energy resources used to generate electricity in the UK (2007).

Figure 3.5 *At the moment renewable energy resources are used to generate less electricity than non-renewable resources.*

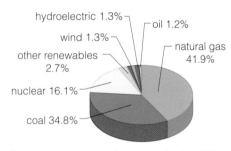

burning rubbish 6.0%
biomass 17.5%
landfill gas 23.8%
solar 0.1%
wind 26.8%
hydroelectric 25.9%

Renewable energy resources used to generate electricity in the UK (2007).

1 Some city councils want to ban people from turning their front gardens into car parking spaces. Why? [Total 2]

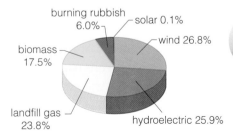

Figure 3.4 *The seaside plant thrift growing by a roadside away from the sea.*

2 Why can dust falling on plants weaken them? [Total 2]

An average person in the UK uses about 80 times more fuel than a person in Bangladesh.

3 What percentage of our electricity is produced using renewable energy resources? [Total 1]

?

4 State two causes of increased levels of carbon dioxide. [Total 2]

5 a) Carbon dioxide is described as being a greenhouse gas. What do you think this means? [1]

   b) Name one other greenhouse gas. [1]
   [Total 2]

6 State two reasons why many scientists think that sea levels will rise. [Total 2]

Burning fossil fuels produces carbon dioxide, which may be causing **climate change**. Carbon dioxide is also produced when forests (biomass) are cut down and burnt. Felling forests also means that there are fewer large plants absorbing the carbon dioxide in photosynthesis. All of this means that carbon dioxide is building up in the atmosphere.

Together with methane (a waste gas from cattle digesting their food), the carbon dioxide absorbs the heat given off from the Earth and this is called the **greenhouse effect**. This makes the atmosphere warmer – **global warming**. Even a small increase in global temperature could have a large effect. For example:

○ wind and rainfall patterns may change
○ ice caps may melt, increasing the sea level
○ sea levels could also rise because water expands when it is warmer.

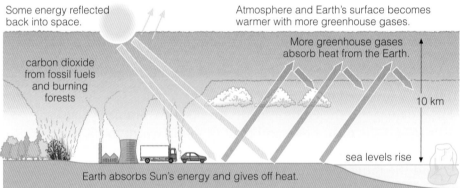

Some energy reflected back into space.

Atmosphere and Earth's surface becomes warmer with more greenhouse gases.

More greenhouse gases absorb heat from the Earth.

carbon dioxide from fossil fuels and burning forests

10 km

sea levels rise

Earth absorbs Sun's energy and gives off heat.

Figure 3.6 *Greenhouse effect mechanism.*

Many people are very worried about climate change. In England and Wales nearly 2 million properties are at risk from river and sea flooding.

About 20% of coral reefs have died or have suffered serious damage. Coral reefs are mainly formed by corals, which are cnidarian animals. They have an outside skeleton that they make from calcium carbonate. Unfortunately, they are very sensitive to temperature changes and if the water gets too warm, they die. Increasing amounts of carbon dioxide in the water also make the water more acidic. The more acidic the water is, the more difficult it is for corals to extract the dissolved calcium carbonate from the water.

If renewable sources of energy like solar, wind, moving water or replanted forests were used instead of fossil fuels then humans would have less effect on the environment. However, renewable energy sources tend to be less reliable and less efficient than fossil fuels.

!

By the year 2100 it is predicted that the sea level will rise between 9 cm and 88 cm and the average global temperature will rise between 1.4 °C and 5.8 °C.

Figure 3.7 *If corals die, they turn white.*

The ozone layer

The **ozone layer** high in the atmosphere stops damaging ultraviolet waves from the Sun getting to the Earth's surface. The ozone layer is being destroyed by a group of substances called chlorofluorocarbons (CFCs). CFCs are man-made molecules, which were used in aerosols and fridges. The chlorine in the CFCs enters the upper atmosphere and reacts with ozone to destroy it. This is most noticeable above the Earth poles. The extra radiation, which reaches the Earth through the thin ozone layer, can cause skin cancer in humans as well as harming all other organisms.

Acid rain

The waste gases from burning fossil fuels also contain sulphur dioxide and oxides of nitrogen. These gases dissolve in water in the atmosphere to form acid rain. Buildings are damaged by the acid. Plant leaves will not photosynthesise properly because the acid in the leaves stops the chloroplasts working properly. Acid rain also reacts with compounds in soil producing substances that poison plants.

When acid rain runs into ponds or lakes many animals cannot survive. Fish get oxygen from water through their gills. The gills are very delicate and if the water becomes acidic, the fish produce extra mucus on the gills as protection. The mucus means that the fish cannot get as much oxygen from the water and they die. Many lakes in Scandinavia have become crystal clear because there are no plankton (microscopic plants and animals) living in the water due to its acidity.

Pesticides and bioaccumulation

Pesticides are chemicals that kill pests such as slugs, insects or rats. Some pesticides do not chemically break down. Wherever the pesticide ends up in the ecosystem, animals are likely to be affected by the poison.

A pesticide may be sprayed onto plants to kill pests. The plants are eaten by other herbivores. The herbivore often stores the poison in fat which it does not use regularly. As the pesticide is not broken down, it will be transferred into the next animal in the food chain. The animal in the next trophic level has to eat many smaller organisms in order to get enough energy to survive. It takes in the stored pesticide from each of its food organisms. The pesticide becomes more concentrated. The process is called **bioaccumulation**. The top predators accumulate so much pesticide that it harms them so they may not be able to breed.

7 Sketch a diagram to show your understanding of the 'ozone layer'. *[Total 2]*

A 'hole' in the ozone layer above Antarctica was first noticed in 1985. In 1987, politicians from around the world met to discuss the problem and signed The Montreal Protocol on Substances that Deplete the Ozone Layer. This 'protocol' phased out the use of CFCs and nearly every country has now signed.

Figure 3.8 *Plants damaged by acid.*

8 a) What is a pesticide? [2]
b) Explain how a pesticide can harm animals that are not pests. [2]
[Total 4]

9 Suggest an advantage for farmers and gardeners of pesticides that do not break down. *[Total 1]*

American biologist, Rachel Carson, wrote a book in 1962 called *Silent Spring*. It was about the damage caused by DDT and led to its ban. However, some people accuse her of distorting the facts. For example, when talking about scientists' experiments she did not mention any results that suggested that DDT was not harmful.

10 Suggest why Rachel Carson's book was called *Silent Spring.* [Total 1]

11 a) Imagine that you have 20 earthworms, eaten by four blackbirds, which are eaten by one sparrowhawk. A pesticide soaks into the ground and is absorbed by earthworms. Each earthworm receives a single dose. Draw a pyramid of numbers of this food chain showing the number of doses of the pesticide at each tropic level. Represent each dose as a spot. [2]

b) How does your diagram help you to explain the idea of bioaccumulation? [2]
[Total 4]

12 Pesticides have never been used in Antarctica. Suggest how DDT has found its way into penguins. [Total 2]

The poison DDT was used widely after the World War II to kill mosquitoes, which carry malaria. DDT is not broken down in the environment and it has entered food webs all over the world. It has even been found in the penguins of Antarctica. It was responsible for the death of many top predators, like the peregrine falcon. The peregrine falcon nearly became extinct in the UK because DDT caused the females to lay eggs with very thin shells. The shells broke when the birds tried to sit on the eggs. DDT has other affects in different birds (see Figure 3.9).

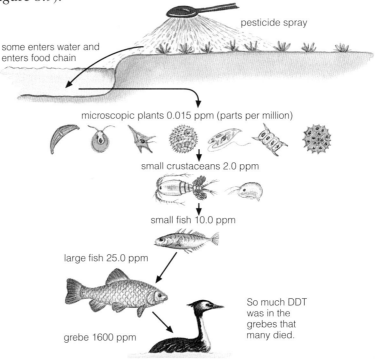

Figure 3.9 *Bioaccumulation of DDT in the community around Clear Lake, California.*

Pollution from accidents

In 1967, the first major oil tanker disaster occurred. The Cornish coast was covered in thick oil from the stricken oil tanker, Torrey Canyon. The birds, cormorants for example, living in the area got covered in oil.

Figure 3.10 *Bird covered in oil.*

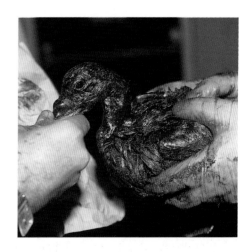

The feathers lost their waterproof layer. The birds could not keep warm and died. Many other marine organisms also died, but after 10 years there was little sign of the disaster. Microorganisms started to decompose the oil and much of it was hidden underneath sand or somewhere under the sea. The process is slow but the natural ecosystem has returned.

Toxic minerals from mines may be accidentally discharged into rivers. The minerals kill most of the organisms in the river because they interfere with enzymes in their cells. All organisms are affected. The mining of precious metals or those needed in industry can have a great cost to the environment.

In January 2001, a dam burst at the Aurul gold mine in Romania. The water released contained cyanide at a concentration of up to 700 times acceptable levels. Once it entered the River Tisza, the effect on wildlife was disastrous. Virtually all organisms in the river were killed, from algae, to fish and otters, and there were fears that the cyanide would enter the food chain. Over a thousand tonnes of dead fish were removed from the river in the first two weeks following the spill. The extent of the disaster was so great that local people declared the river to be 'dead'. The flow continued from Romania, into Hungary and onto Serbia, by which time it had been diluted to near normal levels.

The accident threatened the drinking supplies of over 2.5 million Hungarians and the livelihoods of 15 000 fishermen. Environmentalists have warned that it will take between ten and twenty years for the river ecosystem to recover. However, it is feared that some species of fish may never return.

In 1932, the Chisso factory (near a coastal town in Japan called Minamata) started to make acetaldehyde. This chemical is used in the production of a variety of other chemicals. Production gradually increased. From about 1950 onwards, residents in Minamata noticed that some cats were behaving oddly; they would suddenly behave crazily, have convulsions and then die. There were also reports of birds dying in flight.

Then in 1956, some children started having convulsions and dying. At first, people thought that it was food poisoning or an infectious disease. Later some kind of metal poisoning was suggested. In 1958, a visiting British doctor said that he thought the symptoms were like mercury poisoning. Scientists then discovered that the factory was dumping mercury into the water.

Figure 3.11 *River pollution from a copper mine in Spain.*

13 Why can mining have a great cost to the environment? Give two reasons. *[Total 2]*

14 a) Suggest why people living in Minamata died. *[2]*

c) Suggest why some of the cats developed the so called 'cat dancing disease'. *[1]*

d) Why are animals that are higher in the food chain more likely to develop problems than those lower down? *[1]*
[Total 6]

So, the factory installed a new waste water cleaning plant but it didn't remove the mercury – and the factory officials knew this. They carried on dumping mercury into the sea for another decade. In all, there were 2265 victims, most of whom died an early death. There are still claims for compensation going through the courts today.

Sustainable development

The overgrazing and pollution examples given earlier in the chapter show the way humans change the environment for the worse. The effects usually destroy part of an ecosystem. Sustainable development means continuing to improve and develop standards of living for all people without using up all the Earth's natural resources. For example, we should

- use energy from renewable resources, e.g. wind power and solar cells
- make housing and transport more energy efficient
- use items made from replanted forests
- make sure that mines or any environment that has been changed is renovated after use into productive areas
- recycle all waste substances.

All the living things around us must be respected and conserved. The great diversity of organisms must be protected as each has a part to play in the development of each community. Some of the currently rare species might be useful to humans in the future. Zoos are important in maintaining breeding programmes so that animals can be returned to natural habitats. Other conservation measures include the protection of habitats by creating nature reserves or national parks which help to limit the activities of humans.

15 Suggest three ways in which you could live more sustainably. *[Total 3]*

National Parks are areas of great beauty and special natural interest where people are restricted in what they can do, so that the environments are not damaged. There are 14 National Parks in the UK. Around the world, similar protected areas now cover about 1 million square kilometres.

Summary

- Some animals are becoming extinct because their habitats are being destroyed.
- Some species that can live around humans are increasing.
- Increasing carbon dioxide levels are associated with climate change.
- The ozone layer is being damaged and this could lead to more cases of skin cancer.
- Acid rain is caused by pollutants from fossil fuels.
- Pesticides can accumulate in the food chain so the top predators are accidentally killed.
- Many human activities produce accidents that damage the environment, e.g. oil spills.
- Sustainable development means continuing to develop higher standards of living without destroying the Earth's resources.

Questions

1 Copy and complete the following sentences.
   Human populations are _____ and require extra space to live. New farmland is made by _____ forests. The red panda may become _____ because of habitat destruction. Much of the _____ needed in the developed world comes from _____ sources like coal and _____. Oil spill accidents kill many birds. *[Total 3]*

2 A rodenticide is a pesticide used to kill rodents, such as mice and rats.
   a) Suggest why a farmer would use a rodenticide. *[1]*
   b) New rodenticides were developed in the 1980s. What does the table below suggest about the use of these rodenticides? Suggest one thing. *[1]*

Year	% of barn owl livers containing remains of the rodenticides
1983–1984	5
1985–1986	12
1987–1988	17
1989–1990	22
1991–1992	32
1993–1994	30
1995–1996	38
1997–1998	52

   c) Why are the remains of rodenticides found in barn owls? *[2]*
   [Total 4]

3 Explain how the warming of the seas has an effect on humans? *[Total 2]*

4 Give two different problems caused by deforestation. *[Total 2]*

5 Give two reasons why many seabirds die when there is an oil spillage in their habitat. *[Total 2]*

6 Explain the idea of sustainable development. *[Total 2]*

7 Why are zoos important? *[Total 1]*

8 Write a short paragraph on each of the following points to explain how the action pollutes the environment:
   a) burning fossil fuels *[3]*
   b) using CFCs *[3]*
   c) deforestation. *[3]*
   [Total 9]

9 Look at Figure 3.13.
   a) What trend does the graph show? *[1]*
   b) Suggest two reasons for this trend. *[2]*
   c) Suggest one piece of advice that should be given to people to try to halt the trend. *[1]*
   [Total 4]

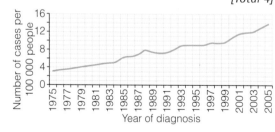

Figure 3.13 *Graph to show the numbers of people with the most serious form of skin cancer, in the UK.*

Farming and the environment

Intensive farming

Intensive farming uses labour-saving methods to try to get as much product out of as small a space as possible. These methods include using machinery, **pesticides** and **fertilisers**. Intensive farming methods produce much more food for each hectare of land than less intensive methods.

Many animals that we use for meat are intensively farmed. The farmer tries to keep energy losses from the animals to a minimum. If chickens or pigs are kept in small pens then they cannot move around as much and so do not use as much energy. If the animals are in heated sheds, they will not need as much energy to keep themselves warm. The cost of heating is cheaper than the extra feed that would be needed by the animals. These factors mean that the farmer does not have to buy as much animal feed. The animals use more of their food for growth. The farmer can then sell the bigger animal at a greater profit.

Crops are also intensively farmed. Huge fields of the same variety of a certain plant are grown. The plants soon take all the mineral salts from the soil which then need to be replaced, using fertilisers. If the same type of plant is grown in the same area for too long, the soil may start to become crumbly and fine. Hedgerows may also be removed, so that large machinery can be used more efficiently. This destroys the habitats of many organisms.

Figure 4.1 *Intensive pig farming.*

? 1 Yellowhammers are birds that eat insects found in hedgerows. They build nests on the ground surrounded by tall plants. The population has fallen 53% since 1970. Suggest reasons for this. [Total 2]

Free range

Some people think that the intensive farming of animals is cruel. They want to buy meat and eggs from animals that have been grown in areas with lots of space. **Free-range** animals have a lot of space in which to move around.

Figure 4.3 *Chickens grown in sheds like this are called 'battery chickens'.*

Figure 4.2 *Free-range chickens.*

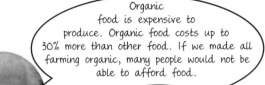

Organic farming

Some people don't like the idea of artificial fertilisers and pesticides being used on the plants and animals that they will then eat. In **organic farming** very few artificial and only natural fertilisers (like manure) can be used. Decomposers break down the manure, returning mineral salts to the soil.

Instead of using chemical pesticides, organic farmers are encouraged to use natural methods like **biological control agents**. A biological control agent is a natural predator of a pest. For instance, ladybirds can be introduced into greenhouses to control greenfly numbers.

The debate

Some people are in favour of intensive farming and some are against it and want farmers in the UK to use more organic methods.

> Organic food is expensive to produce. Organic food costs up to 30% more than other food. If we made all farming organic, many people would not be able to afford food.

A *Prof. Tony Trewavas, plant specialist*

> 31000 tonnes of pesticides are applied to UK farmland each year. In total, organic farms only use about 10 tonnes. many scientists think that pesticides are bad for you

B *Sam Allen, of the Soil Association, which rules for organic farming in the UK.*

> The amount of wheat that the world produces has quadrupled in the last 50 years. It will have to go up about the same amount again in order to feed the world. We either clear rainforests to grow it or we use chemicals to get as much out of farmland as possible. We will protect the wild environment by making better use of farms.

C *Prof. Bill McKelvey, head of the Scottish Agricultural College*

> In our study of 180 farms over five years, we found that organic farms contained over 80% more plant species, 33% more bats, 17% more spiders and 5% more birds.

D *Dr Lisa Norton, of the Centre for Ecology Hydrology*

Figure 4.4 *Some views for and against intensive farming.*

Questions

1 a) How much pesticide do organic farms use compared with intensive farms? Give your answer as a percentage. [1]
   b) Which figure (tonnes or percentage) would you use if you were making an argument for organic farming? Explain your reasoning. [2]
   [Total 3]

Number of turtle doves / Length of hedgerow in UK (thousand km)

— turtle doves   ■ hedgerow length

Year (1984–1998)

2 People can use the same facts and figures to draw different conclusions. For example, some blame hedge removal for the 62% drop in turtle dove numbers since 1972. Others think that droughts in Africa (where the birds spend the winter) are the cause.
   a) What conclusions can you draw from graphs X and Y in Figure 4.5? [2]
   b) How has the data in the graphs been manipulated so that you draw different conclusions? [2]
   [Total 4]

Number of turtle doves / Length of hedgerow in UK (thousand km)

Year (1990–1998)

Figure 4.5

Extinction

Death of the dodo

Sailors discovered dodo birds on the island of Mauritius in about 1507. The birds were not afraid of people. Less than 200 years later they were extinct.

No one really knows what dodos looked like! We generally think of dodos as being fat and clumsy but most of the evidence comes from paintings. The model in Figure 4.6 is based on a painting. Some museums have skeletons but these are made up of bones from many dodos.

Figure 4.6 *Dodo model with stuck on swan feathers!*

?

1 Why don't museum skeletons of dodos provide good evidence for what dodos looked like? *[Total 1]*

2 Does Figure 4.9 provide evidence for or against Kitchener's theory? *[Total 1]*

In 1990 Dr Andrew Kitchener (from the National Museum of Scotland) looked through images of dodos and spotted a trend. Images from before about 1605 showed thin birds, and those after about 1625 showed fat birds. He came up with a theory that the later paintings were of captive birds that had been overfed. He said that wild dodos would have been thin and active creatures.

In 1991 some new drawings of dodos from 1601 were discovered in Holland (Figure 4.9).

Today, geologists and biologists are working together in a swamp in Mauritius looking for dodo bones and **fossils**. They are hoping to find a complete skeleton.

Figure 4.7 *Dodo drawing from an engraving by Carl Clusius in 1605.*

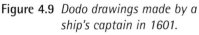

Figure 4.9 *Dodo drawings made by a ship's captain in 1601.*

Figure 4.8 *Dodo painting by Hans Savery from 1651.*

Stopping the decline

Many organisms have become extinct due to humans hunting them, clearing habitats for farms, introducing new species into habitats or using poisons. Dodos became extinct because they were hunted for food, their habitat was destroyed to plant crops and the cats, pigs, goats and rats that sailors brought with them ate their eggs.

In the 1970s governments from 80 countries got together and made an agreement called CITES (Convention on International Trade in Endangered Species). This made it illegal to trade endangered organisms (or their parts) in those countries.

Individuals can also make decisions about how to behave responsibly towards wild animals and plants. Catching whole shoals of some fish like bluefin tuna is not sustainable since it kills the whole of the shoal (and many other animals that get caught up in the net). Since the 1970s the bluefin tuna population has fallen by 70% due to **overfishing**. So some people choose to buy 'rod and line caught' tuna, which is more expensive.

Figure 4.10 *In 1888, to protect farmers' sheep, hunters in Tasmania were rewarded for killing Thylacines. The last one in the world died in a zoo in 1936.*

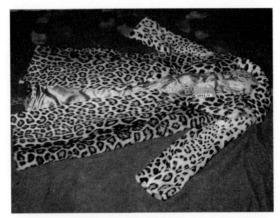

Figure 4.11 *The trade of skins of endangered animals is illegal in most countries.*

Questions

1. a) Animals can become extinct in many ways. List three of these ways. [3]
    b) Suggest some ways in which we can stop extinctions. [2]
        [Total 5]

2. Today geologists and biologists are working together to find bones and fossils of the dodo in swamps in Mauritius. Why do different scientists work together? Give two reasons. [Total 2]

3. a) How is fishing for tuna with a rod and line sustainable? [1]
    b) Why might someone choose not to buy rod and line caught tuna? [1]
        [Total 2]

4. How does CITES help stop organisms from becoming extinct? [Total 1]

5. Quaggas were animals much like zebras and lived in Africa. They were killed by humans and became extinct in 1883. Suggest a reason why they were killed. [Total 1]

Overpopulation

Thomas Malthus

Figure 4.12 *Thomas Malthus.*

In 1798 Thomas Malthus (1766–1834) wrote *An Essay on the Principle of Population*. This was published in London as a pamphlet. Malthus thought that the human population would increase faster than the supply of food could be increased. He predicted that this shortage of food would cause war, starvation and disease.

The world's population

Since Malthus wrote his essay, the world's population has continued to increase. Improved agriculture and medicine, together with our knowledge of how diseases are spread, have meant that people live longer now. When Malthus wrote his essay there were 978 million people on Earth. Today there are 6909 million (see Figure 2.9 on page 208).

The effect on the environment

When the people living in an area consume more food and water than the area can produce, then that area is overpopulated. There are many effects of overpopulation.

Starvation and malnutrition

If the food produced in an area cannot provide enough for its population then some people will starve. Importing food from other areas can solve part of the problem. However, overpopulation often causes wars, which can reduce the supply of food. Table 4.1 shows the numbers of undernourished people around the world.

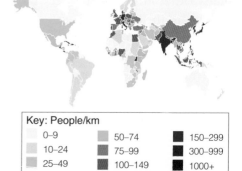

Key: People/km

0–9	50–74	150–299
10–24	75–99	300–999
25–49	100–149	1000+

Figure 4.13 *Density of people living in different countries*

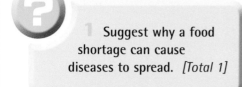

1 Suggest why a food shortage can cause diseases to spread. *[Total 1]*

2 Look back at Figure 2.9 on page 208. When did the human population reach 1 billion (1000 million)? *[Total 1]*

	Number of people undernourhled (millions)	
	1990–1992	1997–1999
Asia (except China)	372.2	380.8
China	192.6	116.3
Latin America	58.6	53.6
Africa	192.8	226.5

Table 4.1 *Numbers of undernourished people. Data source: FAO 2001.*

Pollution and climate change

The more people there are in an area the more energy they will use. The energy is often obtained by burning things. This releases gases into the air that, in large amounts, will damage the environment. There is also a greater demand for products, which require the manufacture of new chemicals that may also cause pollution.

? **3** In which parts of the world are people becoming better nourished?
[Total 2]

Species extinctions

With more people to feed, more land is used for agriculture and housing. This has meant that some species have not got enough space in which to live, and so they become extinct. Other species may become extinct because of pollution, climate change or being hunted. Scientists think that between 30 and 150 species become extinct every day. Of course, most of these are small animals and plants but some scientists think that between now and 2050 we will lose 25% of all vertebrates.

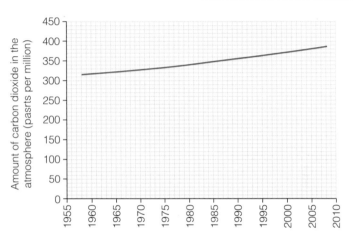

Desertification

Figure 4.12 *Most scientists agree that the rise in carbon dioxide levels in our atmosphere is due to human activity.*

Intensive farming, overgrazing, using too much water and cutting down trees can all turn fertile land into desert. Each year about 21 km² of land becomes desert around the world.

Questions

1 Do you think that Malthus' prediction has come true? Explain your reasoning. [Total 3]

2 a) Name one country where overpopulation may be causing species to become extinct. [1]
b) Explain why you have picked that country. [1]
[Total 2]

3 Lake Chad, in Africa, had an area of about 26 000 km² in the 1960s. Now it covers an area of less than 1500 km². Suggest two possible causes of this change. [Total 2]

4 a) In many parts of China, it is the law that people are not allowed to have more than one child. Why do you think the Chinese created this law? [1]
b) Do you think this law is right? Explain your reasoning. [2]
c) Do you think this law is working? Explain your reasoning. [2]
[Total 5]

End of section questions

1 a) Put the following organisms into the correct order in the food chain. [1]

caterpillar   sparrowhawk   oak tree   blue tit

b) Draw a pyramid of numbers for the food chain. [1]

c) The pyramid of biomass for the food chain is a regular pyramid. Explain why the shape of the number pyramid is different. [1]

[Total 3]

2 Bats can live in caves. They fly out of the cave at night to catch insects. They produce droppings, which are a food source for many organisms. Figure 1 shows part of the food web for the organisms living in and around the cave.

a) In summer, birds enter the caves and eat many of the beetles. Suggest why the population of millipedes might:

i) increase

ii) decrease. [2]

b) Name one herbivore from the food web. [1]

c) Name one parasite from the food web. [1]

d) Name three predators from the food web. [3]

e) Use the information in the question to work out the feeding level of the beetles. [1]

f) Draw the pyramid of numbers and biomass for the following food chain. Estimate the width of the feeding levels. The relative shape is important not the actual number or mass.

flowering plants → moths → bats → fleas [4]

[Total 12]

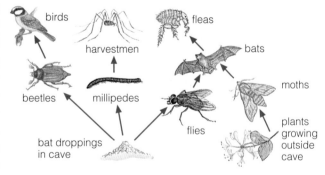

Figure 1 *(not to scale).*

3 Figure 2 shows what happens to most of the energy in the food that a bullock eats in one year.

a) State the word equation for aerobic respiration. [1]

b) Calculate the total energy that remains in the body of the bullock. [1]

c) What is this energy used for? [1]

d) Suggest two different ways that a farmer can reduce the energy lost by each bullock as 'thermal transfer'. [2]

e) Suggest a reason why reducing the 'movement and thermal transfer' losses are cost effective for the farmer. [1]

[Total 6]

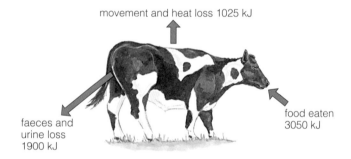

movement and heat loss 1025 kJ

food eaten 3050 kJ

faeces and urine loss 1900 kJ

Figure 2

4 The growth curve of a population sometimes forms an 'S' shape. Sketch the population graph and explain why each part of the graph has a different slope. [Total 5]

5 a) Predict how overgrazing will affect the numbers of plants, other herbivores and predator populations within one season. Give a reason for each prediction. [6]

b) Suggest what might happen after 2 years. [4]

[Total 10]

6 A gardener always grew lettuces every year and he noticed the snails feeding on them. He also found piles of snail shells where he saw thrushes perching. He counted the number of snails and different thrushes in the garden over several years. Figure 3 shows the pattern he obtained.

a) What was the maximum number of snails in year 2? [1]

b) In which year were there most thrushes? [1]

c) Suggest why there were more thrushes in year 4 than in year 2. [1]

d) Write out the simple food chain from the information given. [1]

e) Draw a pyramid of numbers for the food chain. [1]

f) Suggest two reasons why the number of snails did not increase every year. [2]

g) If the gardener used a pesticide to kill the snails, suggest what would happen to the thrushes, giving your reasons. [2]

h) Explain why pesticides are often considered pollutants in the environment. [1]

[Total 10]

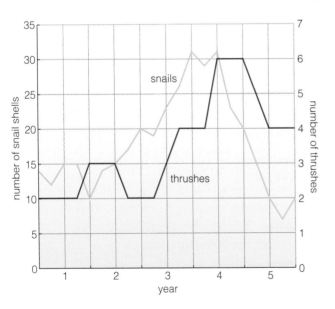

Figure 3

7 Malthus said that the human population increased faster than food supply increases. If a population of one hundred increased by 10% a year and their food supply increased by 10 tonnes per year the data shown in Table 1 are obtained.

a) Plot these data with both lines on the same graph. [5]

b) What trend does the graph show? [2]

[Total 7]

Year	Population	Food produced (tonnes)
0	100	100
1	110	110
2	121	120
3	133	130
4	146	140
5	161	150
6	177	160
7	194	170
8	214	180
9	235	190
10	259	200

Table 1

8 R Find out about the food web in an aquarium. How may it differ from the examples in this section?

9 R Study an area near to your home over a year e.g. a hedgerow, garden, or pond. Record the different types of animals visiting the area. Record the days when leaves and flowers are first seen. Work out a food web for the area.

10 R Find out about Biosphere 2 and what went wrong.

11 P What factors would affect time of leaf growth in oak trees of a small wood?

12 P What factors would affect the growth of yeast cells in a laboratory beaker?

13 P Peacock butterfly caterpillars feed on nettle leaves. How would you investigate the effect of peacock butterfly caterpillars on the growth of nettles in the laboratory or green house?

What are investigations?

A **hypothesis** is an idea about how something works. It can be used to make a **prediction**. The purpose of an **investigation** is to test a prediction and find the answer to a scientific question.

The **data** produced in an investigation can be used to show whether the hypothesis is correct or not. If the data from several investigations support a hypothesis, the hypothesis becomes a **theory**.

New ideas are being suggested and tested in science all the time. Eventually, if an idea is well tested it may be accepted by all scientists. However, even well tested and established ideas can sometimes be proved wrong by further experiments or new ideas.

Many questions can be answered by doing experiments. These involve changing something and measuring the effects of changing it, such as in the example above. However there are other scientific questions that cannot be answered in this way. These questions may involve surveys, or careful observations, without changing anything.

Scientists do not always have to carry out the investigations or observations themselves. A scientist with a new idea diets and obesity could look at observations that have already been made to see if they fit with the idea. Observations made and reported by someone else are called **secondary sources**.

Variables and values

A **variable** is a factor than can change. Each variable can be described in words or numbers (with units), which are called **values**. Variables can be of different types:

- A **continuous variable** is something that can be one of a continuous range of values, and can have any numerical value.

- A **categoric variable** is described in words, or in numbers that cannot be split into smaller values.

In most investigations you will choose a variable to change. This is called the **independent variable**. It is independent because its values don't depend on carrying out the investigation.

The **dependent variable** is what changes when the values of the independent variable are altered. This variable *depends* on the independent variable.

You might wonder how heartbeat rate is affected by exercise. If you were a scientist, you would think up a hypothesis such as 'how hard the exercise is affects the heartbeat rate'. You would use this hypothesis to make a prediction such as 'the harder the exercise, the faster the heartbeat rate', and then design a set of experiments to test the prediction by measuring the heartbeat rate when different types of exercise are being done.

Biologists often want to know the answers to questions like 'What lives in this habitat?' They would come up with some predictions based on what the habitat is like and then test their predictions by doing a survey. The survey might involve taking samples from different areas to find small animals or setting up remote cameras that are triggered when larger animals pass.

The time that someone exercises for is a continuous variable, but the name of the exercise is a categoric variable.

Your year group is also a categoric variable as, although year groups are described using numbers, it can only be 7, 8, 9 etc, and never 7.1 or 8.6.

Investigations involve finding out whether there are **relationships** between different variables.

Fair testing

In most investigations there will be more than one variable that could be an independent variable. Since you only want to measure the effect of one independent variable, you need to stop all these other variables from changing. You need to try to control them. These are the **control variables**. Some control variables are very difficult to control.

Gathering data

The data you gather during an investigation needs to be valid, accurate and reliable.

- **Valid** data is data that is directly relevant to your investigation.

- **Accurate** data is data that is very close to the true value. You need to think about how accurate your data needs to be when choosing the measuring instruments for your investigation. When you choose a measuring device for measuring something you need to think about the **sensitivity** of the device. Instruments that are more sensitive will allow you to take readings with more significant figures which should therefore be more accurate. However, very sensitive instruments are not always needed

- **Reliable** data is data that will be the same if the experiment is repeated, or if someone else does the same experiment. You can make your results more reliable by taking each measurement several times and working out a mean or average value.

You are finding how the speed that someone runs at affects heartbeat rate:
- the independent variable is the speed of running (and is a continuous variable)
- the dependent variable is the heartbeat rate (this is also a continuous variable)
- the control variables are the type of exercise (a categoric variable), the ages and masses of the people (both continuous variables) and their sex (a categoric variable)

A midwife uses a sensitive set of scales to measure the mass of a baby as it grows in the first weeks of its life. Bathroom scales are not sensitive enough for this. But you don't need such a high degree of accuracy to measure your own mass.

Presenting your results

The values of all variables should be recorded in a table, including the values of the control variables. If there is a **relationship** between the dependent and the independent variables in an investigation, there will be a pattern in the results. This is easiest to see by plotting a chart or graph. The independent variable is usually plotted on the horizontal axis. Draw a line graph if your independent variable is a continuous variable. Draw a bar chart if your independent variable is categoric.

If there is a relationship between the two variables, the points on the graph will form a line or a curve. Draw a line of best fit (or curve of best fit) through your points. The line or curve of best fit is the line you would get if all your measurements were perfectly accurate.

If you have gathered data using a datalogger and computer, you can use a spreadsheet program to produce graphs of your results.

The example investigation on the following pages shows you how to plan, carry out and report a typical investigation.

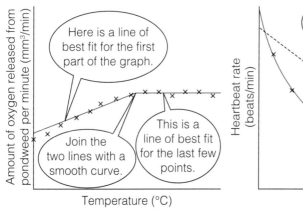

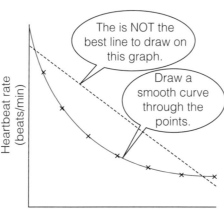

Figure 9.1 *Not all graphs form a straight line*

An example investigation

In many investigations you change the independent variable and measure the effect on the dependent variable, whilst keeping the control variables the same. This can be fairly easy to do in a laboratory but is much more difficult when you do field work because there are a great many variables that are difficult to control. In the example below, the environment has changed the independent variable and so you need to measure both it and the dependent variable to see if there is a relationship between the two.

Plan

What you have to do

1 Think about what you want to find out. What hypothesis do you want to test? Write this down. This is the 'aim' of the investigation.

2 List all the variables that could affect the variable you are measuring (the dependent variable).

3 Choose one variable to investigate – the independent variable.

4 Make a prediction about what you think you will find. You need to explain your prediction using scientific knowledge. It does not matter if your prediction is wrong because the point of the investigation is to find out.

An example from a pupil

I noticed that grass did not grow near the trees at the edge of the playing field. I think that this is because the trees cause too much shade for grass to grow. I am going to find out if there is a relationship between the amount of shade and the amount of ground covered by grass.

The dependent variable is the amount of grass. This could be affected by:

- the amount of light
- the amount of water
- the levels of nutrients in the soil
- how compacted the soil is
- chemicals produced by the trees
- animals or people trampling the grass.

I shall investigate how the amount of light affects the grass cover.

I think that the grass growing near the trees gets less light than those growing further away from them. This causes there to be less grass under the trees. The less light plants get, the less well they can photosynthesise and make food. So, I don't think that grass can make enough food to stay alive when it is growing under trees because there is not enough light.

5 Plan how you will carry out your investigation.
- Choose the apparatus you will use
- State how many measurements you will make
- State whether you will repeat any measurements and why

You might need to do a quick check to make sure that your method gives useful data before completing your investigation plan.

I shall estimate the ground cover of the grass using a quadrat, and show my results as percentages. I will use the quadrat to do a transect, which involves placing the quadrat along a line at 1 m intervals away from the trees for 5 m. I will use tent pegs and string to mark out the line and a tape measure to measure the distances between the quadrats.

There's a type of quadrat that is divided into 100 small squares and I will use that one because it will make estimating the percentage of grass easier. I will repeat this so that I have readings for two transects.

I will place a light meter in the centre of each quadrat and take a light reading.

I will compare the light readings with the percentage of grass cover in each quadrat.

6 Describe how you will make it a fair test.

I will:

- use the same quadrat and light meter each time
- be consistent in estimating the percentage of grass coverage
- choose areas of ground that look similar

7 Describe how you will make the investigation safe.

I will make sure that there are no broken pieces of metal or glass in the area. I will also wash my hands after doing the measurements.

8 Show your plan to your teacher.

Obtain evidence

9 Carry out your investigation. If you make any changes to your method, make sure you write them down.

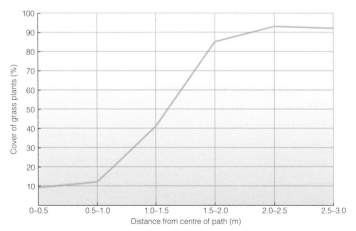

I realised that I had not got a plan for what happens when only a part of a quadrat square has grass in it. I decided that if a square was more than half covered in grass then I counted it as a 'grassy square' and if it was less than half covered in grass then I didn't count it.

10 Record your results in a table. Make sure you include units in your measurements.

Quadrat distance from tree (m)	Transect 1		Transect 2	
	grass cover (%)	light meter reading (lux)	grass cover (%)	light meter reading (lux)
0	0	400	0	600
1	13	3000	24	4500
2	40	11 000	85	15 000
3	95	17 500	100	18 000
4	100	20 000	100	18 000
5	95	19 500	100	19 000

Analysis

11 Plot a chart or graph of your results and describe any pattern that you can see.

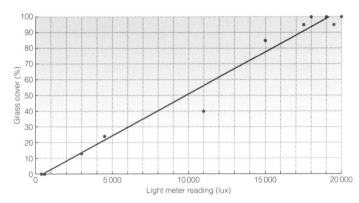

I drew a line of best fit through my points so that I could show the relationship better. Both transects showed the same pattern.

12 State the conclusion that you can draw from your evidence. This is just a simple statement of what you have found together with a scientific explanation for your evidence. Does your conclusion agree with your prediction.

The more light, the more the coverage of grass. This agrees with my prediction. I think that grass plants need to make a certain amount of food using photosynthesis in order to survive and that nearer the trees not enough sunlight gets to the ground to allow this to happen

Evaluation

13 Evaluate your investigation. Think about the following things:

⦿ how reliable were your results? Can you improve the reliability?

Both transects showed the same pattern and most of my points on the graph are near the line of best fit. This shows that my data was quite reliable. I could improve the reliability by doing more transects.

⦿ how accurate were your results? Can you improve the accuracy?

It was quite difficult in some cases to decide whether a square was over half full of grass. This was because in many squares there was an even covering of grass plants but they had gaps between them. I think it would have been better to use the points on the quadrat (where the lines cross) and count it so that if there is a grass plant on that point that counts as '1'. That would have been quicker too.

⦿ how valid are your results? Do they answer your original question?

Yes, my results are valid and can be used to show that there is a relationship between the amount of light and grass coverage.

- do you have any anomalous results (those that do not fit the overall pattern)? If you do, try to explain what you think caused these results.

I guess that the reading on transect 1 for 11 000 lux is a bit low for grass coverage. This could be because the soil was not very good at this point.

- are your results good enough to be certain of your conclusion? How might you be able to be more sure of your conclusion?

There are lots of variables that may affect how well grass grows in a certain area. I can't be sure that it's not moisture levels in the ground that cause the changes and I should have done moisture readings too. However, the whole of this area gets watered by the automatic watering system and I have seen it spray into the trees so I don't think moisture is the problem. But I should have checked. Other variables that could be looked at include pH and soil structure. The pH I could check with a meter but soil structure would need me to dig up the ground, which is not allowed! So, I am confident of my conclusion but to be extra sure, if I did this investigation again I would also use a moisture meter and a pH meter.

Glossary

accurate   A measurement that is accurate is one that is close to the true value.

active transport   Moving chemicals across a membrane against the concentration gradient, using energy.

adapted   Changed to adjust to new conditions. Organisms adapt to changes in their environment.

addicted   When a person always needs a drug.

adolescent   Person going through puberty.

adrenaline   Hormone that prepares the body for action, such as increasing heart rate and breathing rate.

aerobic respiration   The release of energy using oxygen.

allele   Alternative forms of a gene, e.g. blue or green eye colour.

alveolus   Bubble-like structure in the lungs where gas exchange between the air and the blood occurs. (plural: alveoli)

amino acid   Proteins are made of amino acids.

amniotic fluid   Fluid surrounding the developing embryo in the uterus.

ampulla   Small chamber on a semi-circular canal that tells the brain about balance or movement.

amylase   An enzyme that breaks down starch.

anaerobic respiration   The release of energy without oxygen.

angina   Chest pain caused by the heart not getting enough oxygen.

animal   Multicellular organisms that move around and get their food by eating other organisms.

antagonistic pair   A pair of muscles that work in opposite directions to each other, e.g. biceps and triceps.

antibiotic   Medicine that kills bacteria inside the body.

antibody   Proteins produced by lymphocytes that stick to invading microorganisms and make them clump together.

antigen   Protein found on surface of cells that identifies where the cell came from.

antiseptic   Chemical that stops bacteria growing and multiplying.

archaea   Very simple sub-group of monera.

artery   Thick, muscular-walled blood vessel that carries blood away from the heart.

asexual reproduction   Making new individual organisms without involving fertilisation.

asthma   Condition where breathing is difficult.

atria   Chambers at the 'top' of the heart which blood flows into from blood vessels.

auxin   Plant growth substance that allows a plant to respond to light.

axon   The long fibre that carries impulses in a nerve cell.

bacteria   Sub-group of monera, classified by shape. Some are free-living, others are parasites.

balanced diet   A diet containing all that is needed by a person in the amounts needed.

base   A pair of these form the 'rungs' of the DNA double helix.

binary fission   The way in which bacteria reproduce, by growing and splitting into two.

binomial system   Latin two-name system invented by Linnaeus and used to name all organisms. The name includes the genus and species.

bioaccumulation   Increase in the concentration of substances along a food chain.

biological control agent   Natural predator used to control a pest.

biomass   The mass of living material.

biome   An area of the Earth with a particular type of vegetation.

biosphere   The part of the Earth where living things can exist.

biotechnology   Using technology in biology, such as in genetic engineering.

blood   Fluid containing cells that carries substances around an organism.

blood vessel   Tube that contains the blood as it flows around the body.

body mass   What we usually call your 'weight', measured in kilograms.

body mass index   A number that gives a measure of your body mass relative to your height. Used by doctors to determine if someone is overweight or underweight.

bronchi   The branches of the windpipe taking air into each lung.

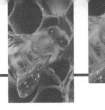

bronchiole Fine branching tube taking air to all parts of the lung.

bronchitis Irritation of the lining of the lungs caused by infection with bacteria.

budding The way yeast cells reproduce by producing a growth on the side of a cell.

capillary Tiny blood vessel connecting arteries to veins that allows exchange of substances between the blood and tissues.

carbohydrase An enzyme which breaks down carbohydrates.

carbohydrate Chemical made up from carbon, hydrogen and oxygen atoms, used for energy by organisms.

carbon monoxide Poisonous gas found in tobacco smoke.

carnivore An animal that eats other animals.

cartilage Tough smooth substance that covers the end surfaces of bones.

categoric variable A variable that has a set of fixed values. These are usually words (e.g. blue green, orange) but can be numbers that only have a fixed set of values (e.g. shoe sizes).

cell The basic unit from which living things are made.

cell body The part of a neurone that contains the nucleus.

cell membrane A structure that surrounds the cell and controls what goes in or out.

cell wall Structure surrounding plant cells giving support. Made of cellulose.

cellulose A chemical found in plant cell walls. A type of carbohydrate made from glucose.

central nervous system Brain and spinal cord.

cervix Neck of the uterus.

characteristic Feature of an individual.

chlorophyll A chemical that traps light energy for use in photosynthesis.

chloroplast A structure in plant cells where photosynthesis takes place. Contains chlorophyll.

chromosome Long strand of DNA found in the nucleus of a cell.

cilia Small hairs on the surface of some cells that wave to keep mucus moving.

circulatory system The organ system that carries substances around the organism.

cirrhosis Damage and scarring of the liver, often caused by excessive drinking of alcohol.

class Level of classification between phylum and order e.g. Mammalia.

classification Arranging organisms into groups according to similar features.

climate change Change in the climate and weather patterns usually associated with global warming.

clone New cell or organism that is an exact copy of the parent cell or organism.

cloning Producing clones.

colony A group of microorganisms.

community A group of organisms of different species that live together in one habitat.

competition When organisms in a habitat compete for limited resources, e.g. food or space.

cone cell A cell found in the back of the eye which allows the eye to see in colour.

consumer An animal that eats another organism.

continuous variable A variable that can have any numerical value. Human height is a continuous variable.

continuous variation Variation in a characteristic that changes in a gradual way, e.g. height in humans.

contraceptive Method of preventing a woman from becoming pregnant.

contraceptive pill Hormone-containing pill taken to prevent unwanted pregnancy from occurring.

contract Get shorter.

control variable All variables in an experiment other than the independent and dependent variables, which must be controlled to stop them changing.

cornea Front surface of the eye which bends light rays as they enter the eye.

cross-breeding When two breeds that have desirable characteristics are bred together.

cystic fibrosis Genetic (inherited) disease that causes thick mucus to be produced, such as in the tubes of the lungs and gut.

cytoplasm   The jelly-like substance that fills a cell and contains most of the cell's chemical reactions.

data   Measurements or other information.

decomposers   Fungi and bacteria that break down dead material.

deficiency disease   A type of disease caused by the lack of a substance in the diet.

denature   When an enzyme molecule changes its three-dimensional shape and can no longer act as a catalyst. Can be caused by high temperatures or extremes of pH.

dendrite   Fine projections from a neurone that connect with other neurones.

dependent   In relation to drugs, when the body always needs the drug.

dependent variable   The variable that you measure in an investigation.

depressant   A drug that slows down the reaction of the nervous system.

diabetes   A disease in which the body cannot control the level of sugar in the blood.

diaphragm   A dome-shaped sheet of muscle that separates the thorax from the abdomen. When it contracts a person breathes in.

diffusion   The net movement of particles from an area of high concentration to an area of lower concentration by random movement.

digestion   The chemical breaking down of food.

digestive system   The organ system where digestion and absorption of food occur.

discontinuous variation   Variation in a characteristic that occurs in separate categories, e.g. tongue-rolling in humans.

disease   When the body does not work normally, due to infection or failure of body cells to carry out their normal processes.

disinfectant   Strong chemical that kills microorganisms outside of the body.

dispersal   Scattering away from a point, as in the scattering of seed away from the parent plant.

DNA   Deoxyribonucleic acid. The chemical that contains the genetic code for each individual.

dominant   Allele whose effect is always seen.

donor organ   Replacement organ for an organ that does not work properly.

double helix   The twisted spiral ladder shape of a DNA molecule.

echolocation   The use of reflected sound waves (echoes) to hunt and navigate.

ecosystem   All the organisms and the way they interact with the physical environment in which they live.

egestion   The removal of undigested food from the gut.

ejaculation   Release of sperm from the penis.

embryo   Early stage in development of a new organism.

embryo screening   Checking IVF embryos for any problems that might stop them developing.

emphysema   Destruction of alveolar cells after irritation by tobacco smoke.

endocrine   System of the body made up of glands that produce hormones.

endoskeleton   A skeleton that is inside the body and is used for support and protection.

environment   The surroundings in which an organism lives.

enzymes   Chemicals that speed up chemical reactions in cells.

epidemic   When many people catch the same infectious disease at the same time.

eradicate   Get rid of completely.

erection   Stiffening of the penis when a man is sexually aroused.

essential amino acid   An amino acid that cannot be made by humans and must be taken in through the diet.

ethanol   The alcohol found in alcoholic drinks.

ethics   Trying to decide what is right or wrong.

evolution   The gradual change of the characteristics of an organism over time.

exoskeleton   A skeleton which is outside the body and is used for support and protection.

extinct   When a species dies out completely.

family   Level of classification between order and genus, e.g. Hominidae.

fats   Chemicals that are used to store energy in organisms.

fermentation   The breakdown of sugar by microorganisms.

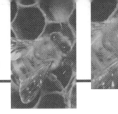

fertilisation When male and female sex cells join together.

fertiliser Chemical used to increase crop production by making plants grow better.

fetus The name given to a developing baby about two months after fertilisation, when it has a head, torso and visible limbs. This name is used up till birth.

fibre The part of food that cannot be digested.

flagellum Fine hair-like projection used for movement in some protists.

flowering plants A group of plants that have broad leaves and produce flowers, which then produce seeds contained in or on fruits.

fontanelle Soft spot at the top of baby's skull where bones have yet to fuse.

food chain The sequence of organisms through which energy flows.

food web A number of interconnected food chains.

fossil The remains of an organism that lived millions of years ago, usually found in rock.

free range Farm animals that are have a lot of space to move around in.

fruit Complete flowering plant ovary after fertilisation. Often fleshy, as in an apple.

fungus Mostly multicellular organisms that form a mycelium of hyphae. Yeast is a unicellular fungus. Most fungi are decomposers.

gamete Sex cell. For example egg and sperm.

gas exchange The movement of gases between the air and the blood in the lungs.

gastric juice The fluid released into the stomach containing enzymes.

gene Small sections of DNA that control a characteristic.

genera Singular: genus. The first part of the Latin name of a species, e.g. *Homo*.

genetic engineering Transfer of a small piece of genetic material from an individual of one species into the cells of an individual of a different species. Also called genetic modification.

genetic testing A technique used when a cell from an IVF embryo is tested for genetic abnormalities.

genetics The study of genes and their effects.

genitals External reproductive organs in animals.

genome All the genes of an individual organism.

germination When a seed starts to grow.

global warming The increase in the average temperature of the air around the world.

glucose A simple sugar formed by plants during photosynthesis and used as an energy source in both animals and plants.

greenhouse effect The natural warming of Earth and its atmosphere due to some substances (e.g. carbon dioxide) absorbing heat that would otherwise escape back into space.

habitat A region of the environment where a particular type of organism lives.

haemoglobin A chemical that carries oxygen in the red blood cells. It gives the blood its red colour.

hallucinogen A drug that causes people to see things which are not there.

heart Organ that pumps blood around the body.

heart attack Health problem caused when a coronary artery is blocked and the heart muscle does not get enough oxygen or glucose to work properly.

herbivore An animal that eats plants.

hibernate To spend the winter in a resting state, when the body temperature is much less than the normal active temperature.

homologous pair Pair of chromosomes carrying the same type of genes.

hormone Chemical that co-ordinates body processes.

hyphae Fine branched threads of cells that are characteristic of fungi.

hypothesis An idea about why something happens but that does not have very much evidence to support it. If more evidence is found to support the hypothesis, it becomes a theory.

immune system The system which protects the body from disease.

immunisation Giving someone immunity to a disease before they are infected with it, often through vaccination.

immunity The body's defence against disease.

immunosuppressants Drugs that weaken the immune system and prevent a transplanted organ from being rejected.

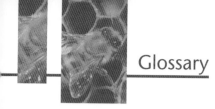

Glossary

impulse   Message carried by the nervous system.

in vitro fertilisation   Fertilisation in a dish, using an ovum removed from the body.

independent variable   The variable that you change in an investigation.

infection   When a disease is passed on to another individual.

infertile   Unable to produce a child.

ingestion   The taking in of food into the mouth.

inherited characteristic   Genetic feature which has been passed on to an individual from his or her parents.

insulin   A hormone made in the pancreas, which controls the amount of sugar in the blood.

intensive farming   Using labour-saving methods to try to get as much product out of as small a space as possible.

invertebrate   Animal that has no backbone.

investigation   Trying to find the answer to a scientific question by making measurements and or observations.

iris   A layer of coloured tissue found at the front of the eye.

joint   A part of the body where bones join together.

key   A biological table or chart that helps in the identification of living things.

kingdom   Largest group that living things are sorted into, e.g. the animal kingdom.

lactic acid   A chemical produced in muscles when they work without enough oxygen.

lens   Part of the eye behind the pupil, which focuses the image on the retina.

ligament   A tough band of fibres that joins bones together in a joint.

lipase   An enzyme that breaks down fats into fatty acids and glycerol.

lymphocyte   A type of white blood cell that produces antibodies which fight disease.

malnourishment   Health problems that are caused by a diet lacking in some nutrients.

marrow   Soft substance in the cavity of bones.

medicine   Drug for treating an illness, to cure it or ease the symptoms.

meiosis   Cell division which happens when sex cells are produced.

membrane   A thin skin or outer surface of a cell.

menopause   When a woman stops ovulating and her menstrual cycle no longer occurs.

menstrual cycle   A series of events lasting about 28 days in the female reproductive system. It includes the production of an egg cell and replacement of the lining of the uterus.

menstruation   When the lining of the uterus and a little blood pass out of the vagina as part of the menstrual cycle.

mesophyll   Tissues in the middle of a leaf which carry out photosynthesis.

metabolism   The release of energy inside cells used for all the actions in the body, including the making of new materials.

microorganism   An organism which can only be seen by using a microscope. Also called microbe.

mineral salt   Soluble chemical needed by plants and animals in small amounts.

mitochondria   Structures in the cytoplasm of cells where respiration occurs.

mitosis   Cell division that happens when organisms are growing or replacing cells.

monera   Very simple, unicellular organisms that have no nucleus. They include bacteria and archaea.

morals   What everyone agrees is right or wrong.

mucus   Sticky fluid.

multicellular   Made of lots of cells.

muscle   Tissue that can contract.

mutation   A change in the genetic code.

mycelium   Mat of hyphae formed by a fungus.

mycoprotein   Protein produced from a fungus.

natural selection   When organisms that are best adapted to their environment survive to pass on their genes to their offspring.

nectar   A sugary substance that attracts insects to plants.

neurone   Nerve cell.

nicotine   An addictive chemical found in tobacco.

non-renewable energy resource   Energy resource that will run out one day (e.g. oil, coal, uranium).

normal distribution   A bell-shaped curve that shows continuous variation of a characteristic.

nucleus   Structure that contains DNA and controls the cell.

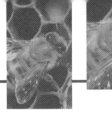

obesity The medical condition of being heavily overweight.

oesophagus Part of the alimentary canal that connects the mouth to the stomach.

oestrogen A sex hormone that helps to control the menstrual cycle and maintain female characteristics.

omnivore An animal that eats both plants and animals.

order Level of classification between class and family, e.g. Primates.

organ A structure that carries out one or more functions in the organism. It is made of different tissues.

organ system A collection of organs working together to do one type of function in the organism.

organelle Structure in the cytoplasm of a cell that can carry out special tasks.

organic farming Farming methods that use a few chemicals as possible and only natural fertiliser (manure).

organism A living individual, which can carry out the seven life processes.

osmosis Movement of water from an area where there is more water to an area where there is less water through a selectively permeable membrane.

ossicle Small bone in the middle ear.

ovary Female reproductive organ. Produces egg cells in plants and humans.

overfishing Taking too many fish from a population so that it risks the fish becoming extinct.

overgrazing When too many animals are eating the plants in an area.

overweight When someone has a body mass that is greater than recommended for their age, height and gender, we say they are overweight.

oviduct Egg tube.

ovulation Release of an egg cell from an ovary in women.

ovum Egg cell. The female sex cell. (plural: ova)

oxygen debt The amount of extra oxygen needed to remove chemicals produced during anaerobic respiration.

ozone layer Layer of ozone, high in the atmosphere, which absorbs a lot of the Sun's damaging ultraviolet waves.

pacemaker Area of the heart that controls the rhythm of the heart beat.

palisade cell Rectangular cells found near the upper surface of a leaf. They contain most of the chloroplasts.

pancreas An organ that produces digestive enzymes and releases them into the small intestine. It also produces insulin.

pandemic Infection that occurs all over the world at the same time.

parasite An organism that feeds on the living tissue of another organism.

passive immunity Getting immunity to a disease from the antibodies of someone else, such as when babies get antibodies from their mother.

pathogen Microorganism that causes disease.

penis An organ in the male that is used for reproduction.

period Another term for menstruation. When the lining of the uterus is lost with a little blood, through the vagina.

peripheral nervous system All the nerves in the body outside the brain and spinal cord.

peristalsis The process of moving something along a tube by a wave of contracting muscles passing along the length.

permanent vacuole Structure in plant cells containing a solution of sugars, salts and water.

pesticide Chemical used to kill pests on crops and farm animals.

petal Brightly coloured part of a flower that attracts insects.

phagocyte A type of white blood cell that engulfs and destroys invading microorganisms.

photosynthesis The process of forming sugars from carbon dioxide and water using light energy.

phylum The first subdivision of the organisms in a kingdom. (plural: phyla)

physical factor A non-living feature of the environment, e.g. temperature.

pituitary gland Small gland at the base of the brain.

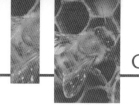

Glossary

placebo   Treatment that contains no drug, used for testing if any effect is due to the drug or something else.

placenta   An organ that attaches to the inside of the uterus and allows the fetus to collect food and oxygen form the mother, and get rid of waste.

plant   Multicellular organisms that make their own food using light energy from the Sun.

plasma   Fluid portion of the blood that carries all the other parts of the blood.

platelet   A type of blood cell that helps the clotting of the blood.

plumule   The tiny shoot in a plant embryo.

pollen tube   A tube that grows from a pollen grain down through the stigma and style and into the ovary.

pollination   Transfer of pollen from an anther to a stigma.

population   Group of individuals of one species in an area.

predator   Animal that hunts and kills other animals (prey) for food.

prediction   Saying what you think will happen in an investigation and why you think it will happen.

pregnant   When a woman has an embryo growing inside her uterus.

prey   Animal that is hunted by another animal for food.

primary consumer   Animals that eat producer organisms.

producer   Organisms that get their energy from sunlight, i.e. plants. They are the starting point for a food chain.

progesterone   A sex hormone that is found in women and prepares the reproductive organs for pregnancy.

protease   An enzyme that breaks down proteins into amino acids.

protein   Chemicals made from chains of amino acids. They are used for growth and repair by the body.

protist   Simple organisms, often unicellular, including *Euglena*, *Paramecium*, *Amoeba* and seaweeds.

protozoa   One kind of protist.

pseudopodia   Feet-like protrusions of single-celled microorganisms.

puberty   The time in humans when physical changes happen in the body, between the ages of about 11 and 15.

pupil   The part of the eye that lets light enter.

pyramid of biomass   The shape describing the mass of individuals at each link in a food chain.

pyramid of numbers   The shape describing the numbers of individuals at each link in a food chain.

quarantine   Keeping infected people apart from non-infected people to stop the infection spreading.

radicle   The tiny root in a plant embryo.

receptacle   Base of a flower.

receptor   Cells or modified nerve endings that respond to a stimulus.

recessive   An allele that codes for a characteristic but can be hidden by another allele.

red blood cell   A specialised cell, full of haemoglobin, which carries oxygen in the blood.

reflex action   An action that does not need conscious thought.

reflex arc   A short nervous pathway that does not include the brain.

rehabilitation   The process of helping someone recover and get back to as normal a life as possible following disease or surgery.

relationship   A link between two variables. If there is a relationship between two variables, one will change when the other changes.

relax   In muscle, to stop pulling.

reliable   A measurement or observation that is reliable is one that will be the same when it is repeated.

renewable energy resource   Energy resource that will not run out (e.g. wind, solar).

resistant   Not susceptible, such as bacteria that are not killed by an antibiotic.

respiration   The process of the release of energy in cells.

retina   The light sensitive layer at the back of the eye.

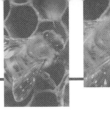

rib muscles The muscles that move the rib cage up and out when breathing in.

rickets Disorder causing soft bones due to a lack of calcium in the diet as a child.

rod cell Receptor cell in the retina that operates in low light conditions.

root hair cell Specialised plant cell for absorption of water and minerals from the soil.

saliva The fluid released into the mouth to start digesting food.

saprobiont A microorganism that feeds on dead matter.

scrotum The bag of skin that contains the testes.

secondary consumer A consumer organism that eats primary consumers.

secondary sexual characteristic Characteristic such as developing breasts in females and facial hair in males, which develops at puberty.

secondary sources A source that contains information that other people have gathered and written about.

selective breeding Breeding plants and animals to obtain desired characteristics.

selectively permeable membrane Membrane that controls the movement of substances across it.

self-pollination The transfer of pollen from anther to stigma in the same plant

semen A mixture of sperm cells and fluids released by men during sexual activity.

semi-circular canal Structure in the inner ear that helps to detect changes in balance.

sensitivity The more sensitive a measuring instrument is, the more accurately it can measure something. A balance that can measure down to 1 g is less sensitive than one that can measure down to 0.001 g.

sepals Small green leaves used to protect the flower in bud.

sex chromosomes The pair of chromosomes that determine the sex of the individual.

sexual intercourse When a man inserts his penis into a woman's vagina.

sexual reproduction Producing new organisms by combining a male with a female gamete.

skeleton A hard and supportive framework of bones found in vertebrates.

small intestine A long, coiled section of the gut where the majority of the digestion and absorption of the food occurs.

solvent The liquid that has dissolved a solid to make a solution.

species A group of individuals that can reproduce to form fertile offspring.

sperm The male sex cell (gamete).

sperm duct Tube that carries sperm from the testes to the urethra.

spore Tiny reproductive cell of mosses, liverworts and ferns.

stamen Male reproductive organ found in flowers. It is made of an anther and a filament.

starch A complex carbohydrate that is stored by plants as an energy supply.

statin A type of medicine used to lower cholesterol levels.

stigma Part of the female part of a flower, where the pollen lands.

stimulant A drug that speeds up the nervous system.

stimulus A change detected by a receptor. (plural: stimuli)

stoma Pores in the leaf surrounding by two guard cells. Allow air to get into the leaf. (plural: stomata)

stomach A bag-like structure to temporarily store food eaten and start to digest the food.

stroke A blood clot in the brain.

substrate A substance that is used in a reaction. In a reaction controlled by an enzyme, the substrate molecule needs to fit into the enzyme molecule.

sugar A group of compounds formed from carbon, hydrogen and oxygen, including glucose formed in photosynthesis. They taste sweet and can dissolve in water.

symptom A sign of a disease.

synapse The junction and gap between two neurones.

synovial fluid Fluid that lubricates joints.

tar Thick sticky substance in tobacco smoke that can block parts of the lung and cause cancer.

taste buds Cells that can sense food in the mouth.

Glossary

tendon   Tough cord, which does not stretch, that attaches a muscle to a bone.

testes   Organs that produce sperm cells. (plural of testis)

testosterone   Male hormone.

theory   An idea about why something happens that has lots of evidence from investigations to support it.

thyroid   Large gland in the neck.

thyroxine   The main hormone produced by the thyroid gland. It controls reactions in cells.

tissue   A group of the same cells all doing the same function.

tissue culture   A procedure used to make many clones of a plant using tiny pieces of tissue.

toxin   A poisonous substance.

trachea   Tube leading from the back of the mouth to the top of the lungs. Also known as the windpipe.

transpiration   The evaporation of water from a plant.

transpiration stream   Movement of water through a plant from roots to leaves and loss from the leaf.

trophic level   A single stage in a food chain.

tropism   Growth response of a plant, e.g. geotropism (growth in response to gravity), phototropism (growth in response to light).

umbilical cord   Carries food, oxygen, and waste between the placenta and the growing fetus.

unicellular   Formed from a single cell.

urethra   Tube leading from the bladder to outside the body.

uterus   Organ in females in which a baby develops.

vaccination   The injection of a vaccine to encourage immunity.

vaccine   Microorganism (or part of one) that usually causes disease but which has been treated to stop it causing the disease. It is often injected into people to protect then against disease.

vagina   Tube in females. The penis is placed here during sexual intercourse.

valid   Valid data are data that are directly relevant to the question that is being answered.

values   The numbers (or labels) that a variable can have.

valves   Structures in veins or the heart which stop the blood flowing backwards.

variable   A factor that can change in an experiment.

variation   Differences between living things.

variolation   Causing a milder form of an infection by transferring the disease from one person to another on purpose.

vegetative reproduction   A form of asexual reproduction in flowering plants, where parts of the plant can produce new plants, e.g. from bulbs or tubers.

vein   Blood vessel which carries blood back to the heart.

ventilation   The flow of air into and out of the lungs.

ventricle   Thick muscular walled chamber of the heart, which pumps the blood to the organs of the body.

vertebral column   Another term for the spine.

vertebrate   An animal with a backbone.

vesicle   Structure in the cytoplasm where food can be stored or other chemicals broken down.

virus   A microorganism which is smaller than bacteria.

vitamins   Chemicals needed by a person in small amounts to keep healthy.

white blood cell   Cells that fight disease and are found in the blood.

withdrawal symptoms   Symptoms that occur in someone who is addicted to a drug when they have none of the drug in their body.

xenotransplantation   Transplanting of cells, tissues or organs from one species to another, such as in the making of organs for human transplants.

xylem vessel   Specialised cell to carry water and mineral salts in a plant.

zygote   The fertilised cell formed when a male gamete joins with a female gamete.

Index

Index

Index

Published by Pearson Education Limited, a company incorporated in England and Wales, having its registered office at Edinburgh Gate, Harlow, Essex, CM20 2JE. Registered company number: 872828

The right of Aaron Bridges, Mark Levesley, Janet Williams and Chris Workman to be identified as the author of this work has been asserted by them in accordance with the Copyright, Designs and Patents Act of 1988.

First published 2002
10 9
15 14

British Library Cataloguing in Publication Data
A catalogue record for this book is available from the British Library

ISBN 978 1 4082 3110 4

Design and illustration by HL Studios, Oxford
Picture research by Kay Altwegg
Cover photo © Pearson Online Database
Printed and bound in Malaysia (CTP - VVP)

Acknowledgements

The publisher would like to thank the following for their kind permission to reproduce their photographs:

(Key: b-bottom; c-centre; l-left; r-right; t-top)

Alamy Images: By Ian Miles-Flashpoint Pictures 126br; Grant Heilman Photography 102; Network Photographers 163; The Natural History Museum 220tl; Bridgeman Art Library Ltd: Glasgow University Library, Scotland 81; British Transplant Games: 24b; Corbis: Amos Nachoum 49; CDC/PHIL 193; PASCAL ROSSIGNOL/Reuters 25; Department of Health: (c) crown copyright 2009 294612 189; Mary Evans Picture Library: 158, 192; FLPA Images of Nature: B. Borrell Casals 205bl; David Hosking 215; MITSUAKI IWAGO 95b; Nigel Cattlin 206; Panda Photo 152tr; Peter Dean 195b; Peter Wilson/Holt 211r; Getty Images: Hans I Savery/Bridgeman Art Library 220br; Shirlaine Forrest/WireImage 99; Sally and Richard Greenhill: Richard Greenhill 166; iStockphoto: Aleksejs Polakovs 107tr; alexander briel perez 3br; Alkimson 107bl; AVTG 6; bluestocking 108; Cathy Keifer 137tc; Clayton Hansen 126tr; Constantine Dimizas 137bc; Donald Erickson 109t; Elizabeth Peardon 169bc; geotrac 152tl; Gez Browning 3bl; Henk Bentlage 144bc/2; ideeone 109c; Inna Looukianova 145l; Jeremy Swinborne 137b; Jim Jurica 203; Kerry Werry 136t; klemens wolf 136t/2; Lev Ezhov 110; Matthias Straka 144bc; Paul Erickson 136b; Rob Broek 138b; Robin Arnold 64b; rodho 8; RonTech2000 144tl; Ruth Ann Johnston 145r; Sandor F. Szabo 107br; Sawayasu Tsuji 135t; Sphotos 3tl; xyno6 107tl; Zuki 136t/3; J. Feltwell/Garden Matters: 70; Jupiter Unlimited: 136c/2, 138t, 145tl, 162, 195t, 207tl, 207tr, 210t, 218bl, 222; Lancaaster Environment Centre: 219br; Mark Levesley: 159bc, 159br, 200, 205tr; NaturalImageBank.com 213; with thanks to Tesco plc 132; Nationaal Archief, The Hague: nummer toegang (1.04.01), inv.nr. 135. 220bl; National Institute on Drug Abuse: 186br, 186tl, 186tr; Natural Visions: Heather Angel 7, 111t, 136c, 157; Nature Picture Library: Anup Shah 3tr; Dave Watts 221r; Pearson Education Ltd: 175b, 176t; GARETH BODEN 92b; Phil Bradfield 233; Trevor Clifford 171r; Photofusion Picture Library: Brian Mitchell 149r; Photolibrary.com: David Dennis 144cl/1, 144cl/2, 152br; Doug Wechsler 144br; Fred Bruemmer 207b; Graham Wren 111b; Larry Crowhurst 144bl; London Scientific 75; OSF/Mike Hill 2t; Oxford Scientific/Herb Segars 84t; Peter O'Toole 175t; Satoshi Kuribayashi/OSF 84b; Tom Ulrich 109bl; Waina Cheng 43; Photoshot Holdings Limited: George Bernard/NHPA 196t; Martin Wendler/NHPA 221l; POD - Pearson Online Database: Digital Vision 135c, 135tc, 137t; Pearson Education Ltd. Gareth Boden 135b; Peter Morris 149l; Photodisc. James Gritz 107tc; Photodisc. Jeremy Woodhouse 90; Photodisc. Photolink 135bc; Studio 8 Clark Wiseman 143; Press Association Images: Chris Radburn/PA Archive 128; EMPICS Sports Photo Agency 211l; John Birdsall 191tr; Reuters: 188tl; Jo Yong hak (SOUTH KOREA) 196c; Marc Serota 196b; Michael Buholzer (SWITZERLAND) 78; Stefan Wermuth (SWITZERLAND) 56b; Rex Features: D Marzolla/Newspix 94; J. Sutton-Hibbert 64t; NILS JORGENSEN 191bl; Science Photo Library Ltd: 54, 98, 159tl, 168bc; ADAM GAULT 56t; ANTONIA REEVE 76; BIOPHOTO ASSOCIATES 85l; CC STUDIO 188r; CHRIS BJORNBERG 86; CLAUDE NURIDSANY & MARIE PERENNOU 109br; CNRI 17; CORDELIA MOLLOY 1, 58, 59, 171l; CURT MAAS / AGSTOCKUSA 218br; DAMIEN LOVEGROVE 69; DAVID M. MARTIN, MD 51; DR GARY GAUGLER 168tl, 188bl; DR JEREMY BURGESS 2b, 27; DR. P. MARAZZI 139t, 169bl; DR. TONY BRAIN 85r; EM UNIT, VLA 176b; EYE OF SCIENCE 139b, 168bl, 168br, 180; PASCAL GOETGHELUCK 129, 136b/2; ADAM HART-DAVIS 92tl, 92tr; J&D ZBAEREN / EURELIOS 21; J.L. MARTRA, PUBLIPHOTO DIFFUSION 184; JAMES KING-HOLMES 100, 190r; JANE SHEMILT 178; JEROME WEXLER 96; JOHN MEAD 34; LIFE IN VIEW 24t; LOWELL GEORGIA 169tr; MANFRED KAGE 14; MARTIN M. ROTKER 164br; NATIONAL LIBRARY OF MEDICINE 156; PAT & TOM LEESON 150; PETER MENZEL 218tl; PETER SCOONES 212; PH PLAILLY/EURELIOS 183; PROF. AARON POLLIACK 20r; PROFESSOR P.M. MOTTA ET AL 20t; SATURN STILLS 179; SHEILA TERRY 127; SIMON FRASER 214; SIU 164tr; ST. MARY'S HOSPITAL MEDICAL SCHOOL 190l; ANDREW SYRED 15, 205br; VOLKER STEGER 103; VOLKER STEGER, PETER ARNOLD INC. 26b; Scottish Agricultural College: 219bl; Soil Association: 219tr; Stephen Hancocks and June Nunn from the Journal of Disability and Oral Health: 186bl; STILL Pictures The Whole Earth Photo Library: Mark Edwards 210b; TopFoto: 164l; Photri 55; Topham Picturepoint 79; US Department of Energy Artificial Retina Project, ARTIFICIALRETINA.ENERGY.GOV: 101; V. Trewavas: 219tl; Wellcome Images: 165; Wellcome Library London 26t, 80, 95t, 119, 124

All other images © Pearson Education

Picture Research by: Kay Altwegg

Every effort has been made to trace the copyright holders and we apologise in advance for any unintentional omissions. We would be pleased to insert the appropriate acknowledgement in any subsequent edition of this publication.